THE MAD DOG

100

THE GREATEST SPORTS ARGUMENTS OF ALL TIME

CHRISTOPHER RUSSO

WITH ALLEN ST. JOHN

DOUBLEDAY

NEW YORK LONDON TORONTO SYDNEY AUCKLAND

PUBLISHED BY DOUBLEDAY

A division of Random House, Inc.

1745 Broadway, New York, New York 10019

DOUBLEDAY and the portrayal of an anchor with a dolphin are trademarks of Doubleday, a division of Random House, Inc.

Book design by Chris Welch

Cataloging-in-Publication data is on file with the Library of Congress.

ISBN 0-385-50898-0

PRINTED IN THE UNITED STATES OF AMERICA

June 2003

7   9   10   8

To my parents, who spent a lifetime trying to
make me a well-rounded individual.
What they got instead was a sports nut.
—C. R.

In loving memory of my brother-in-law, John Esposito,
who bought me my first baseball glove and
took me to my first baseball game.
—A. S. J.

ACKNOWLEDGMENTS

Christopher Russo's Acknowledgments

When you do a sports talk show—or write a sports book—it's a job you prepare for your whole life, so I've got to start by acknowledging some old friends: Grant Napear, Phil Taylor, and Fred Leinfuss, who taught me how to think, talk, and play sports. I can't forget my college advisor, Dr. Charles Edmondson, now the president of Alfred University, or Andy Kowalsky, the best first baseman Rollins College ever produced. Thanks to all the good people who gave me a start in radio at WEXI in Jacksonville, WKIS in Orlando, and WMCA in New York: Pat Hayes, Wayne Mashburn, Mark Davis, Larry Kahn, Jim Philips, Gene Burns, the late Mike Gaier, and the late Rick Sklar. Lee Corso and Pat Williams helped make Orlando a big-time sports town during my stay there. Special thanks to Bob Raissman of the *Daily News*, who gave me the nickname Mad Dog.

My deepest gratitude to everyone who helped bring me to WFAN and helped shape *The Mike and the Mad Dog Show*: Don Imus, Bernard McGuirk, Scott Meier, Mark Mason, Joel Hollander, Bob Gelb, and the good folks at Emmis Broadcasting. What can I say about Mel Karmazin? If there's a more supportive titan in broadcasting, I haven't found him. Giant thank-yous to the rest of my current WFAN radio family, especially general manager Lee Davis, program director Mark Chernoff, marketing director Connie Fitzgerald, and my producer Chris "The Continent" Carlin. Props to all the sports junkies in the WFAN bullpen including Marc Malusis, John Minko, Rich Ackerman, Joe Tolleson, and Bob Heussler. And I can't say enough about Mike Francesa, who's been my on-air partner every afternoon for fourteen years, a great student of so many games who has made me think about sports in a totally different way. And of course thanks to all the listeners, callers, and guests over the years.

On a personal note, I'd like to thank Pat Cosgrove, who has been a faithful listener and confidant, and my friend and agent Sandy Montag of IMG, who encouraged me to do this project. And the biggest thanks of all goes to my wife, Jeanne, and my three children, Timothy, Kiera, and Colin, who have put up with me watching a thousand Giants games.

Allen St. John's Acknowledgments

Thanks to all the good people at Doubleday who made the hard work of turning a manuscript into a book look easy, especially senior editor Jason Kaufman, who's been the Magic Johnson of *The Mad Dog 100*, the guy with the big smile who makes everyone around him better. Thanks also to my agent, Mark Reiter of IMG Literary , who puts together deals like a latter-day Red Auerbach. Karen Brown, Elena Perez, and Francie Hughes deserve a medal—and a bottle of Advil—for transcribing the hundreds of hours of tape that are the backbone of this book. Thanks to WFAN's John Schweibacher, who helped to research this manuscript, and all the good people at the station who made me feel welcome and who helped shape this book in a thousand ways large and small. I have to mention my great friend Allen Barra, who is the Barry Bonds of sports arguments. Thanks to all my magazine and newspaper editors past and present, including Jim Kaminsky, Michael Anderson, Hugo Lindgren, Kyle Crichton, Don Forst, Ward Harkavy, Jonathan Duhl, Erin Friar, Dennis Drabelle, Mark Woodruff, Stephen Tignor, James Martin, Brian Duffy, Martin Hollander, Jerry Beilinson, Jeff Csatari, Alex Straus, Albert Baime, Perkins Miller, and Helen Olsson, who've kept me in business by printing my stories. And finally I thank my wife, Sally, my son, Ethan, and my daughter, Emma, for, well, everything.

CONTENTS

Introduction xv

The Slammer of '41 Which feat was more formidable, Joe DiMaggio's 56-game streak, or Ted Williams's .406 season? 1

Five-on-Five Fantasy If Cousy and Co. took on Michael's Crew, who'd win? 4

The Passer or the Punisher? Who's more important, a dominating linebacker or a great quarterback? 7

Back Nine Nirvana Who'd win golf's ultimate match play challenge, Ben Hogan or Tiger Woods? 8

The Ultimate Baseball Box Seats One game, four tickets, and a time machine. Who would you watch a game with? 10

Off the Record There's a right way and a wrong way to get your name in the record books. What are the rules when you're chasing a record? 13

Dog on Ice How would pro hockey be different if Mr. Russo were NHL commissioner? 16

Sports on the Silver Screen Why do most sports movies stink? 20

Ladies of the Court Topspin, topspin, on the ball. Who's the greatest women's tennis player of them all? 22

The NBA All-Underrated Team Which pro hoopsters don't get their props? 25

Let's Do It Again Is instant replay an annoyance or an educational tool? 28

Kenesaw Mountain Mad Dog How would Major League Baseball be different if Commissioner Russo were in charge? 30

Money Changes Everything Are sports salary caps really necessary? 33

Hoops Hierarchy Which is the greatest NBA team of all time? 36

Same As It Ever Was What are the greatest—and worst—traditions in sports? 39

Dugout Diplomacy What are the dos and don'ts for a baseball manager? 42

Poll Faults What's wrong with college football's national championship system? 47

Diamond Dangerfields Which baseball players don't get the respect they deserve? 49

. . . If You Ain't Got That Ring Does a player need a championship to make a career complete? 54

The Lord of the Rings What's the matter with the Olympic Games? 56

Midsummer Night's Dreaming How can we juice up baseball's All-Star Game? 58

Supe's On How to put the super back in the Super Bowl. 60

Throwing It All Away What are the biggest mistakes managers make when they head to the mound? 62

The Unbreakables Which sports records will stand forever? 64

Burn the Videotape What are the all-time ugliest moments in sports history? 67

Of Black Cats and Seeing-Eye Singles Are there really athletes and teams that are jinxed? 71

Breaking Par How can professional golf be improved? 74

Tools of the Game How would you build the perfect baseball player? 76

Can't Buy Me Love Do women tennis players really deserve equal prize money? 79

They Call It The Streak Whose consecutive games string was more formidable, Ripken's or Gehrig's? 81

Love Shaq? How does O'Neal rank against the all-time great centers? 84

The Big Rewind Button If you could have the ultimate second chance, how would you change sports history? 86

Two of a Kind Which athletes could have been separated at birth? 89

Say It Ain't So What are the most memorable sports controversies of all time? 91

Rep Artists Which baseball players get all the glory but don't back it up? 94

Fighting the Irish Is Notre Dame football awe-inspiring—or just annoying? 98

Gimme an E, Gimme an S, Gimme a P . . . What's right—and wrong—with the biggest sports cable network? 100

Rage On Who would win a fantasy fight between Jack Dempsey and Rocky Marciano? 102

Sideline Einsteins What does it take to succeed as an NFL football coach? 105

The Tracks of My Tears What moments are the biggest tearjerkers in sports history? 107

Making Book What are the all-time best sports books ever written? 111

If Dreams Came True What would the Dog do if you handed him the ball? 114

Monster on the Campus What can be done to clean up college sports? 116

Batter Up Who would prevail in baseball's ultimate fantasy matchup? 120

Serve 'Em Up How can you make professional tennis a big-time spectator sport? 122

The Ultimate Home Run Derby When you absolutely, positively need a tater, who do you want at the plate? 125

All for Love Who would win tennis's Grand Slam face-off? 126

Jocktown, USA Which city is America's best sports town? 128

Fantasy Foursome Which partners would you pick to play the ultimate round of golf? 133

Good Top, Bad Top What make a good owner—and what makes a tyrant? 135

Snap Decisions Who's the greatest NFL quarterback ever? 140

Hearing Is Believing What does it take to be a great baseball play-by-play man? 144

What a Waste Which players got the least out of their talent? 147

Kings of Diamonds Which is the greatest baseball team ever? 151

Braves New World Are the Atlanta Braves baseball's ultimate underachievers? 154

The Unwatchables Which sporting events aren't worth flipping the channel for? 157

Get Backs Who should your QB be handing off to? 159

Goal Oriented Who would prevail in the NHL's ultimate penalty shot? 162

Start Me Up Who are baseball's ultimate aces? 164

Dreams of Fields How can having the right stadium save a franchise? 165

No Guts, No Glory What are the gutsiest coaching calls of all time? 169

Heimlich Time What are the worst choke jobs of all time? 171

The Other Football Why can't soccer make it in the U.S.? 175

Know the Code Should pitchers be allowed to throw inside? 177

Give 'Em the Booth What are the greatest television sports teams of all time? 180

Ice Ageless Which are hockey's greatest dynasties? 183

Punched Out What's wrong with boxing? 186

Russo's Must-Read Is *Sports Illustrated* really indispensable for the sports fan? 188

Down to the Wire What are the greatest pennant races of all time? 190

Next on WDOG How would Mad Dog change sports on television? 192

The Ultimate NBA Draft Who would you pick to start your team with? 196

Willie, Mickey, and the Dog Who's better, Mays or Mantle? 199

Live or Memorex? Are sports really better in person? 203

Oops, I Did It Again What are the greatest vapor locks in
  sports history?   207

Make 'Em Hit Is the designated hitter bad for baseball? 210

The V in MVP What does it take to win an MVP award? 212

The P in MVP Should pitchers win the MVP award? 215

Five Aces Who is the greatest men's tennis player of all time? 216

Caught in the Draft Why can't the pros make the right picks?   219

But Is It a Sport? Can you call a racing driver or a golfer an athlete? 221

Gridiron Greats What are the greatest football dynasties of
  all time? 223

The Hatfields and the McCoys What are the ingredients for a great
  sports rivalry? 227

Hall Passes Which statistical thresholds in baseball are most sacred?   232

My Back Pages What makes a great sports section? 235

Money for Nothing Are professional athletes overpaid? 238

Open and Shut Who is the best closer of all time? 240

For the Love of the Pinstripes Are you a fan of the player—or the
  uniform? 242

Touching Them All Which home run record is the greatest?   243

The Classic Second-Guess What are the biggest managerial blunders
  in baseball history? 247

Tiger, Tiger Burning Bright Is Tiger Woods good for golf? 252

Staff Reflections What are the greatest pitching staffs in baseball
  history? 254

Trade Wins What are the worst trades of all time?   256

Motivation by Armani What makes a great NBA coach? 259

VCR Classics What sports moments are worth watching again
  and again? 261

The All-Century Team Who are the greatest baseball players of
  all time? 265

The Erasables Which sports moments don't hold up under repeated viewings? 268

Do You Believe in Magic? Who's tops in the Lakers-Celtics rivalry? 270

Guilty as Charged What are the greatest guilty pleasures in sports? 273

Heartbreakers, Dream Takers What are baseball's most crushing defeats? 276

100 Years of Swat-i-tude Who was really the top athlete of the twentieth century? 280

INTRODUCTION

Welcome to the candy store. Is there anything more fun and exciting in the world of sports than a good, juicy difference of opinion? No. (Well, except maybe a Barry Bonds homer in the bottom of the ninth.) How do I know? Because for five and a half hours every afternoon, that's what I do. I talk sports. I argue sports. I live sports.

Every afternoon, on the Mike and the Mad Dog show on New York's WFAN, the highest rated sports talk program in the nation's largest market, my partner Mike Francesa and I take dozens of phone calls from listeners, and debate everything under the sun having to do with sports.

A lot of the things we talk about are important today—who's going to win the Super Bowl?—and irrelevant tomorrow after the game is over. Other arguments are evergreen, cropping up week after week, month after month, and year after year. *The Mad Dog 100* takes the best of these classic arguments and puts them in a package you can stuff into your briefcase or take with you to the beach.

I hope you'll get three things out of this book. The first is entertainment. Sports are fun. Sure, the World Series is important and I take it very seriously, but I also realize that we're not mapping the human genome or trying to bring peace to the Middle East. I hope these arguments will make you smile, laugh, and remember some great games and great players.

Second, I hope you learn something from this book. I know I did. Over the years, I've watched thousands of games, talked to hundreds of athletes and coaches, but as I researched this book, I remembered some things I'd forgotten and uncovered some bits of sports history that slipped under my radar.

But most of all I hope this book encourages you to think. This book asks one question over and over again: Why? Why did these teams win?

Why is Bill Russell a better player than Wilt Chamberlain? Why should we ban the DH in Major League Baseball?

I don't expect that you'll always agree with me. But in tossing these questions around, and coming up with the rebuttal, the counterargument, you'll get your brain going in ways that'll make you a better, smarter sports fan.

So when you're done with a chapter, sometimes you'll want to say, "Great job there, Dog." Or you may want to say, "Aw, c'mon, Chris." But either way, if you're a sports fan, I don't think you'll want to put the book down.

THE MAD DOG
100

The Slammer of '41

Which feat was more formidable, Joe DiMaggio's 56-game streak, or Ted Williams's .406 season?

It was one of the most remarkable summers baseball had ever seen. Every day for two months, Joe DiMaggio woke up, put on his sanitary socks and his Yankee cap, and got a hit. And on the last day of the season, Ted Williams wouldn't take a seat even with his .400 average at stake. Sixty years later Mad Dog dissects two of baseball's classic accomplishments.

.406 or 56 games? Two of baseball's magic numbers. They're both amazing feats—made all the more remarkable by the fact that they both happened in the same year. But which feat is really greater?

More than sixty years later, I think baseball fans look on both of these accomplishments with almost equal reverence. But to really compare them, first I think you have to transport yourself back before World War II.

In 1941, people were more in awe of Joe DiMaggio than Ted Williams. Nobody had ever hit in 50 games in a row. The record was 44 by Wee Willie Keeler. And by 1941, Keeler's record had stood for forty-four years, and Keeler had been dead for eighteen years.

But it hadn't been all that long since somebody hit .400. When Williams was taking his shot, there were a few guys still walking around who had hit .420: Rogers Hornsby, George Sisler, Ty Cobb. And the last guy to hit .400, Bill Terry, had been retired only five years. I imagine it was a little like Barry Bonds breaking Mark McGwire's home run record.

So, I think that 56 games captured America's imagination more than .406. After all, they wrote a song about Joe DiMaggio's streak: "He sanctified the horsehide sphere and set our hearts aglow / He's just a man and not a freak / Joltin' Joe DiMaggio." They didn't write songs about Williams.

I think that's because a hitting streak is better theater. America likes streaks. There's drama every single day. Cal Ripken and Lou Gehrig. Even the Orioles losing 21 in a row. And there was drama every day during the summer of '41, from the time the Yankees showed up at the ballpark until Joe D got his first hit. When you're talking about hitting .400, you don't get excited about it until the last few days of the season. When Williams got all those hits on the doubleheader day against Philadelphia instead of sitting down, that was the drama of .406.

But let's get one thing straight. Williams had much better overall stats than DiMaggio in 1941. He hit 49 points higher, hit 7 more home runs, walked 145 times, and his on-base percentage of .553 was then an all-time record. Williams deserved the MVP award. But because DiMaggio had the 56-game streak and the Yankees won the pennant by 17 games, he got it.

The final question is, which one's going to be tougher to break? I think that hitting in 56 games in a row would be quite a bit tougher. I think the pressure of 56 is amazing. It's day after day after day after day. The pressure of the last 20 games will be tremendous. Look at Paul Molitor. He had nine billion reporters following him around and he was still 17 games away.

With .406, it's 500 at-bats, a full season's worth. There's never one at-bat—until the last couple of games of the season—that's ultrasignificant. There's also a way that a guy could back into hitting .400. If he got injured and missed a big chunk of the season, it would be a lot easier to hit .400 in, say, 400 at-bats than 600. That's how Tony Gwynn was able to hit .394 during the strike year of 1994.

When you're going for 56, on the other hand, it can come down to that one at-bat in the eighth inning of game 45. And the pitchers will have a lot to say about whether or not you succeed. Remember how mad Pete Rose got at Gene Garber, who ended his streak? Garber was throwing him junk and Rose didn't like it. Rose thought he owed it to him to throw fastballs so he could keep the streak going. But a pitcher is going to do what he can to stop the streak. So if you go 0 for 2, you've got some pressure on you. The pitcher's going to bear down more.

If a guy's hitting .410 in August, is the pitcher going to bear down? No he's not. Not any more than if the guy is hitting, say, .375. And the guy who's going for .400 can afford to have an off day, a night where he's facing a tough lefty and he can't buy a hit. If he goes 0 for 3, he can get right back on track by going 3 for 4 the next day. The guy on a hitting streak can't afford a bad day. So as impressive as both of these feats are, I think I'm going to have to come down on the side of DiMaggio's streak—.406 is tough, 56 games is tougher.

And by the way, science bears me out. Bill James, the baseball statistician, did a study where he programmed a computer to spit out a thousand seasons' worth of random stats based on Joe DiMaggio's career numbers. The computerized Clipper never had a hitting streak longer than 48 games. James did the same thing with Wade Boggs. The results? Cyber Boggs hit over .400 five times.

WHO COULD HIT .400 TODAY?

A .400 hitter? I really think we'll see one before too long. Here's a guy that I like: Todd Helton. He plays in the right ballpark. He hits it to all fields. Plays first base, so there's not too much wear and tear on him. Plays in a good lineup with Larry Walker hitting behind him, so he'll get some good pitches to hit.

Another guy who could do it: Ichiro Suzuki. Completely different player from Helton. He's also a lefty, but he sprays the ball around. He has great speed, so he'll beat out some rollers to shortstop. Safeco's not a great hitter's park—but it cuts down on the home run more than the single. Suzuki does have a tendency to swing at everything, so he doesn't walk nearly as much as Williams did. But with his speed and his ability to make contact, in a lot of ways he's the prototype of a .400 hitter.

Five-on-Five Fantasy

If Cousy and Co. took on Michael's Crew, who'd win?

If we had an NBA time machine, wouldn't you like to see how the guys from the good old days stack up against modern superstars? Mad Dog analyzes the ultimate hoops dream game.

The old school versus the new school in the NBA. Guys in Chuck Taylors playing guys in Air Jordans. Guys with crew cuts playing guys with shaved heads. Guys with tight satin shorts playing against guys who have them hanging below their knees.

But when you got them out on the court, what would happen? Here's my five-on-five fantasy matchup, with all-time all-star teams from two different eras facing off.

Point Guard: I had Bob Cousy on WFAN one Saturday morning, and he told me the first job for a point guard when he crosses midcourt is to think, "How am I going to get a basket for a teammate?" If I were starting a team today and could pick Cousy or Gary Payton, I'm picking Cousy. I think Payton's more physically talented and he's got guts, but Cousy knows how to play the game. And just about the only modern point guard that I have seen who thinks along the same lines as Cousy is John Stockton. I can't have Cousy going against Magic Johnson, because it's just not realistic to think that Cousy could match up with a guy who's 6'8". Cousy and Stockton are kind of the same guy.

Power Forward: I would love to see Bob Pettit against Karl Malone. Bob Pettit is underrated. He played with the now-defunct St. Louis Hawks in the '50s and '60s, and most people think of him as a throwback to the George Mikan era, but he also went up against Bill Russell and Elgin Baylor. To me the premier power forwards of the last forty years are Pettit and Karl Malone. They both come from Louisiana. Both played in small places. And both were overshadowed—Pettit was overshadowed by those

4

great Celtic and Laker teams while Malone was overshadowed by Michael Jordan's Bulls. I don't think you can come up with two power forwards of any generation who match up better. Their statistics are very similar, both in the mid-20s in points, both 13, 12 rebounds a game. They're both so strong and so physical. There'd be a lot of banging down low when these guys got together.

Center: This is easy. You'd have to take Shaquille O'Neal and Wilt Chamberlain. I don't know how you're gonna get away from it. We've already seen Bill Russell and Wilt. Shaq and Wilt are the two most physically imposing players in the history of the league. They're both over three hundred pounds. They are the two most immovable objects, the most unstoppable forces, in the history of the NBA. Now I think Wilt is better than Shaq. I think Wilt is a better athlete than Shaq. I think Wilt has got better moves than Shaq. He's more refined offensively. Wilt averaged fifty points a game for a season, his rebounding totals are unbelievable, and he led the league in assists. I think Wilt is better.

Shaq relies on his physicality more than Wilt did. But part of the reason for that is that Shaq knows that there is nobody out there who can deal with him physically, so he just gets the ball, bulldozes to the basket, and dunks. Against Wilt he couldn't do that, and that would probably make him go to school and develop a little more of an offensive repertoire. Shaq can make a jump shot. He's a better passer than people think. And he can run the floor fairly well, so it'd be interesting to see what he'd do against a guy who could really defend him. They'd be fouling each other all night because neither of them can shoot free throws. Wilt never fouled out of an NBA game, but you have to wonder if that streak would come to an end against Shaq.

Small Forward: I'd like to see Elgin Baylor go up against Julius Erving. I've always fantasized about that matchup. They both played the game above the rim. Baylor was the first guy with hang time, and Erving kind of took that to the next level. I'd pick the big-Afro, takin-off-from-the-top-of-the-key-and-dunking-at-the-ABA-All-Star-Game Julius. He had some flashes of greatness in the NBA, but basketball connoisseurs know that Julius was at his best as a New York Net or even as a Virginia Squire. It would be a great matchup. I think Baylor is a little better, but it would be fun to watch them both try and stop each other in midair.

Shooting Guard: You can't get away from Oscar Robertson and Michael Jordan. I thought of Reggie Miller and Sam Jones, 'cause they're both great shooters and they both made big last-second shots. I would like to have seen that, but it has to be Jordan and Oscar. Jordan's better than Oscar, but I'd like to see Oscar's big butt backing Jordan down in the low box. Jordan would be putting his hand on Robertson's back, crouching over and trying to knock the ball away from Oscar.

I'd like to see how Oscar could use his physicality against Jordan. Both were very tough on teammates, both were ultracompetitive, both hated to lose. Both had a little mean streak in 'em. I give the edge to Jordan; he's probably a better jump shooter than Oscar was—again, I didn't see Oscar much in his prime, either—and Michael's obviously better in the air, a little like Julius himself. But Oscar's physicality in the low box would cause Jordan a lot of trouble. You'd obviously pay a lot of money to see that one.

So if you got these two teams on the same court at the same time, who's going to win? I think Pettit is better than Malone. I think Wilt is a little better than Shaq. Elgin's better than Julius. Jordan's better than Oscar. I guess I'd have to put Cousy a little ahead of Stockton, but it's close. Who would win that? I think the problem that the new team has is that Erving doesn't match up well against Elgin, so I think the old guys would win.

If it's close in the fourth quarter, 95-95, 46 seconds left, what happens? At crunch time the old guys would have plenty of options. They could go to Wilt if he was making free throws, and they certainly could go to Elgin and probably to Pettit.

For the other team, Jordan's going to take the last shot. Stockton could shoot it, but he's not going to. They're not going to Malone, and Malone's not going to want it anyway. They are not going to go to Shaq, not going to Julius, and that's where they're in a little trouble. So as that clock winds down, everyone in the building knows that Jordan is going to shoot the ball. Especially Oscar Robertson, who's going to be right in his face.

The Passer or the Punisher?

Who's more important, a dominating linebacker or
a great quarterback?

Do you want the quarterback who's going to hit the open receiver? Or do
you want the guy who's going to hit the quarterback? Mad Dog gets to the
bottom of football's perpetual choice between offense and defense.

The NFL has changed a lot in the past couple of decades. Twenty-five years ago you didn't need that dominating linebacker, and now teams build their whole defense around that kind of guy.

So if you were looking for the ultimate impact player on defense, in a kind of all-time fantasy draft pick—who would you choose? Would you go with Dick Butkus? Or Lawrence Taylor? Butkus was the prototypical old-school linebacker. Tough as nails, intimidating, completely stymied your ground game. LT was the first of a new breed, a guy who was always trying to penetrate, constantly trying to create havoc in the backfield.

No offense to that old Monster of the Midway, but I'm taking Taylor. Butkus didn't make game-breaking plays like LT. LT would sack the quarterback, pick up the fumble, and run 80 yards. LT would make a pass interception and run 83 yards down the sideline. You didn't see Butkus do those kinds of things. Butkus was about holding backs to a one-yard gain, while Taylor's specialty was sacking quarterbacks for an eight-yard loss. I'm not trying to say that Butkus didn't keep offensive coordinators up at night as they prepared to play the Bears—he did, no question about it— but LT was so disruptive, so intent on getting to the quarterback, that you had to put two or three guys on him. Which in turn opened up plays for guys like Carl Banks and Leonard Marshall. Butkus and LT were the best ever at their respective positions, so if you want to play a conservative stop-the-run defense, you pick the consummate middle linebacker, Butkus. If you want to play a wreak-havoc defense, you pick Mr. Outside, LT. I'm going with the havoc defense.

Here's the crux of the argument. You could put Butkus on a lousy team and he'd be the great middle linebacker, but the team would still be lousy.

If you put LT on a bad team he would win a couple of games by himself just by making individual plays.

Now LT was the MVP of the league. But if I were drafting and they were both on the board, would I take him over Joe Montana? No way. Always take the QB. The first thing is that the defense by its nature has to react. Which means that offensive coordinators can find a way to neutralize LT—or at least slow him down, by adjusting the game plan, changing formations, throwing double and triple teams at him. Montana on the other hand is going to get his hands on the ball on every play. He can set the tone of a game in a way that even the greatest defender can't. No matter how great LT is, he can't lead a 94-yard drive.

The other point: In the NFL, quarterback is the hardest position to fill. There just aren't many good ones to go around. Linebackers like LT aren't a dime a dozen, but there are other ways to create similar havoc with your defense. You can get a couple of specialist pass rushers. You can even get a cornerback—a Deion Sanders type—who can change a game around. With a quarterback you've either got a good one or you don't. And in every game the quarterback is the most important player on the field.

And one last issue. How many championships did Joe Montana win? He won four. How many did LT win? He won two. I love LT. I love Montana. But I'm picking Montana.

Back Nine Nirvana

Who'd win golf's ultimate match play challenge,
Ben Hogan or Tiger Woods?

Is golf a gentleman's game? Maybe. But it's a little less genteel when it's just you, the ball, the hole . . . and another guy breathing down your neck. Mad Dog chooses golf's two greatest competitors ever and pits them head to head.

If you're setting up the ultimate fantasy golf round—two players, any course, anytime—who are you going to pick? I'm going to go with Tiger Woods and Ben Hogan because there are no two players who've been better at the top of their games. Take Hogan. Between 1946 and 1953 he won nine of the sixteen majors that he played. In 1953 he won three of the four Grand Slam events—the Masters, the British, and the U.S. Open. No other player, not Jack Nicklaus, not Arnold Palmer, was ever that dominant. Until Tiger. So it's a perfect matchup.

Where are we going to play it? I won't do it at Augusta because Tiger's length is too much of a factor there. On those short par fives on the back nine, he's hitting an 8-iron in. Hogan was not a long hitter, but he was a long iron player. I know it sounds wacky, that he didn't drive it unbelievably far, but he did hit a 2-iron far. So I'm going to pick a course where Ben matches up with Tiger, a place where you don't have to hit the ball nine billion miles. I'm going to do it on a U.S. Open course, a place where conservative play is important, where accuracy off the tee and solid approach shots onto the green are rewarded.

So let's do it at Pebble Beach. It's the best course in America. It's Jack Nicklaus's favorite course, and it's a course where the distance isn't intimidating. I've played there, and except for one par five on the back nine, you don't have to go long off the tee. I shot an 88 there hitting 5-woods off the tee. But Tiger can play this course. He won the U.S. Open here, he was 11 or 12 under par, and I don't think anyone else even broke par.

When? Let's do it in 1949, before Hogan's injury in that terrible car accident.

Tiger? Any time in the last five years, you pick. I'm picking these two guys because of their mental toughness. Hogan was a tremendous competitor. He was the first guy who worked out, the first guy who really practiced. He hung out at the driving range for hours and hours and hours. He hit balls until his hands bled. He was a self-made player.

Tiger has more natural ability than Hogan, but you ask anyone who covers golf, and Tiger's the same kind of worker. You go to the driving range and no matter whether he shot a 65 or a 75 the day before, he's the first to get there and the last to leave. So the work ethic is equal.

And Hogan isn't Phil Mickelson. He isn't David Duval. Ben Hogan did not beat himself. Against a lot of the guys today, Tiger has them playing for second before the tournament starts. Hogan, paired up with Tiger in a big tournament, up by a stroke or down by a stroke on the back nine, is not going to hit the ball into the water. He's not going to four-putt a green. He's not going to play scared golf, and he's not going to play stupid golf.

And Tiger Woods is not going to be able to stare down Ben Hogan. Hogan was a tough SOB. There's that classic story where he won the 1951 U.S. Open by two strokes. Clayton Heafner, who finished second, comes up to him and says, "Boy, Ben, great tournament." And Hogan says, "Yeah, not bad. How did you do?" The guy finished *two strokes behind*.

But Tiger's an assassin, too. He's got a little bit of Michael Jordan in him. He wants to rip your heart out. If he sees a chance to make the tough birdie, he's going to take it. If he needs to make a long putt to save par, he'll drain it.

Hogan and Tiger on the back nine, both in their prime—who's going to win? I think Tiger will win. I think it'll come down to shotmaking, and I think he's a better player. He has more natural talent. I think he might have an easier second shot onto a green. He'd be putting for birdies from 12 feet, and Hogan would be putting for birdies from 18 feet. I think sooner or later Tiger's going to make a couple and Ben won't. But would I love to be in the gallery to see it? You bet I would.

The Ultimate Baseball Box Seats

One game, four tickets, and a time machine.
Who would you watch a game with?

It's the classic cocktail party question. If you could hold the ultimate dinner party, would you invite Michelangelo or Genghis Khan? Forget dinner, we're watching baseball. Sit back and find out which all-time greats are going to the game with Mad Dog.

When there's a really huge game, especially one involving my team, I want to be left alone. I want to pace. I want to think. I want to suffer in silence. So that's why when I'm picking a game that's important, but not life-and-death, I like a good, juicy September pennant race game.

Where are we going to watch? Ebbets Field. I want to be in Brooklyn during the Golden Age of Baseball. This is the park that's got the most charm—the Bleacher Bums, the band, the place crammed with thirty-three thousand guys in white shirts.

The first guy I want to watch the game with is Christy Mathewson. Why Christy Mathewson? Because he was college-educated—a Bucknell guy—so you can have a conversation with him. Ask him a question about pitching, and he's not going to spit tobacco juice in a cup, he's going to talk baseball with you. In a lot of ways, Christy was the first big baseball star. At the turn of the century, baseball was sort of a ragamuffin game. People didn't really respect ballplayers, but Mathewson made the game proper. He was a gentleman, a military hero. Everybody loved the Big Six.

And he was sharp. People forget, but he also uncovered the Black Sox scandal. He was analyzing games for the *New York Times* and during the Series he sensed that something was amiss. He was one of the first to see the handwriting on the wall, and that opened up the debate about the 1919 World Series. And there's so much to talk about with him. You can talk about John McGraw, whom he played for. You can talk about Honus Wagner, whom he pitched against. You can talk about Merkle's Boner, which he saw with his own two eyes. He was there for all of that.

The second guy? Leo Durocher. He wasn't much of a player, but boy did he see a lot of baseball history. He was Babe Ruth's roommate on those great Yankee teams of the late '20s. The story goes that the Babe pummeled him pretty good after he discovered that he stole his money and his watch. He was the captain of the '34 Gashouse Gang Cardinals, with all those great players like Pepper Martin, Ducky Medwick, and Rogers Hornsby. He managed the Brooklyn Dodgers in the 1940s, with Jackie Robinson, Pee Wee Reese, and Roy Campanella. Durocher was the first big-league manager to write Willie Mays's name on a lineup card. He managed the '51 Giants through that classic pennant race, coming up with the idea of setting up a telescope in the outfield to steal signs. We could ask him if Bobby Thompson knew what pitch was coming when he took Ralph Branca deep. (Although I don't think he did.) And he managed the '69 Cubs. We could ask him about the black cat at Shea Stadium. It doesn't get any better than that.

Number three, you need a broadcaster. The guy that I'm going to pick is Jack Buck. He was a tremendous storyteller, a part of baseball history for fifty years. Jack Buck could make everybody laugh. One time he said to me, "Dog, are you married yet?" No, Jack, I'm not. "How many kids do you have?" He's got a keen mind, but he never took himself too seriously. He'll be sitting there with a bourbon and ice, just keeping it loose and keeping the conversation going. I just loved the guy.

For the seventh-inning stretch, I want one guy to pop in and say hello. That's Sandy Koufax. You know he likes Buck, you know he can relate to Mathewson, and you know he hates Durocher. Let's face it, he's not going to talk about himself. But I'd love to hear him talk pitching with Mathewson. Let him come in the seventh, and let's hope it's not a 1-2-3 inning. But he shouldn't stay more than an inning. More than that and we'd be bored with him and Sandy would be bored with us.

Let's see, Mathewson, Durocher, Buck . . . and Russo. We've got a pitcher, a hitter and manager, a broadcaster, and between us we've seen just about every bit of baseball in the twentieth century. So wipe off the seats, bring on the dogs, pour us some cold ones, and let's hope for a fifteen-inning game. With lots of pitching changes.

OUTSIDE THE BOX

Here are some guys I respect, but I'm not too sure I'd want to watch a baseball game with them. Babe Ruth would be fooling around too much, eating hot dogs, drinking beer. Lou Gehrig? He'd just be too serious. Joe DiMaggio. Too aloof. Willie Mays would be so busy telling you how great he was that he wouldn't be paying attention to the game. I'll stick with Mathewson, Durocher, and Buck, thank you.

Off the Record

There's a right way and a wrong way to get your name in the record books. What are the rules when you're chasing a record?

Call them style points. When you look at a record book, don't you assign some mental asterisks to those athletes who took a shortcut on the way to a record? The Dog plays Ford Frick and talks about how records should be broken.

To a serious sports fan, records are sacred. No two ways around it. They know the numbers by heart, and they watch day after day as a player gets closer to breaking one. In my opinion, when an athlete is trying to break a record or set some milestone, it should happen in the pace and the rhythm of the game, in the context of winning and losing. Winning comes first, then the record. So when coaches or players start cutting corners, changing the way they play the game just to establish a record, good fans get all bent out of shape, and they should.

It's been happening for a long time. A couple of times Lou Gehrig had a bad back, so he batted leadoff and then left the game in the first inning so he could keep his consecutive games streak going. Sure, he was breaking his own record, but that's still probably not the right thing to do. The idea is to play the game, not just to get one at bat and leave. If Cal Ripken had done that while he was trying to break Lou Gehrig's record, you'd have a major problem with it. And maybe today we'd have more discussions about whether you should let Lou Gehrig get up there in the top of the first inning and take him out of the game in order to keep the streak going.

I'm going to give you a few recent examples that really ticked me off of coaches and players finagling to get to some milestone.

Nykesha on Crutches: Remember a couple of years ago what the U. Conn women's basketball team did with Nykesha Sales? She tore up her ACL and they let her come back in the last game of the season. The two coaches and the players on both teams conspired to let her get a layup at the beginning of the game to set the all-time U. Conn scoring record. That's bogus. It doesn't matter that this is women's sports. If she's hurt and she can't play, she can't play. She had a great career, and getting a record that way only cheapens her other accomplishments. It's like letting Minnie Minoso come back when he's sixty years old so he can say he played in an extra decade. It's the wrong thing to do.

Strahan's Hacky Sack: Then there's Brett Favre a couple of years ago, handing the sack record to Michael Strahan. Again, totally bogus. He rolled out right, but he wasn't even trying to pass the ball. He just wanted to give Strahan the single-season sack record because that's his friend and the game was over anyway. He figured, "No harm. No foul." Wrong. Strahan had the whole damn game to break that sack record. To their credit, the Packer offensive line did a good job of making sure that didn't happen and then Favre gave it away when the game was all but over. That just should not happen. And Strahan got pretty excited about a sack that he knew was bogus.

Dejuan's Hollow Hundred: This sort of stuff happens even in high school. Dejuan Wagner's coach let him score 100 points in a game against a local tech school. The game's over. You've won. It's a blowout. Leaving your best player in there to score 100 points is just unsportsmanlike, especially on the high school level. It's running up the score. In the NBA, when Wilt scored 100 points, it was professionals going against professionals. That's a little different. A lot of Knick players were upset that all the Philadelphia Warriors did was feed the ball to Wilt. At the same time, a lot of Warrior players have complained about the fact that the Knick players were trying to run out the clock so that the Warriors got fewer possessions and Wilt had fewer chances to score. Both sides were guilty there. But letting Wagner—or Lisa Leslie, who did the same thing—score 100 points in a high school game is wrong.

Wade's Day of Rest: And then there's the time back in '86 when Wade Boggs was trying to beat out Don Mattingly for the batting title. He's ahead by a few points, so he figures his best chance to win is by sitting out the last couple of games against the Yankees. He claimed he wanted to make sure he was healthy for the postseason. That's a bunch of garbage.

If that game had had any importance in the pennant race, then Boggs would've played. If Mattingly had gotten six hits in his first seven at-bats, you know darn well Boggs would've put himself into the lineup. Well, the batting title is important enough that Boggs should've played. Especially in Boston. Ted Williams played the doubleheader against the Philadelphia A's in 1941 when he could have guaranteed that he would hit .400 by taking the day off. He got six hits in eight at-bats and ended up at .406. He had everything to lose, almost nothing to gain, and he went out and did it anyway. That's the way you win a batting title—the way Ted Williams did.

Denny's BP Fastball: And finally, we come to Denny McLain laying in a batting practice fastball to Mickey Mantle so Mick could pass Jimmie Foxx for third place on the all-time home run list. I don't care if the game is over. I don't care what the scenario is. It is not an All-Star Game. It's a regular season game. Let Mickey hit the home run the right way. He's a Hall of Famer. He doesn't need charity. As it turned out, Mickey hit a couple more so he ended up with 536 for his career, but what McLain did was wrong. It trivializes Mantle's great career, treating him that way. When you think about the record book instead of the scoreboard, you disrespect the game. It's as simple as that.

DOING THE RIGHT THING

Here are a couple of instances in which I thought the players and managers played it right.

In 2001, Padres catcher Ben Davis caught all kinds of heat for bunting to try to break up Curt Schilling's perfect game. In my opinion, that was the right play. It was a 2-0 game in the bottom of the eighth inning and Davis bunted. The game wasn't over yet. If he gets on, that brings the tying run to the plate. Now if it were 6-0, that's a different story. Nobody bunts when they're six runs down. That's not part of the game. That's being a pain in the ass.

Diamondback manager Bob Brenly got all upset at Bruce Bochy, the Padre skipper, about it. It was funny because a few months later we had Bochy on

(continued)

15

(continued from previous page)

during the World Series and he was really killing Brenly about bringing in Byung-Hyun Kim in both game four and game five. And it didn't dawn on me until later that the reason he killed Brenly so much is because he was ticked off at Brenly for getting on him about Ben Davis.

And in 2002, Luis Castillo of the Florida Marlins got his hitting streak up to thirty-five games. It was the bottom of the ninth inning and they were playing Detroit, and the Marlins rallied from 4-1 down to tie the game. Florida had a man on second and one out. To his credit Marlin manager Jeff Torborg let Tim Raines swing away. After the runner advanced on a wild pitch, Raines won the game with a sac fly, leaving Castillo on deck when the winning run scored. If Torborg had told Raines to take it all the way—and he walked or struck out—Castillo would have gotten another at bat. But Torborg did the right thing and went for the win. But if Raines had made an out, making it two out and a man on third, Luis Pujols, manager of the Tigers, said he would have walked Castillo to set up a force at second, thus preventing him from extending the streak. And I give him credit for that. No, the Tigers weren't going anywhere, but it's still June, and you've got to try to win the game. Even though the Marlins won the game, Castillo was so upset that he didn't get another at-bat that Torborg had to go out and calm him down. The way I see it, Castillo had four chances to keep the streak going in his first four at-bats.

Dog on Ice

How would pro hockey be different if Mr. Russo were
NHL commissioner?

You know the old joke—I went to a fight and a hockey game broke out. It's not all that funny. Mad Dog makes some suggestions for cleaning up—and streamlining—the game.

For starters, I want to say that NHL commissioner Gary Bettman has done some things that you like. He struck a good deal with the union on free agency and compensation. In the NHL, a player can't be an unrestricted free agent until he's thirty-one years of age, and before that, any team that signs a restricted free agent has to give up as many as five draft picks as compensation. And in the NHL, draft picks are gold. As a result of that, there is almost no movement. While it still hasn't solved the competitive balance problem completely, (as we'll probably see when there's a strike after the 2004 season) small-market teams like Montreal, Calgary, and Edmonton have a chance to be competitive. Still, the game itself could be better. Here's what I'd do if I were hockey's head honcho.

Shorten the Season: The NHL season is way too long. Training camp opens in mid-September. I'm at the beach and I'm reading stories about the Islanders opening up preseason in Lake Placid. I'm at a playoff game in baseball and the NHL regular season has started already. Even the NBA's not that stupid. The NHL has no off-season. They finish the playoffs in mid-June and open camps three months later in September. They don't have a window that's all theirs. If they opened up later, after baseball season is over and with football in its regular season, they would have a time where they can get a little buzz going.

And there are simply too many games. You can't play eighty-two games. Nobody pays attention to the NHL regular season. The games mean nothing. In the NHL regular season, there's no correlation between regular season and postseason success. Look at Carolina. They finished seventh in points in the conference, but they got the hot goalie and away they went to the finals. So I'd cut the regular season by about fifteen games or so—play sixty-five regular season games and start the season in late October just after the World Series and before the NBA opens.

Streamline the Playoffs: On the same note, way too many teams make the playoffs. It's a little better than it was—it used to be 16 of 21, now it's 16 of 30 teams—but you can't have more than 50 percent of your teams making the postseason. That's not the idea. In baseball it's 8 of 30, in football it's 12 of 32, and even 12 of 32 is too much. If it were a perfect world and you gave me the NHL job and I could do anything I wanted, I'd slash the number of playoff teams from 16 down to 8. Top four in each conference instead of the top eight in each conference. That would not only shorten the postseason but also put a little juice back in the regular season, because some good teams would be watching the playoffs on television. And I would make it best-of-five in the first round, like Major League Baseball. The NHL becomes such a grind in the postseason with game after game of incredible physicality, that I think shortening the first round would be a plus.

Go to the Games: If you're going to allow pros in the Olympics (see "The Lord of the Rings," page 56), I would definitely send NHL players to the Olympics every four years. I think it's worth it. That Canada-U.S. game at Salt Lake City in 2002 did a 10.5 or 11 rating. That's a great rating. They don't get that for a regular season game. I understand that in Nagano the games were on at three in the morning. I understand that you have to blow off the regular season for a couple of weeks. But the bottom line is that hockey is a sport that needs to do anything it can possibly do to attract publicity. It needs to introduce the casual fan to some new stars. It needs to get eyeballs in front of the screen. Bottom line: Chris Russo is going to watch Olympic hockey in February. Chris Russo is not watching the Kings play Vancouver in February.

Open Up the Game: What I would do if I were Gary Bettman is open up the game more. Play the game the way they do in the Olympics, where the fourth-line guy doesn't get a chance to go out there and be a goon. I would figure out a way to give the stars of my league a better chance to shine. If that means eliminating the red line as they did in the Olympics, I'd do that. Letting those two-line passes go? I would do that. And I'd change the rule so that icing kicks in as soon as the puck crosses the line.

And the game is a lot more fun to watch, more freewheeling, when the players have more space. Olympic ice is a little larger than NHL ice, and if I have to get rid of a couple of rows of seats in order to expand the rink, then I'll do that, too. It would help the game.

Get Tough on Goons: Finally, I want to eliminate the chippiness, which is a much bigger problem in the postseason than in the regular season. There is too little regard for your opponent's welfare in the NHL postseason, whether it's late hits, crashing people into the boards, killing the goalie, or taking out a guy's knees. When something like this happens—and it always does—the NHL is incredibly soft in its discipline. "Oh, boys will be boys." That's their mentality.

Here's my answer: Let's say Tie Domi knocks out Scott Niedermayer on a dirty hit in game six in a first-round series between the Devils and the Maple Leafs. And because of Domi's illegal hit, Niedermayer can't play for twelve consecutive playoff games. Well then, Domi has to miss twelve playoff games, too. If the Maple Leafs get eliminated in the next game, Domi misses the first eleven playoff games of *next year* for the Leafs—or whatever team he's on. That's going to make Domi think twice before taking a cheap shot. And make his coach think twice about sending him out to settle a score with thirty-eight seconds left.

There's got to be a premium on playoff hockey compared to regular season hockey. The NHL doesn't like to do that because that almost admits that the regular season is a waste of time. But if players do nasty, dirty things, you have to punish them severely. This is hockey, not professional wrestling.

CAN DO THIS

I realize that Bettman has his hands tied. I know that he'll give me lots of economic reasons why they have to play 82 games, or why 16 teams have to make the playoffs, or why you can't extend the ice surface because you would eliminate some seats. But he can't give me any reasons for allowing the chippiness in the postseason. Or for not changing the rules to open up the game. The NHL doesn't have to wait for me to become commissioner. Bettman could do those things tomorrow—and the game would be better for it.

Sports on the Silver Screen

Why do most sports movies stink?

Actors who throw like girls. Directors who don't understand the game. And stories that play fast and loose with the facts. It's enough to make you rent Fried Green Tomatoes. *Mad Dog explains why he's got reel problems with most sports movies.*

I'm not big on sports movies. I'd rather watch a Marlins-Brewers game than go to most sports movies. Why? A couple of reasons. First, the subjects they choose don't grab me. Ty Cobb's not very interesting. He's a bad guy, a nasty bigot. I don't need to see a movie about him. Jake LaMotta? I know that *Raging Bull* had Robert De Niro and he gained fifty pounds, and everybody loved Joe Pesci and everything else, but Jake LaMotta was a great fighter whose biggest claim to fame was that he hung tough with Sugar Ray Robinson. Jake LaMotta is not an appealing figure and he probably took a dive for the mob in a fight in the late 1940s. Do I need to sit there in a movie house for three hours listening to two guys cussing each other out? I can see Joe Pesci in about twenty movies, and he does the same thing in every single one. Martin Scorsese or no Martin Scorsese, that movie did nothing for me.

Then there are those "feel good" sports movies like *Rudy*. I liked *Rudy* for what it was—it's a nice story and it makes you feel happy—but he was such a nondescript figure on that Notre Dame football team. He played one play in a blowout. Or *The Rookie* with Dennis Quaid. I know that people loved the movie, but he barely pitched. *Bagger Vance*? Forget it. *Tin Cup*? A waste of time.

And too many directors play fast and loose with the facts. I wouldn't go see *Hurricane* because the director in that film didn't do a good job. The movie is filled with fights that show Hurricane Carter winning, while everybody who saw the particular fights says that Hurricane lost. The problem with going to a sports movie is that you're at the mercy of what the director wants to show you, and nine times out of ten the director is not a big sports fan.

When they get the details wrong, it drives me crazy. *Field of Dreams* I liked a lot. But Joe Jackson was batting right-handed in the movie. Why would you spend millions of dollars on a movie based on a book called *Shoeless Joe*, and go back and create this whole story about the Black Sox scandal, and then have the guy get up from the wrong side of the plate? How do you make a mistake like that?

And what's worse are movies like *The Natural*, where they turn the sports scenes into cartoons. I liked the old-time baseball scenes, but then they made a joke of it by having a guy die crashing into the scoreboard and by having Redford hit a home run that knocks the scoreboard down. I can't take that. Okay, I'm done ranting. There are some good sports movies out there, and here are a few that I can watch any day.

The Pride of the Yankees: Phenomenal movie: eleven Academy Award nominations, deserved every one. It's sad and it hits you. How about the great scene of Gary Cooper walking into that very dank hospital room with that old-time doctor? It gives you goose bumps. Cooper does a perfect job as Gehrig—quiet, unassuming—and Teresa Wright gave a moving performance as his wife. It's a classic and that's all there is to it.

Eight Men Out: John Sayles directed it and did a good job. I had him on the air on WMCA in New York the Saturday after the movie came out. The only problem is that it's an insider movie. I took my parents to the movie and I found out pretty quick that you'd better know who Chick Gandil is before you go in there and see it.

Bull Durham: I loved the story of Crash Davis and the minor leagues. It's got a little bit of everything: big stars, a perfect town, and a great story about the hotshot rookie and the wily old vet. *Bull Durham* is a tremendous movie. And because Kevin Costner's in it, your wife will sit down and watch it with you.

The Champion: Kirk Douglas's tour de force about a boxer who will trample on anyone to be middleweight champion of the world caught all the backroom drama of boxing in the '40s and showcased all its brutality. One criticism: Douglas was a wrestler while at St. Lawrence, and he looks like a wrestler trying to box in this movie.

Hoosiers: Excellent. Gene Hackman is great as the coach, and the film captured the essence of high school basketball in the early '50s in Indiana: the cornfields, the bus trips, the small gyms. It's funny about Milan High School, though. I've had a couple of people, Oscar Robertson included, tell me that Milan High School was a very good team year after year. So the gargantuan upset depicted in the movie is a little misleading, because the team was better than you think it was.

61*: Billy Crystal knew his baseball backward and forward and made no mistakes in the actual depiction of the home run chase between Mickey Mantle and Roger Maris. It's a classic story about their friendship and their rivalry. He also sweated the details, having Tom Candiotti play Hoyt Wilhelm. My wife and my parents loved it. It's a great movie.

Ladies of the Court

Topspin, topspin, on the ball.
Who's the greatest women's tennis player of them all?

She's got a racket. And she knows how to use it. Mad Dog looks back at the greatest women tennis players of all time and comes up with his own all-time top five.

W ho's the best women's tennis player of all time? Well, I'm not going to go back and tell you it's Suzanne Lenglen, or Maureen Connolly, or even Althea Gibson. They were all great players, I'm sure, but 1) I never saw them play, and 2) If there is no depth now in women's tennis (see "Can't Buy Me Love," page 79), how much depth was there fifty, sixty, seventy years ago?

I'm ranking the players I saw, players who played most of their careers in the Open era from 1968 on. Here's my personal top five, in reverse order.

5. Margaret Court: It may seem like I'm slighting Court here—she did win a record twenty-four major singles championships and two Grand Slams, one in singles and one in mixed doubles. Her career is a lot like Roy

Emerson's; they both won so many Australian Opens—Court won eleven, back in the days when nobody played there. You know what else hurts Margaret Court? She was psyched out by Bobby Riggs. A fifty-five-year-old man kicked her fanny. That puts her down a peg in my book.

4. Chris Evert: Evert has longevity going for her as well as her great rivalry with Martina. She was an incredible competitor, so consistent, never gave away a big point. But she lacked that big weapon—her serve was a cream puff and she didn't hit her groundstrokes that hard.

3. Steffi Graf: I think Steffi is a better player than Chrissie is. Graf had a couple of weapons that Evert didn't have. She had a better first serve, a little more lethal off the ground—not as good on the backhand side, but a much better forehand. Plus she won the Grand Slam back in 1988, and won more major singles titles—22 to Evert's 18—than anyone besides Court. I put Graf ahead of Evert, but it's close.

2. Billie Jean King: Billie Jean's my number two. Part of it is an intangible. She's the founder of the women's tennis tour as we know it today, and one of the pioneers in women's sports. She beat Riggs in that Battle of the Sexes match. But she was also a great player. Her combativeness, competitiveness. I can remember the 1975 Wimbledon final where she beat Evonne Goolagong Cawley in about nineteen minutes 6-0, 6-1. I love her volleys, and she was a tremendous net player. And she was a great doubles player with Rosie Casals, and helped Owen Davidson win the mixed doubles Grand Slam.

1. Martina Navratilova: The best player that I've ever seen, top to bottom, was Martina Navratilova. Her serve is the most lethal weapon of any of the top players. When Martina was in trouble, she could serve her way out of it. She had so much confidence in her serve, love-40, 4-5, third set of the Wimbledon final, she's still serving and volleying.

We all know about the nine Wimbledons. But she was also easily the best doubles player of all time, winning a total of 39 Grand Slam titles. She's forty-six and still winning doubles matches on the tour against women half her age.

Martina also had a great hunger. She was a self-made player. She came over here a little, chubby player as a sixteen-year-old and made herself great, lifting weights, rebuilding her body with Team Navratilova, really raising the bar in the sport. At one point in her great rivalry with Chris Evert, she was down 20-4. By the time she was done, she turned that around to lead 43-37. That says something. Navratilova's the best player I ever saw.

NOT SOLD ON SELES

I can't put Monica Seles in my top five, but for a two- or three-year period, Seles was a tremendous tennis player, winning seven of the eight Grand Slams she played. If she doesn't get stabbed in 1993, she probably wins a lot of the majors that Graf and Martina Hingis win over the next few years. One knock I have on Seles, and I'm going to put her down a peg, is that in 1991 she won the French and begged off playing Wimbledon allegedly with a leg injury. "I'm hurt. I need a break." If you are an all-time great and you can walk, you play Wimbledon. It's the most important tennis tournament in the world. And I love Seles. I can remember watching her one time in the early 1990s in Mahwah, N.J. It's in the middle of a 95-degree day at an exhibition that doesn't even count in the rankings, and she was out there practicing for three or four hours in the hot sun, gutting it out. Still, in my book, you've got to play Wimbledon every chance you get, and Seles did not. And I'm not putting Venus or Serena Williams up there . . . yet. By early 2003, they had won nine major singles titles between them, and you've got to expect that they'll win a lot more before they're through.

The NBA All-Underrated Team

Which pro hoopsters don't get their props?

You're choosing up sides in the fantasy game to end all fantasy games. Larry Bird's taken and so's Bob McAdoo. Who's your small forward? Mad Dog tells you who's got game but not fame.

I f you look at pro basketball players today, there's so much publicity, so much hype, so much of an MTV aspect, it's hard to be underrated. There are a few guys who might not get the credit they deserve: Alvin Williams, Malik Rose, maybe Bobby Jackson.

But when you're looking back, you have to ask yourself, "What do you mean by underrated?" He was not the best player on his team, obviously. And if you ask a pretty decent basketball fan about this player, he might have to think for a second about how good he was. But the insiders in the league—the players, the coaches, the scouts—knew how good this guy was. I've tried to come up with players who didn't make a lot of all-star teams, didn't make the Hall of Fame, but they played on winning teams— how can you really be underrated if your team wins twenty games? Maybe he was overshadowed by a Hall of Famer on his own team, got traded a few times, kind of got lost in the shuffle, but when he was on the court he made a difference. Here's my eight-man rotation:

Michael Cooper: He was overshadowed by Magic Johnson and James Worthy, and Kareem and Norm Nixon and Byron Scott, and even his coach, Pat Riley. He never scored a ton of points—people always think of him as a defensive specialist, the kind of guy who comes in to shut down Isiah Thomas or Rolando Blackman. But he always played in the fourth quarter and he made big shots. I'll never forget the fifth game of a seven-game series against Utah in '88, he made a huge fourth-quarter basket, and if he didn't drain it, the Lakers lose the series and don't win back-to-back championships.

Andrew Toney: A tremendous two guard. Toney didn't play long, he only made one all-star team, and he was overshadowed by his teammates

Moses Malone and Julius Erving. And that Sixers team was always kind of overshadowed in the Eastern Conference by those great Celtic teams of the 1980s. Still, Toney had a five-year period where he averaged 13, 16, 20, 20, and 18 points a game. He was a 50 percent career shooter in the regular season, and 48 percent in the postseason. He was called the Boston Strangler, and that says something about his clutch play.

Joe Dumars: He was kind of overshadowed by Isiah Thomas. Did a little bit of everything, made very few mistakes. He averaged 16 points and 5 assists in the playoffs and was 85 percent at the line. He was the youngest player in that group, and once those guys—Bill Laimbeer, Isiah, Vinnie Johnson—got old, you kind of forgot about him. But he held the fort down and nursed Grant Hill along. To me, he's a Hall of Famer.

Dennis Johnson: Another tremendous player. Great defensive player, a five-rebound-a-game guy, which you like to see, not a great shooter, but he wasn't afraid to take big shots and make them. He's not a Hall of Famer but he should be. There are two things that taint DJ's legacy—his rep as a locker room "cancer" in Phoenix, and his 0-for-14 shooting in game seven of the 1978 finals. The other side: Larry Bird called him the best teammate he ever played with, and that tells you something right off. When Bird made that great steal against Isiah in game five of that '87 series against the Pistons, who was on the other end? Johnson going to the basket for the layup. That's typical DJ. We all remember the great pass by Bird, but we forget who caught the ball and scored. That just about sums up Dennis Johnson.

Jeff Ruland: Ruland played only five years, and played a lot in just three of those years. But people don't remember how good a player Jeff Ruland was. He took a little heat for that nickname Johnny Most gave him—he was McFilthy and Rick Mahorn was McNasty. In a three-year period Ruland averaged 14 points, 9 rebounds; 19 points, 11 rebounds; and 22 and 12 rebounds. The Bullets were bad, the nickname hurt him. But he could play.

Jack Sikma: He played for two very good teams, Seattle and Milwaukee. Never missed any games, always hit his free throws. He had that great jump shot, where he released the ball high over his head. He was good for 15 points and 10 rebounds a night. I love Sikma. He played at a small college—Illinois Wesleyan—where you didn't hear a lot about him, so he didn't come into the NBA with a lot of fanfare. A lot of these guys were the same—Andrew Toney from Southwest Louisiana, Dennis Johnson from Pepperdine, Dumars played in Louisiana somewhere, Cooper went to New Mexico for crying out loud. A lot of these underrated guys came from places where you didn't see them play in college.

Jeff Hornacek: He was a very important player on the Suns with Tom Chambers and Kevin Johnson, and he was a very important player on those Stockton-Malone Utah teams. He had some defensive liabilities, but he was smart, made his free throws, made big shots, was a good passer, knew how to play the game. He averaged 16 a game in the regular season. He can play on my team any day.

Bobby Dandridge: The king of the underrated players. Bobby Dandridge was an incredible player. He played in only four all-star games and made only one start in them. Played on two very good teams and won two championships. He played on the Bucks teams and was overshadowed by Oscar Robertson and Kareem. He didn't practice a lot. He adopted the "old bar of soap" theory: The more you use the soap the quicker it wears away. He was silky smooth. He played on those good Bullets teams and was overshadowed by guys like Wes Unseld and Elvin Hayes. He averaged 18.5 in the regular season, 7 rebounds, and shot 48 percent. In the postseason? Even better—20.1 a game and 8 rebounds. In the year that the Bullets won the championship, he destroyed Julius Erving in the Eastern Conference finals. Erving couldn't guard him. You don't realize what a player Bobby D was.

Let's Do It Again

Is instant replay an annoyance or an educational tool?

Let's see the reverse angle. The super slo-mo. The catcher cam. And the high overhead shot from the Pets.com blimp. Mad Dog speaks in praise of replays, telestrators, and expert analysis.

Go to your television and flip on ESPN Classic. Hopefully you'll find a baseball playoff game from the mid-'70s or maybe an NBA finals matchup from the early '80s. If you can get over the culture shock of seeing those Afros, mustaches, and skinny bodies, pay attention to the production quality—or lack thereof. It looks like a local high school game on the cable access channel. Resolution worthy of a surveillance tape, only a couple of camera angles, and replays that are like the food in that Borscht Belt restaurant joke—pretty bad and not nearly enough.

Turn on the game today and it's a different story. Not only do you feel like you're there, sometimes you see more of what's going on than the players do. On the technical front the networks are trying to outdo each other, and that has helped the broadcasts immensely. More cameras. New angles. And some pretty slick visual aids.

For example, I love the overhead camera behind the goal in a hockey game. On a power play in a tight playoff game late in regulation, you can see the action unfold before your eyes and watch the goal being scored. Great work. Even the in-car camera in NASCAR captures some pretty amazing crash footage. I love the first down bar in the NFL, too. It's improved the game immeasurably. You can think about the strategy and the drama of the game instead of just trying to concentrate on the yard markers. It costs money—$50,000 per game—but it's well worth it.

And I just can't live without instant replay. I think that's the one aspect of any sport that you really miss when you're at a stadium or an arena. You never see a controversial replay at an NFL game. You don't see the replay at a baseball game, especially when the umpire makes a bad call that goes against the home team. They don't want to have a riot on their hands, but still. And even when you do get the replay, you've still got to watch a screen that's 500 feet away in centerfield or in the upper reaches of an arena.

On television it's a different story. You want five different replays? You've got it. The amazing thing is that they've got so many camera angles today that the producer can almost always show you the conclusive view. That's pretty impressive.

The telestrator? I'm there. John Madden knows more about football than I do. Tim McCarver knows more about baseball than I do. Doug Collins knows more about the NBA than I do. So when they diagram it, they can show you what to focus on in a particular play. It's one thing to hear about a pick and roll, but it's another to watch Karl Malone and John Stockton run it.

I think it's especially helpful in football. You've got twenty-two players on the field at the same time, plus the refs, and when Madden or Phil Simms or Troy Aikman marks up the replay, he can show me what scheme the offense was trying to run, why this wide receiver was wide open, and who blew the coverage on defense. Why did the quarterback get picked off on third down? The defense went into a zone blitz where the safety blitzes and the defensive lineman drops back into pass coverage.

And as long as they don't overdo it, I even like hearing what goes on in time-outs in the NBA or what a manager tells his pitcher when he visits the mound. You heard Antoine Walker killing Paul Pierce in the huddle before that phenomenal comeback in game three of the Celtics-Nets Eastern Conference final in 2002. That famous Yankee moment when Paul O'Neill hit that home run against the Red Sox and FOX didn't edit the cuss word out of Joe Torre's sound bite as he was welcoming Paulie back to the dugout. It humanizes the game.

Here's my theory. I'm not a big guy for technology for technology's sake. The catcher cam? It doesn't show me anything, so once is more than enough. But I love it when the producer uses his toys—and his good judgment—to show me the game in a way I've never seen it before, to teach me something. That's what I call educational programming.

Kenesaw Mountain Mad Dog

How would Major League Baseball be different if Commissioner Russo were in charge?

It's the best job you wouldn't want to have: being the commissioner of baseball. Sure you get the box seat at the World Series. But you've got more problems than a calculus textbook, and everyone in America thinks they can do your job better than you can. But fearless Mad Dog is ready to throw his cap into the ring.

Okay, Bud's out and I'm in. How is baseball going to change? Let's get something straight up front. The changes I'm suggesting are things I could see getting past the union. So I'm not going to address the big questions here—random drug testing, salary cap, competitive balance—because I as a commissioner can't effect these changes alone. So I'm going to leave them aside for the moment. I'm going to focus on a few things that could get done with the right persuasion, arm-twisting, and a little backroom politicking.

Sunday Doubleheaders: I want each of the thirty teams to schedule one Sunday doubleheader. I don't want any of this day-night garbage, 1:05 and 7:05, two different admissions. None of that. Each team is going to have 80 home dates instead of 81.

It's roughly a twenty-six-week season, so every Sunday I'll have a doubleheader in some city. And I'm going to make sure it's not Yankees-Tampa. No, no, no, no, no. It has to have some juice. Giants-Dodgers occasionally. Mets-Braves. Yankees-Red Sox. We're not going to make this a farce. And to make it more palatable to the union, we'll give those teams Monday off.

I want it because you're giving something back to the fans. It's got tradition to it. Joe D did this. Ruth did this. There's something romantic about it. It's always fun to put the TV on at 1:05, watch the first game, take a little break and come back for the second game. You love that twenty-minute gap, when the manager comes out and talks to the press before the second game. The different uniforms for the second game. You have that opportunity to have a marathon day—the first game starts at one in the afternoon and the second game ends at twelve at night, like the Mets had a couple of times.

Natural Rivalries: I want to streamline interleague play. For every Dodger–Red Sox matchup you get now, you also get Dodgers and the Devil Rays. So instead of going division by division, I want one interleague matchup with each team. Two series. One in each park.

I want the natural rivalries. Reds play the Indians; the Yankees and Mets; Giants and A's; Dodgers and Angels; Cubs and White Sox; St. Louis and Kansas City; Texas and Houston; Tampa and Florida; Montreal and Toronto; Boston and Atlanta; Philly and Baltimore, and rotate the ones that don't work out. I want to eliminate the Mets and the Royals; the Mets and the Twins; and the Giants playing Tampa. Sure, it's fun to see Barry Bonds coming to Yankee Stadium for the first time, or the Diamondbacks visiting Yankee Stadium, or Arizona going to Boston, Pedro Martinez versus Curt Schilling. But it's run its course. I'd rather have one great matchup, and have teams play more against teams in their own league.

Can the DH: I know I've got to negotiate this with the union, but I want to get rid of the DH. If I have to add an extra man per roster, I'll do so. You would think the union would agree to it because it gives them thirty extra jobs. These guys might not be making $5 million a year like a DH would, but I think it would fly. I want to grandfather the DH the heck out of baseball.

Almost any fan will tell you that the classic baseball game is played under National League rules rather than American League rules (see "Make 'Em Hit," page 210). You play along, deciding when to take a pitcher out, when to bunt, when to pinch hit, how you use your bull pen. It's 2-2 bottom of the seventh, two out nobody on, postseason, do you take your pitcher out? We'll grandfather it in, so a guy like Edgar Martinez can finish out his career, but in three years I want it gone. They didn't have a DH for a hundred years and baseball survived. We don't need it now.

Day Games in the World Series: I understand the need to play night games during the week, because the guy who's following the team all year can't watch if it's a two o'clock start.

There's no reason in the world why they can't play some day games on the weekends in the World Series. They've played games in the NFL at one and four in the afternoon. Why can't Major League Baseball play game seven at four in the afternoon so that I don't have to stay up until two in the morning to see the end of the game? The networks want the games in prime time, so I realize that baseball is going to have to take less money from the networks in order to do it.

Contract Some Teams: There are simply too many teams. There aren't enough good pitchers to go around. Get rid of some teams and spread the talent around. Have a dispersal draft and give the worst teams the first picks. Even a team like Tampa has somebody who can contribute on another team. In British soccer, if you finish last in the premier division, the next year you're in the second division. Now you can't send the Tampa Bay Devil Rays to AAA—it'd be nice if you could, but you can't. I say Major League Baseball should be contracted by four to six teams. Tampa should not have a team. Florida should not have a team. Montreal. Goodbye, see you, out.

Who's next to go? I don't want to take teams away from Detroit and Kansas City because they're good baseball towns. I don't want to do that to Minnesota. I don't want to do that to Pittsburgh, even though it's a football town. You want to tick off Bud Selig and contract the Brewers? Go right ahead.

Mediocre talent means longer games, too. A guy who can't really pitch, he tries to get too fine, goes 3-and-2 on every batter, walks guys. Then when he does lay one in, the hitter smacks it for a double. You've got five and six hitters up every inning. And four pitching changes a game. Baseball goes on *forever*: 3-hour, 3½-hour games. Contraction will help with that problem.

Expand the Playoffs: I can't take credit for this one. I heard Steve Hirdt from Elias say this. Add one extra wild card team in each league. Why would you do that? You'd have the two wild card winners play on Monday as soon as the season's over, basically to get into the main draw. One game, go home or go on.

For starters, it would give division-winning teams a real advantage that they don't have now. Under the current system you can have a scenario where the wild card winner gets an easier matchup than one of the division winners—playing, say, Minnesota instead of the Yankees. It would eliminate what we saw in 1996 with San Diego and the Dodgers, where they were playing for the division in the last weekend with nothing on the line. Under this scenario they would have played that series very differently. Why? The winner gets to rest their pitching staff and doesn't have to face that one-game-and-out deal on Monday. It's a great idea. It would add juice to your divisional races. You'd start your postseason with a tremendous bang.

BASEBALL ON SPEED

Here's one little in-the-game rule I would implement. How many times do you see teams stalling so they can get a guy in the bull pen warmed up, and the catcher walks to the mound, talks to the pitcher, goes back behind the plate, and by the time he gets back there, here comes the pitching coach. I would limit the number of trips to the mound by both pitching coaches and catchers. Let's just play ball, okay?

Money Changes Everything

Are sports salary caps really necessary?

Sometimes when you're reading the sports section, you'd think that you opened the Wall Street Journal *by mistake. Luxury taxes. Base year compensation. Salary slots. But is the sports world better off because of salary caps? Mad Dog, as usual, has an opinion.*

When people ask me if you need a salary cap in professional sports, here's what I say: In basketball, where you have a salary cap, the Sacramento Kings win. In football, where you have a salary cap, the Green Bay Packers win. Can that happen in baseball? Can the Kansas City Royals compete year in and year out? No, they cannot.

If you want to give small-market teams like the Royals a legitimate chance to be competitive every year, not a blip on the radar screen like the Twins in 2002 or the A's the last couple of years, you must have a salary cap.

If you don't have a salary cap, the teams with the big revenue—whether it's the Yankees with their big TV contract, or the Dallas Cowboys, who sell more T-shirts than the Jacksonville Jaguars—will dominate. It's that simple.

People say, "This has been going on forever, Chris. The Yankees dominated in the 1930s and '40s and '50s. They won all those championships." Well, there were 16 teams in baseball when they won. There are 30 teams now, and the Yankees were still in the World Series four years in a row. The Yankees are now more dominant than they've ever been. What does that tell you? That tells you that the Yankees are living on an energy rock. The way Saudi Arabia is sitting on oil, they're sitting on a cable TV gold mine. Good for the Yankees. They're playing by the rules. But it's bad for baseball.

When NFL camp starts in July, people ask me who's going to win the next Super Bowl. My answer: Anybody. The Patriots are the perfect example. This is a team that went 5–11 the year before, lost their quarterback, lost their first two games, and came back to win the Super Bowl. That can't happen in baseball.

In baseball, when spring training opens, twenty teams know they've got no shot. And before you say, it, no, in baseball having the money isn't enough. You've got to have good management, too. The Yankees spend their money wisely, the Dodgers do not. The Orioles do not. But by the same token you can have the best owner, the best general manager, and the best manager, and if you've got a $50 million payroll you can't win consistently. And that hurts the sport.

I know there's another side to it. There are negatives to having salary caps. In football, for example, it's a hard cap. Teams have got to be at $71 million or whatever the figure is, and that's it. So one year Bryan Cox is the starting outside linebacker for the New England Patriots and the next year he's playing for the New Orleans Saints. Friends one minute, enemies the next. There's no continuity, no chance to build up loyalty. And a guy like Jerry Rice doesn't get the chance to end his career with the 49ers. The Niners have too many receivers, so off goes Jerry Rice to end his career with the Raiders. That's a bad thing. To the sports fan he'll always be a 49er, not a Raider.

And the hard cap works against building up a dynasty—or even just staying competitive year in and year out. The Baltimore Ravens can win the Super Bowl in 2001, and not even two years later they're average at best.

In the NBA, which has a soft cap, there are some different problems. The cap forces general managers to be visionaries. You've got to make big decisions about your own players, and if you pay that kind of money and you're wrong—Allan Houston's $100 million deal with the Knicks, Big Dog Robinson getting all that money in Milwaukee—you're dead. For a long time. Years. You can't make mistakes.

The soft cap also places incredible importance on the draft. If you want to win a championship, you had better get lucky with a lottery pick and have the ping-pong balls come up right in a year when there's a great player coming out. The Spurs were terrible for a year, they got Tim Duncan, who's a Hall of Famer, and they won the championship. The Rockets got Hakeem Olajuwon. The Bulls caught a break when Portland made the mistake of drafting Sam Bowie ahead of Jordan.

And any kind of salary cap makes it very difficult to pull off trades. You've got to match up the salary slots to make a deal, which makes the off-season pretty dead. In the NBA you'll even see teams trading a better player for a guy who is worse but who'll come off the cap sooner.

But there are tradeoffs in everything. The bottom line is that in any sport it's a fact of life that there are going to be some franchises that make more money than others. If those teams buy up all the cream-of-the-crop free agents, they're going to win every year. And when the same teams win year after year, that's a problem. If we want to give that well-run small-market team a chance to compete, a chance to win, a chance for their fans to have a ticker tape parade, you've got to have a salary cap. No two ways around it.

Hoops Hierarchy

Which is the greatest NBA team of all time?

Over the last fifty years, the NBA has changed immensely, from Chuck Taylors and two-handed set shots to Air Jordans and 360-degree reverse dunks. But when hoops aficionados get together, one question remains: What's the greatest team ever?

When you rate the greatest NBA teams of all time, there are a couple of different factors that you've got to consider. You've got to look at the number of Hall of Famers that were on the teams. You look at how many All-NBA first team and second team candidates they had on the club. And then you have to look at the competition: How many Hall of Famers were on the other teams that they beat in the postseason? Here's my top five in reverse order:

5. 1985-86 Celtics: They had three Hall of Famers on the front line—Larry Bird, Kevin McHale, Robert Parrish—with another one, Bill Walton, on the bench. (To be fair, he wasn't playing like a Hall of Famer by then.) I think Dennis Johnson should be a Hall of Famer, too. Obviously, Bird was at the peak of his career. They were 67–15, which is a phenomenal record, and they were unbeatable at home: 40–1. The knock on them? They did lose two games to the Rockets in the finals, and the Rockets were not a great team. And the Celtics had only one guy—Bird—who made All-NBA first or second team. It's a great all-time team, don't get me wrong. I love the club. But I'm putting that team as number five.

4. 1982-83 76ers: They had two guys All-NBA in Moses Malone and Julius Erving, and both of them are Hall of Famers. Andrew Toney and Bobby Jones were great, great players. You throw in the fact that they had Mo Cheeks as a point guard and that's a hell of a team. They were 65–17, so they were four or five games away from the top, recordwise. But they lost just the one playoff game, and that's as close to running the table in the postseason as any team has ever come. They went "Fo-Fi-Fo" as Moses Malone might have called it, losing only one game to the Bucks. And they swept the defending champion Lakers in the finals. Los Angeles had Bob McAdoo and Norm Nixon hurt, but they still did have Magic and Kareem. I can't put them any higher than fourth, but they slip ahead of the '85–'86 Celtics because they beat a better club in the finals.

3. 1963-63 Celtics: It's tough trying to decide which Bill Russell–led Celtic team to put into the top five. I originally liked the '60–'61 Celtics because that club had both Bill Sharman and Sam Jones and they lost only two play-off games after a 57-win regular season. But when I looked a little closer, I chose the '62–'63 team primarily because it's the only Celtic team that had both John Havlicek and Bob Cousy. It was Hondo's rookie year and Cous's last, and both played well, if not at their absolute peak. The '62–'63 team lost five playoff games and actually had to play a game seven against Cincinnati in the Eastern Conference finals. It's close, but the Cousy-Russell-Havlicek troika wins out.

2. 1966-67 Sixers: The choice between two and one is very hard. When you're trying to rank the '66–'67 76ers and the '71–'72 Lakers, you're splitting hairs. Both teams had three Hall of Famers: Wilt Chamberlain, Hal Greer, and Billy Cunningham for the Sixers; Wilt, Jerry West, and Gail Goodrich for the Lakers. They both had the same representation on the All-NBA Team: the Lakers had West on the first team, Wilt on the second, while the Sixers had Wilt on the first and Greer on the second. Virtually the same record: 68–13 for the Sixers, 69–13 for the Lakers.

They both had a distinctive streak during the season. Sixers won 46 of their first 50 games. The Lakers won 33 straight.

Plus the fact that you have Wilt on both teams. Wilt was better in '66–'67 than he was in '71–'72. He had to do more things on that '66–'67 team. He averaged 24 a game, 24 rebounds, and 8 assists for the Sixers, while in '71–'72 he was a little more of a role player, averaging just under 14 points and 19 rebounds a game.

The other interesting thing is that they both beat the defending champion in the postseason, and did it relatively easily. The Sixers won in five over the Russell–Havlicek Celtics. The Lakers won in six over Kareem Abdul-Jabbar's Milwaukee Bucks.

And both teams were even coached by Hall of Fame players: the '71–'72 Lakers by a Celtic, Bill Sharman; Alex Hannum, who won with the Hawks as a player, coached the Sixers. So you've got the same record. The same number of Hall of Famers and All-NBA players. This one is very close.

1. 1971–72 Lakers: But I'm going to lean to the Lakers for three reasons: They were more prolific offensively. They set the record for the most games in which a team scored more than 100 points—81. Chamberlain led the league in field goal percentage and rebounding. Goodrich and West finished one-two in scoring.

The Laker team also set a lot of records. Thirty-one wins on the road. Thirty-eight wins at home (a mark that was broken later by the Celtics). They had that 33-game winning streak that lasted November through January.

And finally, I like the quality of the competition just a little bit better. When the Lakers won 69 there were eight NBA teams over .500. When

WHERE'S MICHAEL?

Okay, start yelling and screaming: "What about the 1995–96 Bulls?" They went 72–10. They had Michael Jordan, arguably the greatest player of all time. They had a future Hall of Famer in Scottie Pippen, although I think he's a little overrated because he can't score in the fourth quarter of big games. And a defense and rebounding specialist in Dennis Rodman. But then look at the rest of the roster: Tony Kukoc, Luc Longley, Ron Harper, Steve Kerr, Jason Caffey, Dickey Simpkins, Jack Haley. Are those guys all-time greats?

I think that Chicago's great record is a product of a watered-down league. And they lost two games to a not-so-great Seattle team in the final, a team with one borderline Hall of Famer in Gary Payton. I would argue that the '90–'91 Bulls might be even better. I like Horace Grant better than Rodman, B. J. Armstrong better than Harper, Bill Cartwright better than Longley. They won a lot of games, but I just don't love that 72-win Bulls team.

the Sixers won 68, there were only three teams with a winning record. In the playoffs, the Lakers beat the Bulls, who won 57 games, in the first round of the playoffs. They beat the Bucks, who were the defending champs. And they beat a championship-caliber Knicks team in the final. Yes, Willis Reed was not 100 percent, but they killed the Knicks in the final. They lost the first game but beat them four straight times after that. So I'm going to lean to the Lakers, but it's very, very close.

Same As It Ever Was

What are the greatest—and worst—traditions in sports?

Admit it. One of the reasons you love sports is the fact that there are things you can count on every year. Traditions that roll around as dependably as the seasons. Some you love as much as the Fourth of July. Some you hate as much as mowing your lawn. Mad Dog separates one from the other.

I'm a sucker for tradition in sport. I'm a history buff and I love those events, places, and things that have been around for longer than you can remember, that take me back fifty years, a hundred years, and make me think about the way they played the game way back when.

But it's a fine line. While I love tradition, I'm not into pageantry for pageantry's sake. That stuff drives me crazy. I think it's for the housewives out there who don't even watch the actual sporting event. Here are four sports traditions I love every year and five others that I can leave.

Love 'Em

Lions on Thanksgiving Day: Here's my Thanksgiving Day tradition. Play a touch football game in the morning, then go watch the Lions. I don't care how bad the Lions are—and sometimes they are an awful football team—they always come out and give you everything they've got. It's always a very competitive game. It was even okay when it was at the Silverdome—but I really used to love it when it was outside in the cold against Green Bay at old Tiger Stadium. And they should get a little bit of that mystique back with Ford Field. Outside, in November, in Detroit, that's football.

The Stanley Cup: Out of all the trophies in sports, this is the one that everybody can relate to. You don't talk about the NFL's Lombardi Trophy or the Commissioner's Trophy in baseball. The Cup has got all the names of all the players on all the winning teams engraved on the base. And watching player after player put that Cup over his head and skate around the ice, that's a real goosebump moment. You might stay up until two o'clock in the morning watching the seventh game in a Cup final just to see it. ESPN has a field day with it. And the Stanley Cup is a really public thing, too. Players take it home, show it to their friends, let their kids play with it, let the hometown fans have their pictures taken with it. There's just something about that trophy that gets you going.

Wimbledon: Where else in the sports world do you have to curtsy? That's Wimbledon. The players bow or curtsy to the royal box, wearing all white on the green grass of Center Court. There are fifty other weeks in the year when a twenty-two-year-old girl can express herself with nine different colors in her outfit or the guy can wear all black. Wimbledon is history. And I even love it when they break with tradition—like letting the public in for the Goran Ivanisevic–Pat Rafter final in 2001.

The Masters: I understand that's a restrictive club. But I'm a sports fan, and it's the only major in golf where we all know the holes, because unlike the PGA, the British Open, or the U.S. Open, it's played on the same course every year. And for those of us who watch on TV, they give you only four minutes of commercials, which means fifty-six minutes of action every hour. There are some things that I don't like about it. It's stuffy. I wish they would show all eighteen holes on television. I don't get crazy about the green jacket. If I don't see Doug Ford hit the ball at the first tee, I'll live. But it's just something about Augusta on a Sunday in early April. It's Bobby Jones. It's *golf.*

Hate 'Em

The Opening Ceremonies at the Olympics: That's a total TV event. I don't need to see little kids skating. I don't need to see all these different countries that have no chance to win an Olympic gold medal waltz in with their flags. I don't need to see the politicians out there. If it's such a big deal how come half the athletes don't even show up? They did the opening ceremonies in Salt Lake City and none of the hockey players were there. I didn't see Mario Lemieux walking with the Canadian team. To me it's a total, total waste of time. I never watch it.

"Gentlemen, Start Your Engines": As Jim Murray said, they ought to begin the Indy 500 with "Gentlemen, start your coffins." Maybe it's because I don't like auto racing, but the only good thing about hearing "Gentlemen, start your engines" is that they've started the race and the pain is going to be over in three or four hours.

The Ceremonial First Pitch: Let's face it. It's a yawner. They bring the politicians down, and half of them can't reach home plate. You go to some Yankee postseason games, you're going to see Whitey Ford throw out the first ball ten straight times. Whitey can't throw the ball anymore—he's bouncing the ball to home plate. And then you've got to watch that ridiculous Challenger the Bald Eagle fly in from center field. Enough already. Occasionally you'll get a little goose bump, like when President Bush threw out the first ball at Yankee Stadium after 9/11. But day after day after day, when they bring in an advertising executive for Arizona Ice Tea or the salesman of the year for IBM to throw out the first ball at the Mets game in June against the Padres, you know what? Wake me up when it's over.

Cutting Down the Nets: This could be like the Stanley Cup ceremony, but it's not. It's too far removed from the championship game. It happens an hour after the game is over. When there is a victory lap in track and field, or the Stanley Cup ceremony, it happens right away. It feels spontaneous. In college basketball you've got to wait for all the celebration and the interviews; it takes forever for them to cut down the nets. And they do it too much. They cut down the nets at the end of the regular season, after a conference tournament, and when they win a regional to advance to the Final Four.

"My Old Kentucky Home": I've been waiting *weeks* for the Kentucky Derby. Get the darn horses on the track, get them in the gate, and let's go. I'm not sitting there with my mint julep waiting for the song. The song takes longer than the race. I turn the race on at 6:05, and I can't wait until they get to 6:12.

Dugout Diplomacy

What are the dos and don'ts for a baseball manager?

It's as much a part of baseball as the seventh-inning stretch: second-guessing the manager. But what really separates the great skipper from the guy who doesn't deserve his double knits? Mad Dog clues you in.

I hear it every day.

"Why on earth didn't he bunt here?"

"Only an idiot would go to the bull pen there!"

"He stinks, get him out of there!"

I think that fans give baseball managers too much credit sometimes and get on them for the wrong things at other times. In a lot of ways, understanding what a good manager really does is difficult. You put a great manager in a lousy team and they are still going to be a lousy team. And with the right players, even a lousy manager can steal a pennant. But what's the difference between a great manager and a lousy one? Well, I don't think it's making the right call on the hit-and-run.

Joe McIlvaine, former GM of the Mets, once told me that in-game decision-making is about eighty-eighth on the list that GMs look for when they're hiring a manager. It's important that your manager made the little moves that gave you a chance to win last night. But it's far more important what he does over the course of the 162-game schedule. Here's a list of dos and don'ts any good manager has to keep in mind.

Do Sell the Star: That's the first thing he's got to do. He has to have his best player—a Mike Piazza, a Sammy Sosa—respect him and believe in him, because if he doesn't he's got a problem. In a lot of cases the team takes its cue from the best player. If the best player is just going through the motions because he doesn't respect the manager, that manager is as good as gone. Even if the best player can be a pain in the butt, like Barry Bonds, then you've still got to deal with him. Dusty Baker might have had some problems with Barry Bonds, but Dusty could do one thing. Dusty could count. He could count to 73. And even if Barry was difficult to deal with, all those homers helped the Giants win.

Don't Bury the Bench: A good manager needs to get everybody involved. It's a 162-game schedule, day after day, for six months. You need to get the backup infielder involved, play your fourth and fifth outfielders occasionally. Guys like Ron Coomer, Jose Vizcaino, David Dellucci, Marquis Grissom. You don't play them every day, but you've got to keep them sharp and ready because there's going to come a point where you might have to rely on that guy to help you win an important game.

Do Be a Diplomat: What did Casey Stengel used to say? You've got five guys who like you, five guys who don't, and fifteen guys who are undecided. Your job is to keep the guys who don't like you away from the guys who are undecided. There's a lot of truth to that. A good manager has to be part psychologist. He has to understand the dynamics of his clubhouse. Who gets along. Who doesn't. Who he can depend on to chew out a teammate who's not hustling. Who's trying to be a clubhouse lawyer. That way he can address a problem before it becomes a full-blown mutiny.

Don't Be an Undertaker: I never want my manager to get down on a player to the degree where he buries him. You never know when you're going to need that player again. Now listen, if a guy is making $15 million a year and he's not hitting, you've got to play him anyway. But if you have a guy who's a regular player, but he's not high-priced, it takes guts to keep that guy on the field. But that loyalty is rewarded. Like Yogi Berra said, 90 percent of baseball is mental and the other half is physical. Put a player who's struggling in a big spot and he'll think, "If the manager thinks I can do it, then I can do it." And out of the clear blue sky a guy who's done nothing all year goes in there and gets a couple of big hits and you've won a huge game. J. T. Snow's 2002 postseason is a perfect example of this. And don't think that the other players don't notice when a manager shows faith in a guy who's not doing well.

Do Manage the Media: Especially if you're in a big city, you've got to make sure the media is on your side. That way you can sort of shield your players from reporters poking around looking for the negative story. There is an art to talking to the press without saying anything at all. It's not all that hard, really. Be accommodating. Be nice to the beat guys. Call them by their first names and get to know who they are. If you do that the media will cut you some slack when it comes to benefit-of-the-doubt time.

Don't Panic: A good manager stays on an even keel, which is why I could never be a manager. I'd lose a game in April and I'd be going nuts. Managers can't do that. You've got to be consistent with your approach—don't get too high after a win or too low after a loss. A good manager shields his players from the expectations of the press and the fans, even when it's a crucial game. He doesn't want them to get nervous. He doesn't want them to get down on themselves if they lose.

Do Go for the Jugular: At the same time, I do think that there are certain games that are more important than others, games where you match up with an opponent head-to-head, games with a two-game swing. When Joe Torre tells you that a game against the Royals in early July means as much as the Red Sox game in late August, don't believe him. A good manager will quietly set up his pitching rotation and rest his bullpen with an eye toward these big games.

Don't Worry About the Second-Guess: A lot of managers are too worried about being second-guessed in a big game. They are worried about the fans and the media getting all over them if they make a move that backfires. In big games, I think that managers who get conservative and stick too close to the book end up losing. You know—playing for one run late in a tight game on the road, maybe bunting a guy over and looking for that one-out or two-out hit. Making pitching changes, looking for the platoon matchup. I say stay aggressive. You see it in other sports all the time. If a golfer has got a five-shot lead and he starts nursing the lead and managing the course to a fault, he ends up losing. When a football team is trying to protect a ten-point lead early in the fourth quarter by running the ball all over the place and playing a prevent defense, a lot of times that backfires. A manager should go for the kill and not mess around with spotting his middle relievers too much. Aggressiveness wins.

Underrated Managers

Here are a few guys who seem to get the most out of their teams year in and year out.

Bruce Bochy: He's not a big fanfare guy. He doesn't toot his own horn, but players love playing for him. When he had a good ball club, look what he did. He beat Houston and he beat the Braves in the playoffs in '98. You never see players bitching and moaning about him. Trevor Hoffman stayed there, Tony Gwynn stayed there, Ryan Klesko signed a contract there. Padres are still a pesky team, and they never quit.

Art Howe: Every time you look up in October, there is Art Howe without a big contract, playing in a lousy ballpark, sort of a second-class citizen in his own town. Billy Beane got all the credit for the A's success, but Art Howe knows what he's doing. His handling of the A's pitching rotation in the 2002 division series against the Twins wasn't great, but Howe did a good job with the Astros, and he did a great job with the A's. He's not a sexy choice. He's a survivor. Howe can manage my team any day of the week.

Davey Johnson: He is a very underrated manager. He can be a little arrogant. He does things a little differently. But when Davey goes to manage a team, he wins. He won with the Mets, he won with Cincinnati, he won with the Orioles. And he dealt with some difficult owners—Marge Schott, Peter Angelos. When he was in New York he brought along young pitchers like Dwight Gooden, Ron Darling, Sid Fernandez, and David Cone, and gave jobs to young guys like Len Dykstra and Kevin Mitchell.

He also got along with veterans like Gary Carter and Keith Hernandez. He's a stand-up guy. He had the guts to move Cal Ripken from shortstop to third. And while he was in New York, he did that manager's show every day on WFAN with Howie Rose. Great show. After every game, Howie second-guessed him and Davey sat there and took it. Give him credit, he answered the questions.

Overrated Managers

Here are some guys who should be managing a Dairy Queen someplace.

Don Baylor: I'm not a big fan. I don't think he knows how to run a ball game. He's the sort of guy, when his sixth-place hitter gets a leadoff hit, he'll have his seventh-place hitter bunt with his eighth-place hitter and his pitcher coming up. Stupid. And getting Sammy Sosa ticked off wasn't too smart either. No wonder he got fired.

Jimy Williams: He totally got out-managed by Joe Torre in the '99 playoffs when he was managing the Red Sox. The only reason Williams beat the Indians is that Mike Hargrove was even worse, pitching Bartolo Colon on three days' rest with a 2-1 lead. And the players can't stand Williams. It's no coincidence that the Blue Jays started winning championships after he left.

Phil Garner: He had one year where he was decent, the '92 Brewers. That's it. How this guy kept getting jobs, I don't understand.

Poll Faults

What's wrong with college football's national championship system?

You can almost hear the Gipper rolling over in his grave. Leaving it up to computers to determine who's the national champion? There's got to be a better way. And Dog's figured it out.

I love college football, love it. There is nothing like a Saturday afternoon big-time college football game. I love games in those places like Tuscaloosa, Norman, Happy Valley, the Swamp. But college football's got some huge problems, too. College football has to devise a better system of determining the national champion. Has to. Now you say, "Hold on. Why?" Bob Griese argues that the one thing you love about college football is that if you lose a game in August, you know you could be in huge trouble as far as winning the national championship. If that's the case, he reasons, why do you need the playoff system, because it's almost like the whole season is single elimination—you lose and you're out.

Well, it doesn't work that way. In the year 2001 Nebraska got destroyed on Thanksgiving weekend, losing to Colorado 62-36, but six weeks later they played in the national championship game. In the year 2000 the Miami Hurricanes beat Florida State, regular season head-to-head. Guess what? Florida State, not Miami, played in the championship game against Oklahoma. The BCS formula is a joke. I know they are going to try to tweak it here and there, but the bottom line is when you are using ten computer services to determine your championship game, you are in huge trouble.

My idea is to eliminate the BCS poll we just discussed, take the computer out of the mix, and get Division 1-A college football focused on a tournament. At the same time, we'll close the gap between Thanksgiving and the start of the year, in which there is no college football, and make sure that the season ends on January 1.

Here's how it'll work. Take the champions of the six big conferences: the SEC, the Big East, the ACC, the Big 10, the Big 12, the Pac 10, and two at-large teams, which keeps Notre Dame, the WAC champion, or a strong number two in any of the other conferences in the mix. (If some athletic director is upset because he didn't get one of the at-large bids, let him play a tougher schedule next year and then maybe his team will get in.) Seed them and number one plays number eight, two plays seven, and so on.

We can play the four first-round games at four different sites on December 1, and if you want to incorporate some of the old bowls like the Cotton Bowl in the first round, that's fine. The top four bowls—the Sugar, Rose, Orange, Fiesta—are going to rotate the semifinals and the final. We are going to have four games on December 1, we're gonna have two games on December 15, and we are going to have the championship game on January 1. So every two weeks we are going have a huge college football game. If the Weedeater Independence Bowl in Shreveport still wants to have their bowl game, well then fine. They can take the fifth-place team in the Big 10 and match them up with the fourth-place entry in the ACC, and they can have their twenty-five thousand people on New Year's Eve. If one of these small bowls wants to take one of the first-round losers, that's fine. And if you want to have other games on New Year's Day, go ahead, just play the championship game at seven o'clock at night. Stop

PACKING THE SCHEDULE? POPPYCOCK

Here's one gripe I'm ready for. College presidents will squawk about adding more games. C'mon. This isn't about academics. Division I-AA, Division II, and Division III teams—nonscholarship programs—have been doing playoffs forever. I understand that many schools have exams in early December, but they don't give tests on Saturday, do they? And how many more games are you really adding? For the eight teams that make the tournament, they would be playing in a bowl game anyway, and four of those teams are going to lose in that first round. So that leaves only four teams that are going to play an extra game, and two teams have to play an extra two games. What's the big deal? If this system means that a team doesn't start its season on August 15 at some Pigskin Classic or if Florida doesn't play UCF, what's the big deal?

with this January 4 championship game. People have had their fill of college football by then. The college football season should end on New Year's Day. That's the plan.

Of course, none of this is going to happen because there are too many people out there who are only looking out for their own selfish interests, so they are going to veto this every time. The bowl committees would lobby hard against this. Coaches are going to oppose it because it increases the pressure on them—the alumni are going to ask them every year, "Why didn't you make the top eight?" So I don't care if Chuck Rowe or John Junker and the other big bowl guys are going to be annoyed at the fact that they don't get to drink their martinis with the coaches on bowl week. Who cares? A playoff system would make major college football a lot better than it is right now.

Diamond Dangerfields

Which baseball players don't get the respect they deserve?

I went to the trainer and said, "My arm hurts." And he says, "You're fine." So I said, "I want a second opinion." And he says, "Your change-up stinks." Bada-boom. Which major leaguers are punch lines—until they step on the field? Mad Dog tells all.

Did you ever notice that there are these guys in baseball who do the job year in and year out but don't get any credit for it? Sometimes it's a guy who plays well for a bad team. Sometimes it's a guy who gets overshadowed by his teammates. Sometimes it's a guy who just doesn't look like a baseball player.

Who are guys that I see as underrated? I'm going to go from 1967 forward. I'm not going back before 1967 because I didn't see the guys play. So for me to sit there and tell you about who was underrated in the 1950s isn't fair because I'd be basing it strictly on statistics. So here's my list of the baseball players who, in my humble opinion, don't get the respect they deserve.

Mel Stottlemyre: It's hard to be underrated when you're a Yankee, but Mel's that rare case. He won twenty games three times and has a lifetime ERA of 2.97. He always had a lot of decisions. He pitched an incredible number of innings—over 250 in every full season.

But Mel was born at the wrong time. He was 9–3 in 1964, his first year, and helped the Yankees win the American League pennant. He pitched in the World Series that year and was a big shot in the arm for the team. But after that he was always on lousy teams. If he had been born ten years earlier, pitching for teams that won a hundred games and made the World Series every year, he might be in the Hall of Fame. His problem is that he pitched on a team that was just awful, with a lot of Fritz Petersens and Stan Bahnsens behind him. The Yankees had a great run during the '50s and early '60s, but once '65 came around it was lala land for them. And for Mel.

Dave Stewart: Here's a guy who can start a playoff game for me any time. He won twenty games four straight times, but he never won a Cy Young. He pitched well for Toronto, great for the A's, but he was overshadowed by guys like Roger Clemens and guys who had one big year like Bob Welch. He was a real big-game pitcher. He had a 2.84 ERA in the postseason and a 10–6 record. He's a hell of a pitcher.

Part of the reason that Stewart doesn't get the respect he deserves is that he kind of came out of nowhere. He started out as a middle reliever in the Dodgers system. And those A's teams are remembered for their great offense with Jose Canseco and Mark McGwire and Rickey Henderson and all the other great hitters, so you kind of forget about the pitching staff. The fact that the A's won only the one world championship hurt him, too. The bottom line is that Dave Stewart was a very, very good pitcher.

Al Oliver: Scoop was a tremendous offensive player, a lifetime .303 hitter. He wasn't a tremendous home run hitter and he didn't put up big RBI numbers, but Al Oliver was a guy you'd want up there two outs, bases loaded, ninth inning down by a run. He's going to get a base hit. He's not a Hall of Famer because he didn't reach the magical 3,000-hit mark, but had 2,743 career hits, which is an amazing amount of hits. He played on those great Pirate teams that had Roberto Clemente, Willie Stargell, even

Dave Parker. And the whole team was kind of overshadowed by the Reds in the '70s. But Al Oliver could just plain hit.

Reggie Smith: Most people remember Reggie Smith as a National Leaguer, but they don't realize that Reggie Smith played on the '67 Red Sox. He was a good outfielder and a very good hitter, .287 lifetime. He hit over .300 seven times. He had over 2,000 hits in his career. He had 314 career home runs. He played in four World Series, played in big games. That's a tremendous career, but who talks about Reggie Smith? Maybe people forget about him a little because he bounced around from team to team, got traded a lot, had a reputation for being a troublemaker. But Reggie could play.

Darrell Evans: He was a great guy to have on your team. Evans was a dangerous left-handed hitter. Not a high-average hitter. Lifetime of .248, but he was a very good home run hitter. He had a great eye at the plate. He walked a lot—eight seasons with 90 or more walks. And he played two different positions—third and first. He was good in the clubhouse. He played on the 1984 Tiger team and Kirk Gibson loved him. He hit 40 homers for the 1973 Braves, that great team along with Hank Aaron and Davey Johnson. His managers loved him. Did you realize that Evans has 414 career home runs? That's more than Duke Snider. That's more than Johnny Mize. That's more than Joe DiMaggio. How many people know that? I love Darrell Evans.

Keith Moreland: People don't realize what a good hitter he was. But the big thing about Moreland that I like is this: He played a lot of different positions, outfield, first base, catcher. He was the sort of guy that you say to yourself, "He's not a great defensive catcher. I'm going to play Bob Boone or Jody Davis." But managers like Dallas Green and Jim Frey, when they won the division, found a way to get Keith Moreland in the lineup. In 1980, his rookie year with the Phillies, he played in only 62 games but he hit .314. In '84 with the Cubs he hit .279, 16 home runs, and 80 RBIs. And he was a clutch hitter: 6 for 18 in the playoff series against San Diego that year. He wasn't a great defensive catcher so you had to find a spot for him, but he could get a big hit for you.

Paul Molitor: I know it's kind of weird to put him in an underrated category because he's going to go to the Hall of Fame, but I don't think that people realize how good he was. Maybe it's because he spent so much time as a DH. He's got 3,300 career hits. He is a lifetime .303 hitter. He was a tremendous baseball player. He hit. He ran the bases well. When he had to play defense he did that properly. He was smart. He was one of those guys who understood the situation. In other words, if he's down by a run in the ninth inning on a 3-0 pitch, you know he's going to take a strike, take two strikes to try to get on base.

He also had that great hitting streak. And remember how it was stopped? He was on deck when Rick Manning got a base hit to win the game. He was all excited about the Brewers winning and wasn't thinking about the streak. He was thinking about winning the ball game. Then he signed a baseball for John Farrell and said, "Great job stopping my streak." Compare that to Luis Castillo, who was all upset when he had his 35-game hitting streak stopped in 2002 with the Marlins. Molitor's a legit Hall of Famer.

Here are a few contemporary players who are underappreciated as far as I'm concerned:

Steve Finley: He is a great defensive center fielder. He played on three good teams, the Astros, the Padres, the Diamondbacks. He played in a couple of World Series and a lot of playoffs. He's a better clutch hitter than you think he is. He knows how to play the game. He can run the bases. He's not afraid of the big spot. He hits some home runs when you don't expect him to—he hit 30 three different times. And between 1995 and 2000 he scored at least 100 runs five times. He's a great defensive center fielder, too. He's had a heck of a career.

Garret Anderson: A very underrated player, at least until the 2002 postseason. You don't hear that much about him. For most of his career the Angels were bad and he was overshadowed by guys like Troy Glaus and Darin Erstad. He doesn't say anything. He doesn't have a big contract. But he's got a career average close to .300 and over three years averaged 31 homers and 121 RBIs. Not shabby at all.

Ellis Burks: He was supposed to be a superstar when he first came up with the Red Sox, and when he didn't turn into Barry Bonds, people kind of forgot about Ellis Burks.

Ellis Burks is a very good hitter. People don't consider him a tremendous home run hitter, but at the end of the 2002 season he had 345 round trippers in his career. He's not thought of as a tremendous average hitter, but his career average is .293. And he hits situationally. He did a tremendous job on the 2000 Giants backing up Bonds and Jeff Kent. I would make the argument that he was the MVP of that team, not Kent (who won the NL MVP) or Bonds (who has a trophy case full of awards).

Craig Counsell: You don't realize how good a little player Counsell is. Counsell will play two different positions for you. He won't get himself out. He'll make you work. He responds in the clutch. He was the MVP in the NLCS for the Diamondbacks in 2001, and in game seven of the '97 World Series he had a big sac fly to tie the game in the ninth inning and scored the winning run in the eleventh for the Marlins. He's a pain in the butt—if you're playing against him. Counsell is one of those guys who, as the season begins, a manager says, "You know what? He's my third infielder. I'll get him some at bats." And as the year progresses, when you have an injury here or there, you plug him in at third or second or shortstop, Craig Counsell is playing every day. I'd love him on my team.

Jamie Moyer: He doesn't blow you away when you watch him, and part of that is the way he pitches—change-ups, breaking balls. He kind of throws you soft stuff and then softer stuff. He uses the ballpark. He's a little bit like Kirk Rueter of the Giants. Did you know that Rueter is

---

SO UNDERRATED, HE'S OVERRATED

Fans talk so much about Ron Santo being underrated, he almost gets a little too much publicity. Santo is a good guy, not a great broadcaster, but a good guy. He was a good third baseman. But he's not a Hall of Famer. I'm sorry, he's just not.

fortysomething games over a .500 career? Moyer too. Moyer's probably a little better than Rueter is, but he's the same kind of guy. He can pitch in big games. I know he's over forty, and he's blossomed late, but Jamie Moyer is underrated.

. . . If You Ain't Got That Ring

Does a player need a championship to make a career complete?

"All I want is to win a title." If you had a dollar for every time you heard an athlete say that, you'd be a rich man. But it doesn't always work out. Mad Dog examines when a player gets a pass—or not—for a ring-free career.

Players love to talk about how important it is to win a championship. But what about those guys like Karl Malone or Dan Marino, who've had Hall of Fame–type careers but never got that ring? How important is a championship to validate an athlete's place in history? Take Patrick Ewing, a guy who is in the top fifty NBA all-time list. He is a sure bet Hall of Famer, won a college championship, played in an NBA final, and could have played in another one if he hadn't gotten hurt. How much does that lack of a ring tarnish his reputation? There are a lot of great and near-great players who never got that champagne shower—Charles Barkley, Dan Fouts, Fran Tarkenton, Ted Williams, Ernie Banks, and even Ty Cobb.

First off, just winning a championship doesn't make you a great player. Look at the quarterbacks who've won Super Bowls. Doug Williams. Mark Rypien. Jim McMahon. Tom Brady. Even Brad Johnson. In the NBA, Bill Wennington has as many rings as Patrick Ewing, Hakeem Olajuwon, and David Robinson combined. Lonnie Smith has more rings than Ty Cobb and Ted Williams put together.

So when you're talking about that great player, there are two things to look at. First, you evaluate his performance in big games. Did he do his part? Take the case of Karl Malone. Whenever he had a big game against Jordan, he rarely responded. It's one thing to have a bad shooting night, but with Malone there were moments where he almost looked a little afraid, had that deer-in-the-headlights look.

Charles Barkley never won a title either, but I don't remember too many moments when Barkley came up small in the big game. Barkley scored 44 points and grabbed 24 rebounds to beat the Sonics in game seven of the 1993 Western Conference finals, and he played very well against the Bulls in the Finals. I don't know of a moment where anyone can say that Barkley choked, and I can't say that for Malone. To me, Barkley is an all-time great.

In baseball, regular season performance is much more important than the postseason. Take Ted Williams. Should the Red Sox have won the World Series sometime between 1946 and 1950? Probably. There were probably fifteen games that, if they would have won one of them, they could have won the championship.

But how much of the blame do you lay on Williams? I think the only real knock you have on Williams is that he was such a scientific and disciplined hitter that there probably was a spot or two in those games, say, in the eighth inning, instead of taking that 3-2 pitch on the outside part of the plate, he should've tried to hit a game-winning home run. But that's really nit-picking.

On the other hand, I think the other way to look at it is to switch the guy with some of his contemporaries. For example, if you put Stan Musial on the Red Sox in place of Williams, I don't think they're going to win the World Series. I'm not even sure that DiMaggio or Mantle would have gotten them over the hump. If you did that kind of a flip-flop in Super Bowl XIX and put Dan Marino on the Niners and Joe Montana on the Dolphins, I still think San Francisco wins 38-16.

But if the Knicks traded Patrick Ewing for Hakeem Olajuwon, the Knicks might have won a title or two. And that's got to be a knock on Ewing.

So sure, you've got to look at the rings when you're evaluating a player's place in history. But at the same time you've got to decide whether a player did everything he could to give his team a chance at the brass ring. There may not be an "I" in "team," but there is one in "win."

The Lord of the Rings

What's the matter with the Olympic Games?

The Olympics is a great event—despite the judging scandals, the creep-
ing professionalism, the rampant commercialism, and the "plausibly live"
television coverage. Here's how Mad Dog would make the Games work for
the real sports fan.

If I get a call tomorrow morning over breakfast, telling me that I'm the new chairman of the International Olympic Committee, here's what I'm going to do. I'm going to turn back the clock. I want to make the Olympics more traditional, get rid of some of the excess garbage that we have in it now and make it more like the original Olympic ideal, both the ancient games of Greece and the modern games of 1896. Now I understand that the world has changed and the genie's out of the bottle. It's a global event, there's big television money on the line. But I'd still like to make the Olympics a little purer. Here's what I'd do.

Streamline the Sports: First off, we are going to eliminate the sports where the ultimate prize isn't the Olympic gold medal. For a runner or a gymnast or a ski jumper, that medal is the reason to get up in the morning and train every day for four years. Do you think that Serena Williams is thinking about the 2004 Olympics today? Here's the test: If you gave Barkley a choice, "Charles, you can have an Olympic gold medal or an NBA championship?" you know he's going to choose the NBA championship. Charles probably can't *find* his gold medal in his closet.

Ask Marion Jones the same question and she'll take the Olympic gold medal over the world championships or any big-money match race in Oslo or even an NCAA basketball championship. (She played hoops for North Carolina, you'll remember.) For a weight lifter, the Olympics represents his moment of glory. It's not a moment of glory for Charles Barkley to play on the Dream Team and beat Angola by sixty points. So I want to eliminate sports like baseball, tennis, and even basketball and soccer that have their own history that's separate from the Olympics. And that's why I'm not adding golf. Do you really think Phil Mickelson or David Duval wants to win an Olympic gold medal more than the green jacket?

Ax the X-Games: Get rid of these made-for-TV sports. Snowboarding. Mountain biking. Freestyle skiing. Beach volleyball. Did Jim Thorpe play beach volleyball? The Olympics is not supposed to be about attracting the nineteen-year-old viewer. The Olympics is supposed to be big enough to stand on its own, and if a sport's been around for only fifteen or twenty years, I'm sorry, it doesn't belong in the Games.

Cut the Commercialization: I don't want it to be the Coca-Cola Atlanta Olympics. We get enough of that all year long. I know that you need sponsors, but let's not guarantee them that they'll have billboards on every damn stadium for every single event. Make us feel that we could be watching something that the ancient Greeks could have watched. You know that Samsung did not sponsor the 776 B.C. Olympiad.

Tighten the Regs: I don't want some swimmer from North Dakota whose great-grandfather who played on the Olympic curling team for Canada to compete on the Canadian Olympic team just because he can't make the U.S. team. I don't want to see Americans playing on the German or Israeli basketball team, and I don't want to see Kenyan runners competing for the United States. If you live there, if you carry a passport from a country, that's fine. But it's a joke when you see some of the athletes participate for these countries where they've hardly ever set foot.

Go Live: I want to show as many of the events live as I can—forget this "plausibly live" stuff. But we're not going to hold the host country hostage in the process. So NBC, we're gonna do the Olympic basketball final at eight o'clock at night local time and if you don't like it, tough. We're going to do the swimming at three o'clock in the afternoon and if you don't like it, tough. We're going to do track and field at six at night, and if you don't like it, put on a James Bond movie. We're not gonna start these events at these incredibly wicked hours locally just so you can televise them back in America. We're gonna schedule it so the athletes can be at their best and so fans in the host nation can watch their own Olympics at a decent hour. That's the Olympic spirit.

Eliminate Artistry: One last thing. I would like to try to eliminate the impact of judging as much as possible. I understand that you can't get rid of figure skating completely, and you can't eliminate gymnastics, as tempting as it might be. But I think they should tighten up the rules so that you're judging the technical merits of an athlete's performance, and not just the artistic impression. If one skater lands a triple-triple combination and the other does a triple-double, the one who landed the triple-triple should win regardless of who has the prettier dress or waves her arms more elegantly between jumps. I want to eliminate the possibility of a judge waking up in a lousy mood and having that affect how he scores. I want to eliminate the idea that the favorites always get the high artistic marks, which makes it almost impossible to beat them. Most of all, we want to eliminate the disaster we had this past Olympiad in Salt Lake City, with the French judge making a deal so the Russian pair could win. I want the events to be fair for everyone. And I want the Olympics to be about the athletes, not the judges.

Midsummer Night's Dreaming

How can we juice up baseball's All-Star Game?

"He's struck out Ruth, Gehrig, and Foxx and Simmons and Cronin . . . in succession." But as you're watching an All-Star Game today, does Carl Hubbell's classic performance seem as far away as the Hubble Space Telescope? Well, the Dog has a plan to restore the luster to baseball's All-Star Game.

For years and years and years the one All-Star Game in professional sports that had some juice to it was the baseball All-Star Game. The NFL Pro Bowl is a total waste. It comes at the end of the season, after the Super Bowl. It's really more for the players. The NBA All-Star Game is all run and gun, 155-150. The NHL All-Star Game is silly, too. There are so many goals, and no defense, and the old system of the American players against the World didn't work.

In baseball you looked forward to the All-Star Game. You had a long cycle of the National League winning these games. The NL players were all pumped up—Bob Brenly was on the show and told us how Gary Carter and Ozzie Smith stood up before the 1984 game and made a Gipper speech in the clubhouse—and they won 19 out of 21, an incredible streak.

There have been some memorable All-Star moments in the last twenty-five to thirty years. Fred Lynn's grand slam against Atlee Hammaker. The 2-1 fifteen-inning game. The game at the new Yankee Stadium in 1977. And even Pete Rose flattening Ray Fosse.

But the problem with the baseball All-Star Game is that it's lost all its juice. Part of it is the fact that thirty or forty years ago, if you lived in an American League town, it might be your only chance all year to see National League superstars like Willie Mays, Hank Aaron, and Sandy Koufax. Now you see Barry Bonds, Sammy Sosa, and Randy Johnson every other week on cable.

Even the players don't care. League pride used to be a big deal, but now half the All-Stars—Johnson, Roberto Alomar, Ken Griffey, Rob Nen, Pedro Martinez, and it goes on and on—have played in both leagues. If they've been to a couple of All-Star Games already, they'd rather have the three days off.

You can't turn back the clock, but I want to make the game meaningful again. And the way I would put value on the game is to have the winner get home field in the World Series. Currently the American League and the National League alternate home field in the World Series. They don't do it by who had a better record like they do in the NBA. It's just luck of the draw.

So if it were up to me, to put a little juice in the game I would have the winning league get the seventh game at home in the World Series. I think if that were the case, you'd see most of the players get into it. If Randy Johnson knew that playing in the All-Star Game could mean the difference between the Diamondbacks playing game seven of the World Series at home or at Yankee Stadium, he might have second thoughts about blowing it off to go to the ESPY awards. If the All-Star Game was important from a home field advantage standpoint, don't you think that Joe Torre might manage the game to win instead of just trying to get everybody involved?

Now most fans flip on the All-Star Game, and after their favorite player gets a hit they turn it off. But if I knew that the game had some bearing on what league would host the seventh game, I as a fan would watch. Because it would be a real game, not just an exhibition.

DECISIONS, DECISIONS

If you really wanted to improve the selection process for the All-Star Game, you'd do two things. First you'd take the responsibility for selecting the reserves away from the managers. Now they feel like they've got to take care of their guys, so you end up with Joe Torre taking six Yankees and Bobby Cox emptying his own clubhouse. Do something. Poll the GMs. Poll the players. Let the fans select the reserves. It would be an improvement. Second, eliminate All-Star bonuses in contracts. Some players have them and some players don't. Major League Baseball has long outlawed performance incentives—you hit thirty home runs and you get an extra million. Taking money out of the equation would make the selection process less political—this guy should get picked because he's having a great year, not because he's getting an extra hundred thousand dollars.

Supe's On

How to put the super back in the Super Bowl.

Starting with the three hours of pregame shows, the Super Bowl is the biggest day in sports. But the best? Hell no. Mad Dog wants to tweak Super Sunday so the game will be worthy of the hype.

As I've said many times before, there's nothing better than being at a Super Bowl in the stadium a half hour before kickoff. The problem with the Super Bowl is, 90 percent of the time that's the highlight of your day.

And there are a variety of reasons for this. The cycle has been that one conference has been dominant—the AFC with the Dolphins and the Steelers back in the '70s, and more recently the NFC with the 49ers and the

Cowboys. Add to that all the hoopla that makes the Super Bowl a bigger event but less of a football game and, well, you've got a recipe for a blowout. Here are a few ways that the NFL could make its biggest day one of its best.

No Week Off: The NFL wants to have the extra week off between the championship games and the Super Bowl so they can gear up the hype machine. But the upset, the close game, usually occurs when they play the Super Bowl the Sunday after the conference championships. Giants-Buffalo, no week off. Redskins-Miami in the early '80s, no week off. Patriots-Rams, no week off. Why is the game better without the week off? Teams are in rhythm. They go right from one game to the next the way they've done it all year long. They don't get stale. They don't get wrapped up in the hype. And if you give the better team an extra week to prepare, they'll almost always find a way to win the game, usually by a big margin.

Seed for the Playoffs: Yes, there is something to the NFC against the AFC, conference pride, style of play, all that. But here's the problem with the way the Super Bowl is now: If the two best teams are in one conference, then they can't play each other in the ultimate game. In a lot of cases in the last twenty-five years, the real Super Bowl occurred in the NFC or AFC championship game: Pittsburgh-Oakland. San Francisco-Dallas. San Francisco-Green Bay. If your goal is to have the best teams in the Super Bowl, then there's a lot of merit to the idea of putting the team with the best record in one bracket, the team with the second-best record on the opposite side.

Keep the Neutral Field: There's a part of me that likes the idea of playing the game at the home stadium of one of the teams. You'd give the average fan a little better chance of scoring tickets. You might even have one of those great cold weather classics like the 1962 Giants-Packers or the 1967 Packers-Cowboys. The problem is, home field advantage is just too big in the NFL. The favorite is going to win almost every time. If the Patriots had played the Rams at the RCA Dome in 2002, the Rams would have won the game. Abandoning the neutral site is just going to make the game less competitive, and that's what we're trying to avoid. And no cold weather sites, please. No one wants to sit in the Meadowlands on February 3.

Play It Earlier: I'd move the game up to four o'clock on the East Coast, one o'clock on the West Coast. It would make it easier for the players. It disrupts their schedule when they have to get ready for a 6:18 game. They've been used to playing at the same time all year long, so let them play then at four. And shorten the darn game. It lasts four hours. The kickoff goes on and on and on. There's a 28- to 30-minute halftime. Because the NFL tries too hard to justify the $400 price of a ticket. The real football fan doesn't want to hear Britney Spears sing at halftime. The real football fan wants the score to be 17-14.

Throwing It All Away

What are the biggest mistakes managers make when
they head to the mound?

They say that pitching is 95 percent of baseball. It's not, but it might be 95 percent of the conversation about baseball. Mad Dog discusses the traps that managers fall into in handling their pitching staffs.

There's an art to handling a pitching staff. I've spoken to a lot of players about this, and it's all about the details. I was with an infielder at the Super Bowl a couple of years ago and he told me that his manager's big problem is that he gets the bullpen up and down too much. Subtle stuff.

Handling a pitching staff is all about making decisions. What do you do when a pitcher is struggling in the early innings? Do you go to the bullpen? Do you show confidence in the pitcher and let him battle through bad periods? Do you keep your pitchers on a pitch count and at the first sign of trouble, out he comes? It is a very tricky thing. I don't think there is a blueprint you follow. You sort of do it on a hunch.

But I think there are a couple of mistakes that I see managers make over and over. First, I think that sometimes managers get trapped into making too many moves, trying to show you how smart they are. Sometimes simple is better.

Here's an example—tie game, eighth inning on the road, two out, nobody on. You know what? If he's pitching a good ballgame and his pitch count is not terrible, my pitcher's hitting. What are my chances, top of the eighth, two out and nobody on, of my pinch hitter starting a rally or hitting a home run? His chance of getting a hit is maybe 25 percent. His chances of hitting a home run are about 5 percent. Not great odds. I say, keep your better pitchers in the game as long as you can.

And too many managers follow a blueprint that their closer is pitching the ninth inning no matter what. Well, why? Why can't he come in for the eighth inning occasionally if it's the heart of the order? Their number two hitter gets on to lead off the eighth and your setup guy is not doing a good job, so why can't you bring your closer into the game? Let him pitch two innings that night. You never know what is going to happen the next couple of days. Maybe you'll score twenty runs or get rained out, and all of sudden the guy gets his full rest anyway. Joe Torre uses Mariano Rivera like this all the time. I don't even mind using my closer in the seventh inning every now and then. Dick Williams did that with Rollie Fingers all the time. In the 1972 and '73 World Series he put Fingers in the game in the sixth inning or earlier four times.

Ninth inning, 4-4, bases loaded, two out, and your setup guy is getting rocked? Get the closer in the damn game. Who knows what's going to happen in the top of the tenth. I think that managers are too cautious with their closers. Use them. I'm not bringing Robb Nen into a game in the fifth inning, 5-5, but I say use him in the ninth because you don't know what the next day is going to bring.

I'm not a big believer in sticking to a strict five-man rotation, either. I know that GMs are worried about a guy hurting his arm. But remember those stories about Whitey Ford and all those guys from thirty, forty, fifty years ago? They didn't pitch in a five-man rotation. And yet those guys pitched forever. Their arms were strong. Look at the Atlanta Braves' pitchers. They pitch a lot. They never get hurt. As a manager, if I can take a few starts from my number five guy and give them to my number one and two starters, I'll do it in a heartbeat.

I think the overall theme with the pitchers is that too many times teams lose games with pitchers who stink. For the most part, if these long relievers or spot starters could really pitch, they'd be starters or closers. Too many times over the course of a season your favorite team will lose an important game because the middle relief guy gives up three runs in the eighth inning, or the number five guy got roughed up in the second inning. Avoid that as much as you can. Try to not use your lousy pitchers. Makes sense, doesn't it?

The Unbreakables

Which sports records will stand forever?

They say that records are made to be broken. But in the world of sports some marks are like Eliot Ness—untouchable. Mad Dog tells you which ones will stay on the books.

The one thing you learn about sports is to never say never. If this was ten years ago and I was making a list of records that will never be broken, it would have been pretty different. I didn't think Lou Gehrig's consecutive games record would be broken. I didn't think the Lakers' 69-win season would have been eclipsed, but the Bulls did it. And I didn't think that we would have had three guys hitting more than 61 home runs. I'm going to set aside some of the career records—I think we can all agree that no modern pitcher is going to win more games than Cy Young. Here are six streaks or single-season records that are under constant assault, but should stand the test of time.

The Perfect NFL Season: I don't think any team is going to go through an NFL season unbeaten again. The Dolphins did it in '72 when they went 17–0, going 14–0 in the regular season and winning two playoff games and the Super Bowl. That feat was made all the more impressive because the NFL had no best-record incentive back then, so the Dolphins actually had to play the AFC championship game on the road in Pittsburgh.

Here's why no team will ever do that again. First of all the regular season is longer. A perfect season is 19–0 now instead of 17–0. Beyond that I think that because of the salary cap, there's much more balance in the NFL. There are fewer dominant teams. It's much harder to stockpile talent the way the Dolphins did, so injuries hurt you more. And finally, I'm not sure that running the slate would be a big priority for a coach today. It's almost like coaches *like* to lose a regular season game now and then to get their message across to their teams. Look at the 1998 Vikings, who went 15–1 but lost in the NFC championship game.

Yes, I know that the Bears lost only once in 1985, and the 49ers lost only one game in '84. But the 49ers lost to Pittsburgh by a field goal, pretty early on, in the seventh week of the season. And the '85 Bears and their vaunted defense got beaten up pretty good in that historic Monday night game against the Dolphins. They came in 12–0 and lost 38-24. If a team gets to 12–0 now, there's going to be a lot of pressure.

130 Steals: I don't think anyone's going to break Rickey Henderson's single season record of 130 stolen bases that he set back in 1982. All the elements were there. He was a cocky young player, leading off, walking all the time. He had Billy Martin as his manager who wanted to play go-go baseball, and he gave Rickey the green light all season, letting Rickey steal just for the sake of stealing bases. He had 172 steal attempts. There are plenty of guys who don't *get on* 172 times in a year. Rickey set the record for caught stealing that year, too. Now baseball has changed. The ballparks are smaller. The pitching isn't as good. Guys are hitting more home runs. So managers don't want to run themselves out of a big inning. The stolen base just isn't as important as it was twenty years ago. I know that base-stealing could make a comeback, but it won't happen any time soon.

Back-to-Back No-Hitters: Forget about any pitcher breaking this record. That would take *three* no-hitters in a row. No chance. It could be tied, though. If Johnny Vander Meer did it twice, why couldn't somebody else? But 1938 is a long time ago. When a record stands that long, it usually lasts for a reason. First off, Vander Meer didn't have a lot of pressure. After they pitched the first no-hitter, did they go and flock to his second game and see him pitch? No, because nobody had ever done it before, and Vander Meer wasn't a great pitcher anyway. Now, if a pitcher pitches a no-hitter, he hears about Johnny Vander Meer for four days. And remember Vander Meer's second no-hitter came in the first night game at Ebbets Field, so the hitters had their hands full just seeing the ball.

100 Points in a Game: Nobody's scoring 100 points in an NBA game today. Teams would not allow it. They'd foul all twelve guys out before they'd let someone get close to Wilt Chamberlain's record. And the game has changed a lot. In 1962, Wilt averaged 50 points a game, so him scoring 100 was a little like Kobe Bryant scoring 55. Consider two other things: Wilt scored more than 70 points five other times. And the NBA record for a guy not named Wilt is 73 by David Thompson way back in 1978. Compared to forty years ago there's much more emphasis on defense. Zones. Lots of fouls, some that get called, some that don't. Those are some of the reasons why whole teams don't score 100 every night anymore. For one person to put up that kind of big number would take a physically dominant player like Shaq on a night when he was hitting all his free throws, going to the basket early, and getting fouled to stop the clock. But it might take quadruple overtime.

UCLA's 88-Game Winning Streak: That's never going to happen again, because college basketball teams don't stay together long enough. These days, a player like Bill Walton would stay around a year, maybe two, and then leave for the NBA if he didn't declare for the draft straight out of high school. And now there's so much parity, so many teams that are halfway decent. Even a team like Duke loses some tough road games in the ACC. The bottom line is that you haven't had a team go undefeated since Bobby Knight's Indiana team did it in 1976—you might argue that *that* won't ever happen again—and 88 games is almost *three* full seasons.

56 Games: I don't think Joe DiMaggio's 56-game hitting streak is going to be challenged (see "The Slammer of '41," page 1). Pete Rose came the closest in my lifetime and he was still 12 games shy, which is a decent streak in itself. You'd have to be so consistent, and you'd have to be more than a little lucky. This is a record that's constantly under assault—every player tries to get a hit every day—but nobody has ever come close.

163 Assists: Gretzky owns a lot of single-season records—goals, points—but the one number that's untouchable is 163 assists. That's more than two assists a game in a league where only the best players average one assist a game. Wayne assisted on 100 or more goals eleven times in his career. Only Mario Lemieux, who had 114, and Bobby Orr, who had 102, reached triple digits even once. The reason Gretzky put up those numbers is that he was the greatest player of all time on a team chockful of Hall of Famers. And over the last two decades, hockey has changed in a way that keeps scoring down. You clutch. You grab. You play traps. You don't play the freewheeling style that the Oilers did back in the day. Gretzky's going to take this record to the old-age home.

Burn the Videotape

What are the all-time ugliest moments in sports history?

Turn it off. Some moments in sports history are just too gruesome to watch again. Mad Dog dredges up some sports lowlights that you'd probably rather forget.

There are lots of ways to define ugly in sports. A baseball beaning. A dirty, vicious hit in football. An on-court meltdown in tennis. I'll define it more viscerally. I've seen it once, and if it comes back on, I'm going to change the channel. Here are a bunch of moments that made it tough to be a sports fan.

Boxing: Mike Tyson biting a chunk of Evander Holyfield's ear off. Nothing gets nastier than that. Tyson was frustrated, he had just gotten head-butted by Holyfield, who's a head-butter nonpareil. He was all ticked off, and he did a Vincent van Gogh on him. What could be worse than seeing Holyfield with half his earlobe falling off because it's in Tyson's mouth? Think about how gross that is. This episode is up there all alone as the ugliest moment in sports.

Dishonorable mention: No, it's not in the same class, but do you remember the Riddick Bowe–Andrew Golota fight in Madison Square Garden in the summer of 1996? First you had Golota landing low blows in a fight that he's winning. Then after the fight you've got Rock Newman—that idiot—and all his morons coming into the ring, throwing chairs, beating each other up, starting half a riot. And you wonder why people have problems with boxing?

Baseball: It was unbelievable for Pete Rose to do what he did to Ray Fosse, barreling headfirst into him at home plate in the 1970 All-Star Game. He broke Fosse's shoulder and his career was never the same after that. I've had Fosse on many a time to talk about it—he's now a broadcaster for the A's. He takes the high road, saying, "That's baseball." And yes, I know that the All-Star Game was a bigger deal back then, and there was more of a rivalry between the two leagues. But Rose was so into his little macho trip that he just went over the line. I mean, c'mon. It's an exhibition game. Rose would have scored the winning run anyway. Do you have to send a guy to the hospital, too? Not necessary.

Dishonorable mention: Mike Piazza and Roger Clemens in 2000. Not the bat-throwing in the World Series, which was really blown out of proportion. I'm talking about that game in the regular season, the second game of that historic day-night, Queens-Bronx doubleheader. Clemens is a headhunter, we all know that. What he did was out of line. Now I don't think he hit Piazza in the head on purpose. If you go back and look at a replay, you can see Clemens actually recoil when the ball hits Piazza. He gave him one of those looks like when you see a big black bug in your bathtub.

But it wasn't completely an accident either. Piazza had owned Clemens. He'd hit a grand slam off him in the past. So Clemens wanted to come inside and dust Piazza and make him hit the dirt. That was nasty, to see a guy concussed on the field like that's just terrible.

NBA: Kermit Washington punching Rudy Tomjanovich during a brawl in 1977. Anything that you've seen a guy like Karl Malone do, everything pales in comparison to that one. The doctors compared the impact to getting thrown through a car window at fifty miles per hour. It almost cost Rudy his life. Now Kermit Washington didn't know he was hitting Rudy T—he just happened to walk into the punch. And Kermit Washington didn't have a reputation before that. In fact, I had a basketball coach at my high school who'd played with Kermit Washington at American University and said he was a great guy, loved him. After all these years Rudy T has forgiven Kermit. Washington blames the whole incident on Rudy's teammate Kevin Kunnert—gimme a break—and thinks he's been railroaded. That punch just sticks in your mind as much as you wish it wouldn't.

Dishonorable mention: Latrell Sprewell choking P. J. Carlesimo: Okay, we don't actually have this one on videotape, but you've heard so much about it that you almost *think* you saw it. And let's give Sprewell some credit—he's been a good citizen since then. I never wanted Sprewell with the Knicks, and I'll say I was dead wrong. But I don't care how much a guy's yelling at you, you can't do something like that. And Sprewell came back a second time. He choked P.J., settled down for fifteen minutes, then came back and had to be restrained again. Strangely, the whole incident had much more of an effect on P.J. than on Sprewell. On the one hand, it probably kept him in the Golden State job longer than he might have been otherwise. They couldn't fire him after that. But the fact that Sprewell basically rehabilitated himself and got along so well with Jeff Van Gundy, that really hurt P.J.'s career.

NFL: Dirty play in football drives me crazy. The Jack Tatum hit that paralyzed Darryl Stingley is in a class by itself. Even today, there's one hit a weekend in the NFL where you say that's just not necessary. But the worst one is what Bill Romanowski did to Kerry Collins in preseason. He just drove his helmet into Kerry Collins's face and shattered his jaw. In preseason. In preseason. I've talked to Kerry Collins about this and he doesn't have any problems with it, but trying to ruin a guy's career in an exhibition game? That's out of line. And you'll remember that in a *Monday Night Football* game against the 49ers, Romanowski spit in J. J. Stokes's face, and even some of his own teammates thought it was a racial thing.

Dishonorable mention: In one of those Steelers-Browns battles back in the mid-'70s, Joe "Turkey" Jones of the Browns sacked Terry Bradshaw. After the whistle he slammed him headfirst to the turf and flipped him around six or seven times. Bradshaw got a concussion on the play and Jones got nailed with a $3,000 fine. They hated Jones in Pittsburgh so much after that he had to stay in a different hotel than the rest of the team.

Tennis: Martina Hingis in the French Open in 1999 against Steffi Graf. She's winning the match, gets a bad line call, and she runs around the net and wipes away the mark on the clay. In the third set she calls for a bathroom break, then comes out with a new outfit and a new hairstyle. She served for the match at 5-4 in the third, and from there on in she basically collapsed. And after the loss, her mother had to all but drag her out of the locker room and out onto the court for the awards ceremony.

Dishonorable mention: In the early '80s, the radio station where I was working, WKIS in Orlando, held an exhibition tennis match to raise money for the Adam Walsh Foundation. Jimmy Connors and Ivan Lendl were playing. Lendl, who had the reputation of having no personality, could not have been better. Came on the radio, was absolutely phenomenal. Even though John Walsh was Connors's friend and the exhibition was Connors's idea, Jimmy wouldn't come on the radio. As a matter of fact, Connors was so upset about being there that weekend, after a close call went against him, he picked up a ball and smacked it at a lineswoman and hit her. He got defaulted. In an exhibition match.

NHL: It's one thing to get called for a penalty. It's another thing to get convicted of assault with a weapon. What Marty McSorley did to Donald Brashear in February 2000 was just terrible. Brashear had cleaned McSorley's clock in a fight earlier in the game, and then told him he wasn't going to give him a rematch because his team was up 4-0. So McSorley comes up and tries to decapitate Brashear with his stick. He's lying on the ice with a concussion, his eyes rolling around in his head, and McSorley says it was an accident. C'mon. Even the judge said that a kid playing T-ball couldn't miss that badly.

Dishonorable mention: Tie Domi knocking out Scott Niedermayer with an elbow to the face in the 2001 playoffs. Typical NHL playoff chippiness. Final seconds of the game, a goon taking out one of the other team's good players. Any time Pat Quinn's Leafs are in the playoffs, nastiness follows. According to Niedermayer, Domi's hit was premeditated. He said that Domi had told him two games before, "I'm going to take a suspension on you." Given Domi's track record, that's no surprise.

Of Black Cats and Seeing-Eye Singles

Are there really athletes and teams that are jinxed?

Sports fans are superstitious types. The Curse of this. The Jinx of that. But should teams hire astrologers . . . or just get better players? The Dog examines this otherworldly issue.

Fans love to talk about jinxes. When they can't figure out why a team loses—or just can't face it—they call it a jinx: The sports gods don't want us to win. To me, I think that there are relatively few real jinxes in sports.

The Utah Jazz aren't jinxed. They had two chances and lost to a better team both times: the Bulls. It's not like the Jazz have lost to nine billion teams. To have a jinx you have to have an all-time great player or a classic franchise that has had ample opportunity to win a big event. They've been the favorite, or should have been. But they haven't been able to get over the hump for a variety of reasons. And it helps if there are some bizarre circumstances surrounding the losses. Here are six legitimate jinxes.

Sam Snead at the U.S. Open: This one's a no-brainer. Sam Snead was a great golfer. He won seven major championships. He beat Ben Hogan and Byron Nelson. He won golf tournaments when he was sixty. He played in the U.S. Open for twenty-five years. But he just couldn't win the tournament. And he lost in crazy ways. In 1939 they didn't have a leaderboard, so he thinks he is losing when he's actually got a one-stroke lead. He heads to the eighteenth trying to make a birdie when a par would do. He ends up with an eight when a five would have at least gotten him into a playoff. Another time he lost in St. Louis in 1947 when there was a controversy on the green over who was away. They ended up taking fifteen minutes to measure it, and Sam got out of rhythm, missed the putt, and ended up losing in a playoff. Now Slammin' Sammy always hit the ball beautifully, but he didn't always use his noodle when he was out there—think of Phil Mickelson today—but he was a great golfer. And he lost in the U.S. Open in such crazy ways that it was a big-time jinx, one that bothered him to no end.

Björn Borg at the U.S. Open: Borg was an all-time great player. Won eleven majors—six French Opens and five Wimbledons. He played the U.S. Open on three different surfaces—grass, clay, and hard court. He played in four finals. He lost to Jimmy Connors. He lost to John McEnroe. Sure, these are great players, but he led the career rivalry with Connors 13–5 and was even 7–7 against McEnroe. In '79, which might have been his best chance, he lost in the quarters to Roscoe Tanner in a night match when he could barely see Tanner's rocket serve. Borg just seemed to be jinxed by New York City—the noise, the environment, the different surfaces, whatever it was. But you figure that somewhere along the way between 1974 and 1981, he should have won one.

Roy Williams: The jinx guy in college basketball right now is Roy Williams at Kansas. For years it was Dean Smith, but he got the monkey off his back. I don't want to hear about Guy Lewis, he's not a great all-time coach. I don't want to hear about Jim Boeheim because Jim Boeheim hasn't had the best team year in and year out. But year in and year out for a decade or more, Roy Williams has had a Final Four–quality club. Since he's been at Kansas they've won twenty or more games thirteen seasons in a row. His winning percentage is the best among active coaches. He's been to three Final Fours. He's played in the championship game. And no title. Roy's not Dean Smith but he is a big-time coach. He's had plenty of NBA players, it's a great all-time program. I can't say that KU's jinxed because they won for Larry Brown. But they should have won an NCAA championship during Roy's tenure.

Elgin Baylor: The NBA player I think about is Elgin Baylor. As a rookie in '58–'59, he comes in and leads a pretty bad Minneapolis Lakers team to the finals, where they get swept by the Celtics. Okay, he's got to be pretty happy with that: he's been on the doorstep. In '61–'62 the Lakers get to the finals again, lead the series three games to two, and have a chance to close it out at home. Can't do it. Back to Boston for game seven, it's tied at 100 as time's running out, and Frank Selvy has an open twelve-footer for the championship. His shot bounces off the rim, and Elgin and the Lakers lose in overtime. The next year? Again, game seven against the Celtics. Again the Lakers lose by three. In 1964–65, another final against

Boston, and Elgin's Lakers lose in five games. In '65–'66, again they push the Celtics to seven, and again they lose by a basket in the Boston Garden. In '67–'68, same old story: Celts-Lakers and Boston wins in six. Finally in '68–'69, Elgin's got Wilt Chamberlain to match up against Bill Russell, and Los Angeles has home court advantage in the finals. They win the first two games, but they lose game seven at home, again by two points. In '69–'70, Russell's retired and the Celtics are out of the way. This time the Lakers lose to the Knicks in seven games. In his first twelve years in the league, the great Elgin Baylor makes eight finals. Four times the Lakers get to a decisive game seven, where just a couple of timely baskets would have gotten him a ring. And it's not Elgin's fault, because he's played great. Now here's the ironic part. The year that Elgin gets hurt, the Lakers win thirty-three straight and win the finals with Jim McMillan playing every day. Baylor is the very definition of snakebit.

The Red Sox: This is a classic. The Red Sox have had plenty of years where they were right there—1946, 1949, 1967, 1975, 1978. And, of course, 1986. This is a franchise that has been loaded with Hall of Famers—Jimmie Foxx, Ted Williams, Yaz, Lefty Grove, Roger Clemens, Pedro Martinez. There have been a bunch of opportunities where the Red Sox could have won a championship if the ball had bounced right. They lost the 1946 World Series when Ted Williams hurt his elbow in a tune-up game against the American League All-Stars, and Enos Slaughter scores from first on a base hit in game seven. In 1949 they could have easily beaten the Yankees, up by half a game with two left, and they lose both games. They lost a seventh game in '75. In '78 they won ninety-nine games but lost that playoff game on Bucky Dent's homer and Lou Piniella's play in right. Lost game six to the Mets in 1986, when they had a two-run lead in the bottom of the tenth inning while up three games to two. Somewhere since 1918, there should be a year where Boston should have won a World Series. After all, if the Florida Marlins managed to win a championship, why can't the Red Sox?

The Minnesota Vikings: Somewhere, somehow, the Vikings should have won a championship, too. They lost four Super Bowls under Bud Grant. Grant is a Hall of Fame coach, better than Marv Levy, who everybody compares him to. Now they lost to good teams—the Dolphins, the Raiders, the Steelers, and the Chiefs—but it wouldn't have been a huge upset if they had won any of those games.

Remember, they also beat a lot of good teams in the NFC: the Cowboys, the Rams, the Redskins. And since then, they've been in the playoffs plenty of other years. It really went into jinx territory in 1998. They went 15–1, and a team that loses only one game in the NFL almost always goes all the way. Never in a million years should Minnesota have lost to the Atlanta Falcons in the NFC championship game. Gary Anderson, who hadn't missed a field goal all year, missed one that would have put them up ten with two minutes to go. Randy Moss dropped a touchdown pass. And they lost in overtime. Sure, Randall Cunningham and Dennis Green did their part by running out the clock at the end of the game and playing conservatively in overtime, but they should have never lost that game.

THE UN-JINXED

When it comes to guys who always seem to collect rings like they were Cracker Jack prizes, I think about Lonnie Smith. In the early 1980s he bounces from the Phillies to the Cardinals to the Royals and collects three rings in five years, then lands in two more Series with the Braves. He's always been in the right place at the right time.

Breaking Par

How can professional golf be improved?

Okay, you can't do anything about the ugly shirts, the bad hats, or Craig Stadler's beer gut. But pro golf could be better. Here are a few things that has Mad Dog, um, teed off.

Watching a pro golfer is pretty impressive. They hit the ball a million miles. They can get up and down and save par from the Okefenokee Swamp. But I don't think there's quite enough balance in the pro game today. It's a little too extreme. Guys are hitting too far off the tees. The courses have roughs that are ridiculous. I'd like to bring the game back a little, make it a little more like the game that you and I try to play on Saturday afternoon. If I'm Tim Finchem, PGA Tour commissioner, here are a few things that I would do to make pro golf a game that the average duffer can relate to.

Standardize the Golf Ball: Players are already hitting the ball too far off the tee, and companies are still trying to make balls that'll go 15 or 20 yards farther. Listen, if a guy's clubhead speed is 125 miles per hour and the ball goes 350 yards, that's one thing. But I can't have the guy swing the club 100 miles per hour and still have his drive go 350 yards. After all, the balls in every other sport are standardized, so why can't they standardize them in golf?

And it's really threatening the integrity of the game. Augusta had to buy land to make the course longer so guys like Tiger Woods don't turn it into a pitch and putt. We are going to end up doing that to every golf course in America if we're not careful.

Keep the Hazards Hazardous: This idea of raking traps is crazy. It's gotten to the point where traps aren't hazards anymore, that golfers actually want to put the ball in traps rather than in the rough. Maybe it's okay to rake the trap before the day starts and that's the end of it. Ball lands in the trap, play it the way it lands.

Tweak the U.S. Open: Too many times at the U.S. Open the USGA likes to make the course the star. They grow the rough until it's twenty feet deep, make a tough course into the kind of course that humbles golfers, brings them to their knees. There's a happy medium. I don't wanna see them 16 under par, but I don't want to see them 3 over, either.

And get rid of the Monday playoff. Sports in America are made to conclude on Sunday nights. People don't want a playoff on Monday afternoon. It's anticlimactic. Can anyone name me a dramatic eighteen-hole playoff in the U.S. Open? On the other hand, I don't like the sudden-death playoff because I think it's unfair to the guy who's been sitting around for an hour—he makes one bad swing and he's out. We'll do what the British Open does: a four-hole playoff and then sudden-death after that.

Juice Up the PGA Championship: The problem with the PGA right now is that it's last in the pecking order among the majors. Ask fifty pros and some will say the Masters is more important, some will say the U.S. Open is more important. Ask the Europeans, they'll say the British Open is more important. Nobody says the PGA. So I would love to try match play at the PGA. They did it for fifty, sixty years there and it made the event unique. Match play is something that recreational golfers can relate to, playing hole to hole, trying to beat your partner. I know that TV hates the idea because it leaves them with only two golfers on Sunday afternoon and a lot of dead airtime. But I think the networks could find a way around it. After all, they love the Skins Game.

Tools of the Game

How would you build the perfect baseball player?

Ever wonder what would have happened if Lee Majors's boss on the Six Million Dollar Man *were a baseball scout? The Dog gets bionic and assembles the ultimate position player.*

Leo Durocher said it first: "There are only five things you can do in baseball. Run. Throw. Catch. Hit. And hit with power." Now every decent prospect is called a five-tool guy. But what are the benchmarks for these tools? Which guys were the best ever at each one of these fundamental skills?

Run: I'm not talking about running wind sprints down the foul lines. If that's the test, I'd take the A's designated runner Herb Washington, the sprinter who stole twenty-nine bases and got caught sixteen times. I'm talking about a guy who can use his speed in the context of a game. So Lou Brock's my guy. I thought about Rickey Henderson, but I can't pick him because too many times I saw Henderson watch what he thought was a homer bounce off the wall and have to settle for a double.

Brock scared the hell out of you. Great base-stealer. Left-handed hitter, another advantage. The only thing that bothers me about Brock is that he got thrown out at the plate against Detroit in the fifth game of the 1968

World Series. The fact that he didn't slide in that spot probably cost the Cardinals the World Series. That bothers me, but I love Lou Brock.

Throw: When you think of throwing arms in Major League Baseball you think of two spots on the field: in the hole at short and the right field corner. And although there are a lot of shortstops who can gun it, gunning it from short to first is one thing. Gunning it from the right field corner 250 feet to home plate is something entirely different. And nobody had a better throwing arm than Roberto Clemente. Strong. Yes. But accurate, too. A guy like Vladimir Guerrero has Clemente-like arm strength, but he overthrows cutoff men and things like that. Roberto had a legendary arm. You couldn't go first to third, and if you tried to tag up on a short fly, you'd be dead at the plate.

The ultimate compliment is that opposing players stopped running on him. In 1961 he had 27 assists, and after that his numbers tailed off, not because his arm weakened, but because runners were afraid to challenge him. He intimidated opposing base runners and third base coaches by his mere presence.

Catch: I know there are lots of Willie Mays fans, as well as fans of guys like Andruw Jones and Devon White. But I've got to go with Joe DiMaggio. There was one play back in 1937, recounted in Richard Ben Cramer's biography, where Hank Greenberg crushed a ball to the deepest part of Yankee Stadium. It was out past the monuments, which were on the field of play back then, probably 450 feet. Everyone's in awe of how

---

THE YANKEE SLIPPER

Yogi Berra talks about how he never saw DiMaggio make a mistake. What do you call what DiMaggio did to Mickey Mantle in 1951? You know that famous scene. Willie Mays hit the ball to short right center field and DiMaggio waited until the last second to call Mantle off. Mantle tried to get out of the way because he didn't want to hit the great DiMaggio, and Mantle ripped up his knee on a drainpipe. That was Joe D's mistake. Joe was always concerned about looking like, well, Joe D.

hard Greenberg hit the ball, and then out of nowhere, DiMaggio glides under the ball and makes the catch. He didn't dive, he didn't sprawl out, his hat didn't fly off. He just ran and caught it. There's a word you always hear about Joe D: effortless.

Hit for Average: I thought of three guys here: Ty Cobb, Ted Williams, and Rod Carew. Cobb hit .367 lifetime, but he played in the dead ball era, so I'm going to eliminate him for that reason. Williams, we all know he hit .406, but I don't think of him as hitting purely for average. So if it's the ninth inning, tie score, guy on second, two outs, game on the line, I'm going to give you Carew. The man won seven batting titles. He was a magician with that bat. Pitch him outside of the plate and he'll bloop it over the shortstop's head. Pitch him inside, he'll find the hole between first and second. Pitch him over the middle and it's a line drive up the middle. Carew was a tremendous batsman. He flicked that bat anywhere he wanted. He was like a cricket player who can direct the ball where he wants it when he's trying to avoid the wickets. That's Rodney Carew. He could use the bat as a defensive weapon, almost like a goalie stick: kick it out foul, kick it out foul, two strikes on him, he hits a little bloop down the left field line. He won't hit the home run, but I'm not looking for that. But if you want a guy who can handle the wand, that's Rod Carew.

Hit for Power: I'm picking Mickey Mantle. Nobody had power like he did from both sides of the plate. He hit a 565-foot homer to *left* field at Griffith Stadium in Washington in 1953, literally the first tape-measure home run. In 1960 he hit one over the *right* field roof in Detroit that was measured at 643 feet. And then there was the shot he hit against the A's at Yankee Stadium in 1963. When Mantle hit the ball, Yogi Berra popped out of the dugout and yelled, "This is it!" because he thought it was going to be the first ball hit out of the Stadium. Instead, the ball ricocheted off the upper deck facade in right field so hard that it bounced back onto the field. One computer projection estimated that this ball would have traveled 734 feet if it hadn't clipped the facade. Hank Aaron didn't have that kind of power, Willie Mays didn't have this kind of power. Even guys like Jose Canseco, Mark McGwire, and Frank Howard, who hit some long,

long home runs, couldn't jack 'em like the Mick. My father used to tell me that nobody hits a longer ball than Mantle, and I gotta believe him.

THE SIXTH TOOL

I'm going to add one category to Durocher's list: instincts. And I think Willie Mays had a better feel for the game, could beat you more ways than any player in the history of the sport. Base running, fielding, positioning himself on defense. Whatever it might be, there were situations where Mays just knew how to play the game. It's really applied intelligence. You know that play in the seventh game of the World Series against the Yankees, when Willie doubled down the right field corner. After the game somebody asked Willie if he would have scored if Willie McCovey's scorcher had gone through. "I would have been showered, dressed, and out of the ballpark by the time that throw came into home plate." And The Catch. Sure he caught the ball. But he didn't fool around and show the ball to everyone. He had the presence of mind to throw a strike back to second base. If ever a player was born to play baseball, whom God put on this earth to play baseball, it was Willie Mays.

And today, no one else understands the way the game is supposed to be played—reading pitchers, playing the outfield, running the bases, moving runners over, looking for a certain pitch—better than Barry Bonds. Who did he learn from? He learned from Willie.

Can't Buy Me Love

Do women tennis players really deserve equal prize money?

It sounds harsh, but women's tennis has about as much depth as an Adam Sandler movie. So Billie Jean King be damned, Mad Dog tells you why Andre should have a bigger purse than Venus.

I 'll admit it. I'm not big on women's sports. Maybe I'll watch a U. Conn–Tennessee basketball game, but I couldn't care less about the WNBA or the LPGA. Still, when the important women's matches at Wimbledon or the U.S. Open roll around, I'm in front of the TV.

The problem that I have with women's tennis, and the reason why I do not believe in equal prize money for the women, is that the depth in the sport is an absolute disgrace. I know John McEnroe has gotten off this argument. I'm sticking to it.

Right now there are basically five top women's tennis players, at best. You have the Williams sisters. You have Jennifer Capriati. Maybe Kim Clijsters and Justine Henin. And when they're healthy, Lindsay Davenport and Martina Hingis. I know Mary Pierce has had her moments, too. But, at any big tournament, there are really only a handful of women who can win.

So if you're at a Grand Slam during the first week, you're wasting your time watching a women's tennis match because it's never, ever competitive. You watch Serena play a couple of games while she's beating someone 6-2, 6-0 in forty-one minutes, and that's the end. It's a disgrace. Her route to winning that title is far easier than for the men's champion. She's got to play two matches where she could lose. Two.

On the men's side the competitiveness is very, very good. If you go and watch a second round men's match at any of the majors, the big player, say, Pete Sampras, can get knocked off by a guy like George Bastl, who's ranked eightieth in the world. That's not the case in women's tennis.

Because of this competitive imbalance, I don't believe that equal prize money is warranted for the women. To me the Grand Slam is a two-week endeavor. It's not a four-day endeavor. The idea of the Grand Slam is that you've got to win seven matches to win a championship. And the problem with the women's game is that in the first four of those matches, maybe five, you can write down the score before you go out and watch. And to me, that's not worth my money as a fan, a spectator of the sport.

I know that people are going to argue, "Hold on, Russo. You're nuts. You're just a male chauvinist who knows nothing about women's sports." That's not true. I've followed women's tennis for a long, long time. I have loved every minute of it. Martina Navratilova is the best player I've ever seen. I'd watch her play any day of the week. I'd watch Billie Jean King play any day. Steffi Graf, Monica Seles, Margaret Court, same thing. But I'm not watching two women on the bottom end of the draw.

Would I watch Karel Kucera against Hicham Arazi? You betcha.

The men's game is simply much better than the women's game. I'm amazed that everybody goes gaga over the women's game, but people who do are the casual fans who sit there on a Saturday night and watch Venus and Serena in the U.S. Open final instead of watching a rerun of some sitcom. While they play great tennis, the matches between Venus and Serena aren't compelling because there's no sense of rivalry. Who do you root for? The bottom line is that there are five women who are worth paying money to see. That's my issue with the sport, and that's why the men deserve more money than the women.

BEST OF THREE, BEST OF FIVE

I can certainly make a bigger deal about the fact that the women play best two out of three while the men play best of five. In a perfect world, you'd like to see the women play best of five. The potential for drama—for a big down-two-sets-to-love comeback—is much greater than in best of three. But the way the women's game is now, if you've seen Venus win the first two sets 6-1, 6-1, do we have to stay around to see the extra set at 6–2? Is it a big deal to you?

They Call It The Streak

Whose consecutive games string was more formidable, Ripken's or Gehrig's?

They're two of baseball's singular accomplishments, separated by almost sixty years. But who gets the most credit for showing up every day? The Iron Horse or Cal, Jr.? The Mad Dog weighs the argument.

This was one record I thought I'd show my kids in the record book. I never thought that Lou Gehrig's consecutive games streak would be broken. But day after day, season after season, Cal Ripken went out there and chipped away at the number. Both Ripken and Gehrig did remarkable things. But which accomplishment is really greater? I put both of them under the magnifying glass and here's my take.

The Case for Cal

Obviously Gehrig is playing a much easier position. He's playing first base while Ripken's playing shortstop. Rip's got much more of a chance to get hurt, jam a finger, sprain an ankle turning a double play, get a sore arm.

The second thing is the scheduling. Ripken played eight more games a season, 162 to 154. The travel is much harder today than it was then, too. Although they can fly on planes and they have four-star hotels and they have night games instead of only day games, the fact is that players today have to go coast to coast, maybe play in Anaheim on a Thursday night then back in Baltimore on a Friday night. In Gehrig's day you didn't have to go west of St. Louis and you had a lot of teams right in one area— Philadelphia, New York, Boston, and Washington—that were easy to get in and out of.

I think Ripken also gets a bonus in that he was breaking a legendary record. Gehrig broke Everett Scott's record early on, not a big deal, and for most of the streak he was just adding on to it. Now I know that it takes great motivation to go out there every single day when you already have a record: "I got 2,000. I'll just take a day off today." But I think breaking that kind of gargantuan record is going to be harder than setting it. When he got to 1,500, Ripken knew he still had four or five seasons to play before he got past Lou. So I think you've got to give Ripken a big plus on that.

The fourth edge I'll give Ripken is the fact that there were a couple of games where Gehrig did bat first because he had back problems. He left the game after the first or second at-bat to keep the streak going. I can't think of too many situations where Ripken took the easy way out to keep the streak going. The difference is that Gehrig could afford to do that because he's breaking his own record. Ripken had to be aware of the asterisk, and Gehrig didn't.

The Case for Lou

The main thing going in Gehrig's favor is that he was an incredible baseball player. Most people agree that Gehrig is the greatest first baseman of all time. Lou's hitting cleanup behind Babe Ruth, knocking in 184 runs a year.

Ripken was not that kind of player. Yes he won a couple of MVPs, but they're not at the same level at all. It's almost an insult to Gehrig to even compare him with Ripken. To have that kind of consecutive game streak while you're an all-time great is an incredible accomplishment. So the fact that Gehrig is a better player than Ripken, far better, is a huge factor.

In a lot of ways Ripken is about the streak. Lou Gehrig would be one of the greatest players of all time if he never played even one hundred consecutive games. That's not the case with Ripken. That's another big plus for Lou.

The other knock on Ripken is that he became consumed by the streak, almost selfish. There were a lot of times where a day off would have done Ripken some good, where the Orioles would have been better off if he had taken three or four days a season off to rest. There were years in the middle of Ripken's streak where he hit .250.

And there's no question it affected his career in a negative way. Here's a guy who wins an MVP his second year, hits .318 with 27 home runs, and wins a World Series. And except for that one blip during his MVP year of 1991, he never even got close to those numbers again. What great player reaches his peak at age twenty-three? His career was a ski slope for crying out loud, all downhill.

Then look at Gehrig. He had one season where maybe you could say he tailed off significantly and that was in 1938, and that was because he had the early symptoms of ALS and didn't know it. He still hit .295 with 114 RBIs, and it wasn't because he was tired, it was because he was *dying*.

I dare anybody to find a game in the heart of Lou's career where the Yankees would have been better off to give him a day off and not play him. You can't find one.

I can give you a million games where Ripken hurt his club by forcing himself to go out there and play.

The Verdict

I give Ripken an incredible amount of credit. I know he was great for baseball when he broke the record in 1995, coming off that strike. At the same time, I have always felt that Ripken was a little overrated as a player. He's a Hall of Famer but he's not an all-time great. Gehrig is one of the greatest players to ever step on the field, so to be an all-time great and play 2,000-plus games is more significant than being very good and playing more than 2,000 games. I'm going with Gehrig.

Love Shaq?

How does O'Neal rank against the all-time great centers?

He's the world's largest rapper and he's got a fistful of rings. But can Shaquille O'Neal compare to the best big men in the history of the game? Mad Dog elaborates.

We had Tommy Heinsohn, the great Hall of Famer from the Celtics, on the Mike and the Mad Dog show during the 2002 NBA playoffs. He was ranking the all-time best centers and here's what he said: Bill Russell's in Boston, Wilt Chamberlain is in Newton, Kareem Abdul-Jabbar is in Buffalo, and Shaquille O'Neal is not even in the country. That's tough.

So where does Shaq really stack up against the great centers? Shaq has a couple of negatives compared to the all-time greats. First off, the way he plays the position doesn't have the grace and beauty of some of these others. Shaq's game is all power, and it can be pretty ugly at times. He's a bull in a china shop. He's not pretty, he's not fun. Kareem could show you the sky hook. Wilt was such a great athlete, and when he couldn't dunk, he'd use the dipsy doo, the fadeaway, the finger roll. Hakeem Olajuwon wasn't as great a player as Wilt, but he had those ballet dancer's feet and a tremendous repertoire offensively.

Russell wasn't quite as spectacular as these other guys, but he had the brains of a surgeon. He'd be a power forward today, but he positioned himself beautifully and blocked shots like crazy. He was a thinking man's player. Moses Malone falls into the same category. He was a tireless offensive rebounder, a great free throw shooter, and he had a relentlessness about him that set him apart.

Shaq's got some tough competition when it comes to cracking the upper echelon of all-time centers. Each of the top three centers had something distinctive going for him. Kareem has the career scoring record. Chamberlain put up all kinds of crazy numbers—averaging 50 points for a season, leading the league in assists, scoring 100 in a game. Russell won like no one ever has before or since. And each of them played against other great centers on a nightly basis.

And when you're evaluating O'Neal you have to remember the fact that he's playing in an era when there aren't any other great centers. On a night-to-night basis he is not going up against other all-time greats. Kareem was going up against Wilt, Bill Walton, Willis Reed, Dave Cowens, Bob Lanier, and Nate Thurmond. Russell and Wilt were going up against each other, and you can throw in Zelmo Beaty, throw in Walt Bellamy. They were both going up against great, great centers. Hakeem had Patrick Ewing and David Robinson.

Shaq is going up against Rik Smits, Vlade Divac, and Todd MacCulloch on the way to a championship. Name me a great center that Shaq is going up against right now? Tim Duncan's a power forward and Robinson, Ewing, and Olajuwon were at the tail end of their careers when Shaq was winning titles.

So Shaq isn't on the same level with Russell, Wilt, and Kareem. And he's probably never going to get there because he's never going to have that guy who can challenge him. You've got to rank him ahead of Moses Malone. And he's close to Olajuwon already. If you like finesse, you take Hakeem; if you like power, you take Shaq.

It's going to be tough for O'Neal to crack that top three. But I will say that Heinsohn was unfair to Shaq when he made that comparison: Shaq is definitely in the country. If Russell's in Boston and Kareem's in Buffalo, let's say Shaq is in Chicago with Olajuwon, and moving eastward.

The Big Rewind Button

If you could have the ultimate second chance, how would you change sports history?

Remember when you were playing ball as a kid, and you got into a fight about the rules? You'd play a do-over, right? Well, what if you had the same kind of chance to change sports history. Would you give your team a couple more championships? Or take the high road like Mad Dog.

What if you had a cosmic sports rewind button? You could press a button on your remote, back things up a few seconds or a few minutes, and let them play it again. I'd like to think that I'd use it for the right reasons. Not just to erase the outcome of a game that my team lost. So sorry, Raider fans, we're not going to replay that Tom Brady fumble. And sorry, Red Sox fans, Bill Buckner had his chance. My idea of the rewind button is to erase the kind of bad moment that cheated us, and give us a second chance that could bring some kind of closure to a great event, or a career, that kind of left us hanging.

Freddy Brown's Turnover: The 1982 NCAA final between Georgetown and North Carolina was an all-time great game. A bunch of future NBA stars on the court: Michael Jordan, Patrick Ewing, James Worthy, Brad Daugherty, Sleepy Floyd. That game deserved a better outcome than Georgetown's Freddy Brown not paying attention and throwing the ball to Worthy, who was out of position near half court. That game deserved a Georgetown final shot to win.

To refresh your memory, Georgetown was up one, and North Carolina had the ball on the second-to-last possession of the game. Time out Dean Smith. The Tar Heels pass the ball around the perimeter, and Jordan without blinking an eye drains a jump shot that puts UNC up by a point. It was a sneak preview of what was to come for Michael.

Anyway, Georgetown gets the ball back, down by a point, with maybe thirteen, fourteen seconds left, and comes down the court to set up their last play. Classic end to a championship game. And then the turnover. Now if Ewing misses a 10-footer or Floyd bricks a 20-footer, that's one thing. But this was an anticlimactic ending to one of the greatest college basketball games ever. I want to press the rewind button right at that point and play that last possession clean.

Herb Score's Line Drive: In the mid-'50s with the Indians, Herb Score posted these numbers. His rookie year he was 16–10 with a 2.85 ERA and led the league in strikeouts. The next year he was even better: 20–9, 2.53 ERA, and again led the league in strikeouts. Lefty, young, struck a lot of people out on a good team, Herb Score had a chance to be an earlier version of Sandy Koufax. And then early in his third year he gets hit in the eye with a line drive by Gil McDougald. Herb Score was never the same. He was 19–27 the rest of his career. The magic ended with the line drive. Wouldn't you like to press the rewind button and have that line drive go over his head into centerfield? To see what kind of pitcher Herb Score could have become—would he be Koufax or Vida Blue? Damn right you'd like to know.

Knicks-Heat WWF: Remember game five in the Eastern Conference semis when the Knicks went out on the court and got nine million guys suspended after that fight between Charlie Ward and P. J. Brown? I'd like to rewind that for a couple of reasons. One, the Knicks players didn't participate in the fight, they just kind of drifted onto the court. The rules are the rules, but this was a tough one. Second, assuming that a full-strength Knicks team would have won game six at the Garden and gotten past the Heat, I think they could have made it interesting against the Bulls in the Eastern Conference final. The Bulls were a little more vulnerable than they had been the year before, and the Knicks beat them late in the regular season in Chicago. The Heat got swept by the Bulls, and that wouldn't have happened to the Knicks. So I would like to press the button and see if we would have had another classic Knicks-Bulls series.

The Dempsey-Tunney Long Count: I say hit the button and let's start that count right away. I understand that Jack Dempsey didn't go immediately to a neutral corner, but Gene Tunney got an extra seven seconds. That's a lifetime in a boxing match.

This was a huge fight. Chicago 1927. The largest fight crowd in history: 103,000 people in Soldier Field on a summer night. Everyone was there. Jess Willard. Jack Johnson. Dempsey was a little past his prime, and Tunney had beaten him the first time they fought. Tunney was beating Dempsey and then he got knocked down. Tunney has said that it took him seven seconds to clear his head. So if there wasn't a long count, that would have given him three seconds to get on his feet. So wouldn't you like to press that rewind button and see Tunney have to get up within three seconds? A couple of afterthoughts: A lot of people argue that Dave Barry, the referee, did not make a mistake here. He ushered Dempsey into his corner and started the count in accordance with the rules. And people forget that Tunney not only got up, he took control of the round and the rest of the fight. I have trouble believing that would have happened if he'd had to get up in a regular ten count. So the long count to me is a classic rewind.

Monica Seles's Stabbing: It's easy to forget what a great player Monica Seles was. Just before she was stabbed in 1993, she had won seven of the last eight Grand Slams she played. And she won only one more after the attack. So the first reason you want to hit the button is to see what might have happened, how many majors she might have won, if she didn't miss more than two years in the prime of her career. The second reason is that Gunter Parche, the wacko who stabbed her, was obsessed with Steffi Graf and attacked Seles just so Graf could become number one in the world again. And not only did he get what he wanted—with Seles out, Graf dominated the game for another four years—the judge let him off and he didn't even end up going to prison. A great career is ruined and a bad guy gets off scot-free. A sad story and a perfect rewind scenario.

Two of a Kind

Which athletes could have been separated at birth?

Unlikely connections. That's what makes sports so endlessly fascinating. The tennis player who reminds you of a baseball star. The point guard who reminds you of a hockey center. Mad Dog shows you how to think outside the box.

Do you ever watch a game or a highlight show on ESPN Classic, and it strikes you. Doesn't he remind you of such and such? A guy in a completely different sport. Sometimes it's a physical resemblance. Sometimes it's the way their careers went. Sometimes it's the way they played. Here are some that have always intrigued me.

Tiger Woods and Kobe Bryant: With their prodigiousness, their will to win, their competitive juices, and the way they're motivated by championships, not money, these guys are like brothers. All Kobe's got to do is sign with Nike. Actually you could make this a trifecta. Kobe reminds me so much of Michael Jordan, and Tiger is Jordan on a golf course. All three have ice water in their veins. And they've got a certain similarity of personality—on the one hand a little guarded and on the other they've always seemed mature beyond their years.

Pete Rose and Jimmy Connors: Talk about feisty, neither of these Midwestern guys would give an inch to their grandmothers. They both are self-made, busted their fannies, always gave you 100 percent, and had more hustle than Van McCoy. They would spill their guts every time out. They could also be petulant, argumentative, and difficult to deal with. They both played forever, too, hanging on well into their forties. Hell, they even had the same hairstyle.

Willie Stargell and Mean Joe Greene: Either one of these guys could have run for mayor of Pittsburgh. Both were big, powerful men, but it was more than that. They were both Hall of Famers, both father figures, both elder statesmen. And both did well by their adopted hometown—between them they helped bring six championships to Steeltown in the 1970s.

Wayne Gretzky and Magic Johnson: Physically they couldn't be more different. But both of these guys raised the assist to an art form. Both could dominate a game without scoring, through their ability to get their teammates involved, making everyone around them better. Both were so much fun to watch, the stars on great offensive teams. Gretzky camped behind the net, flicking the puck off a guy's back and scoring a goal. Magic running the three-on-two Showtime fast break, ending it with a behind-the-back dipsy doo pass to Byron Scott or an alley oop to James Worthy. The real common thread is the vision thing. Both of these guys had eyes in the back of their head. They saw openings that no one else did, saw how the play could unfold before anyone made a move. In a phrase: unteachable intangibles.

Tom Landry and Tom Osborne: Both stoic, both legendary, and both should have won more championships. Landry was 2–5 in championship games, losing two NFL title games to the Packers, two Super Bowls to Pittsburgh, and one to the Colts. Osborne knocked at the door forever, but did manage to win three national championships. Old-fashioned guys with old-fashioned values, but they sometimes had a little trouble controlling modern athletes. Armen Keteyian wrote that book about the problems in Nebraska, and of course Peter Gent wrote *North Dallas Forty*. Mostly I think these coaches each should have five, six, seven championships.

Say It Ain't So

What are the most memorable sports controversies of all time?

We all make mistakes. But sometimes you get caught. Big-time. When it happens in the world of sports, the results usually transcend the sports section. Mad Dog weighs in on the greatest and most enduring controversies in sports history.

The world of sports is full of controversies. This guy gets arrested. This guy gets caught cheating. This guy gets suspended. And by next week it's forgotten. The controversies that stick in my mind are the ones with legs. The ones that everyone remembers as if they were yesterday. The ones that have had a lasting effect on their sports. And often it's been a positive effect, a silver lining from the black cloud, so to speak. Here are five controversies that had an impact that reached way beyond the next day's sports section.

The Black Sox: This is the biggest sports scandal of the twentieth century. Everybody—my mother, my wife, my four-year-old—has heard of the Black Sox scandal. Look at the ramifications. A World Series that was compromised, players banned for life from the sport, a legendary player like Shoeless Joe Jackson still barred from the Hall of Fame.

A couple of things that people forget. This all started when Charles Comiskey, the old Roman who owned the White Sox, ordered the manager to sit Eddie Cicotte down at the end of the season two starts short of collecting his bonus. Cicotte, who went 29–7 that year, lost the money and then probably fell in with gamblers. Now I'm not trying to make excuses for Cicotte because he should have known better, but you can understand why the players don't trust the owners, even today. And don't forget that these players were brought to trial and acquitted in a court of law. People think, well, they must have gotten kicked out right away. No. They played in 1920, and it wasn't until a year later that Kenesaw Landis kicked them out in spite of the court decision.

The Aftershocks: After the Black Sox scandal the owners got serious about corruption in baseball. That led to the formation of the powerful commissioner in Landis. They also felt the need to juice up the game to revive people's interest, so this also marked the end of the dead ball era and the birth of modern baseball with Babe Ruth.

Pete Rose's Betting on Baseball: Pete Rose sort of represents what America is all about; a guy without a lot of talent, combative, competitive, a hustler, a self-made baseball player, that's Pete Rose. Pete Rose embodies a lot of what America loves: individuality, playing to win, fighting until your last breath. That's why he has always been so popular. Then all of a sudden you had Pete Rose in trouble with gambling. And even though he was gambling as a manager, not as a player, and he was gambling on his team to win, so far it has cost him a Hall of Fame induction ceremony.

The Aftershocks: Pete Rose is a magnet. If we want to do a talk show today, we bring up Pete Rose and the Hall of Fame, and the phones light

---

PUT PETE IN

Pete Rose should be in the Hall of Fame. Why? Because his Hall of Fame credentials aren't based on his managerial career. He bet on the Reds to win while he was a manager, and there's no evidence that he bet on baseball as a player. And he's going to get into the Hall of Fame as a player.

Remember, Major League Baseball doesn't control the Hall of Fame. It's a separate institution. To me being banished from Major League Baseball and being eligible for the Hall of Fame really ought to be two separate things. But the Hall of Fame connects them. "If you're on baseball's suspended list, you can't be on our list." It shouldn't be that way.

And while we're at it, Joe Jackson should be in the Hall of Fame, too. How is he not? It's stupid. He had a .355 career batting average, third best all time, Ty Cobb said the best pure hitter he ever saw. Why isn't he in? Because he took $5,000 in 1919 for the Black Sox? He wasn't the smartest guy who ever walked the face of the earth, so it's possible he didn't know what he was doing. More to the point, he had a great World Series. And finally, he was acquitted in court. This has gone on long enough. Put him in.

up. When Jim Gray grills Pete Rose at the World Series—Gray was totally out of line by the way—that grabs headlines and completely overshadows the Fall Classic.

The Heidi Bowl: Remember back in 1968, NBC leaves a Jets-Raiders game with the Jets leading 32-29 to switch to the movie *Heidi*? The Raiders score two touchdowns in the last forty-two seconds to come from behind and beat the Jets 43-32? Whoever made that decision in the control center at NBC won't be telling his grandchildren about that one.

The Aftershocks: The fact that the Heidi game has legs thirty-five years later is unbelievable. Imagine them doing that today. You can't, and that's a good thing. The Heidi Bowl was kind of a watershed event for sports on television. The networks learned their lesson with that one, and now they'll never ever cut from a live sporting event to some kind of regularly scheduled programming.

George O'Leary's Fudged Résumé: I would never fudge my résumé, would never even think about doing it. But the fact that a football coach fudged his résumé to say that he played in New Hampshire as a running back and had a graduate degree from NYU is mind-boggling to me. And for holier-than-thou Notre Dame to hire O'Leary without checking his résumé. Unbelievable. It took a guy writing for the Syracuse newspaper, just trying to get a little more detail about O'Leary's college playing days, to bring this to light.

The Aftershocks: I think that in a lot of ways this will prove to be a blessing for Notre Dame. Never in a million years would athletic director Kevin White have hired Tyrone Willingham under normal circumstances. But since he was so embarrassed by the O'Leary fiasco, bringing in the first black coach at Notre Dame took a lot of pressure off him. But it says here that Willingham should have gotten the job originally.

The 1972 USA-USSR Gold Basketball Game: Play it again, Sam. That was the theme in the final seconds of the Gold Medal game between those two superpowers. The officials kept adding time back onto the clock, playing that three seconds over and over again until Aleksander Belov scored the layup, the Soviets won, and the 63-game U.S. winning streak was ended. The Americans didn't play great that night, but they won fair and square. It was a travesty.

The Aftershocks: The U.S. never picked up those silver medals. The team voted to skip the medal ceremony, and the medals are still sitting in a vault in Switzerland somewhere. It was also one of those moments where we saw the ugly, political side of sports, coming only a few days after the Israeli massacre. And it certainly put some juice in the 1976 Games; Dean Smith *had* to win that gold.

WHEN IS A FUMBLE NOT A FUMBLE?

Here's hoping that the controversial Tom Brady fumble in the 2002 playoffs has some legs, too. You remember, closing seconds of the game against the Raiders, late fourth quarter, Brady gets hit and seemingly coughs up the ball. But upon further review it's ruled an incomplete pass because of the NFL's obscure Tuck Rule, and the Patriots go on to win in overtime.

Listen, the Patriots earned their Super Bowl. They beat the Steelers on the road, and they beat the Rams. And it was poetic justice in a way. On their way to the Super Bowl in '75–'76 the Raiders beat New England thanks to a very controversial call on a late hit by Ray Hamilton on Ken Stabler.

But the Brady play was a fumble, no ifs, ands, or buts. I think it's a terrible rule, and the NFL had better get around to changing it.

Rep Artists

Which baseball players get all the glory but don't back it up?

Everybody is a star. That's more than just a Sly & the Family Stone song— it's also the status quo in Major League Baseball. But who's the real deal and who's just a pseudostar? Just ask Mad Dog.

D id you ever listen to an announcer talk about a player—he should be an All-Star, he should be a Hall of Famer—and wonder if he's watching the same guy that you are? It happens to me all the time. I look at the stats, watch him play, and scratch my head, but the guy's name is in the lineup day after day. My list of overrated players includes a bunch of Hall of Famers and All-Stars—it's no fun trashing utility players. I'm not saying that these guys can't play. It's just that they're not as good as everyone seems to think they are. And my list only includes players from 1967 onward. Ernie Lombardi may have been overrated, but since I never saw him, I can't say.

Let me start with two overrated Hall of Famers.

Carlton Fisk: Mr. Four-Hour Ball Game, Carlton Fisk played twenty-four seasons, hit .269 lifetime. He knocked in 100 runs only twice. Gary Carter did it four times. How is that possible? Fisk hit 30 homers only once. Carter did it twice. And while Fisk's total of 351 homers is a record, for a catcher Carter hit 298 homers so it's not like there's a big difference. But it took Fisk twenty-four years.

I also think the magnitude of Fisk's big home run in game six of the '75 World Series was overrated. Bernie Carbo's home run was more important because his came in the eighth inning with the Red Sox down 6-3, six outs from losing the World Series. And let's not forget, the Reds won the next day, so Fisk's homer didn't really change anything.

Eddie Murray: A little bit of a compiler, a guy who just racks up stats. He played forever. Here's a guy who hit 504 home runs lifetime, which is an automatic ticket to Cooperstown, but his career high is 33. He had 3,000 hits, but never more than 186 in a season. He never won an MVP. In the '79 World Series against the Pirates he was 4-for-26. Made out after out after out. He had only five great years, 1980–85. And five great years does not make you a Hall of Famer in my book.

Dwight Evans: I get the idea that people look at Dwight Evans as a borderline Hall of Famer. Stop. He was a hell of a right fielder and he had a great throwing arm. But he played eighteen years at Fenway Park on great offensive teams and averaged 21 homers. He knocked in 100 runs only four times. His lifetime batting average is .272. I never thought, when I had to go face the Red Sox, that Dwight Evans was going to hurt me. On the '78 Red Sox he was the fifth or sixth most important offensive player. Jim Rice, Fred Lynn, and Yaz were better. George Scott was more dangerous. I'm not putting him in the Hall of Fame.

Harold Baines: I know he had 2,800 hits. But he's also a .289 hitter who never scored 100 runs and drove in 100 only three times in twenty-two years. He was a DH from the day he was born, so he never had to play the field. A good hitter, but that's about it. A Hall of Famer? Well, the Rangers once traded one—Sammy Sosa—to get him.

Lou Whitaker: He gets so much credit for being a part of that great double play combination with Alan Trammell. At Tiger Stadium where he played, if you hit a routine fly ball to right field it's a home run. But Whitaker hit only 244 homers. Only twice in his career—he played forever—did he reach triple digits in RBIs or runs scored. And his lifetime average of .276 is just that—average. He made the All-Star team every year in the mid-'80s, but I just never thought of him as more than a decent player.

Bo Jackson: Great athlete? Yes. A great running back? No doubt. A great baseball player? No way. His lifetime batting average is .250. In 694 career games, he struck out 841 times. That's more than a strikeout per game, sports fans. He gets an incredible amount of mileage out of a few *SportsCenter* moments: the catch where he's running up the wall, that monstrous leadoff homer in the All-Star Game against Rick Reuschel in Anaheim. No, you didn't go to the bathroom when he was up at the plate. But if you wanted to win, you didn't want him in your lineup, either.

Lee Smith: He leads the universe in career saves, but he would never get my vote for the Hall of Fame. I always thought he was extremely hittable. I never thought he had an overpowering presence, despite his size. He never had the Mariano quotient, the Bruce Sutter quotient, the Rollie Fingers quotient. It was never lights out when Lee Smith came in the game. You still think Lee Smith is a Hall of Famer? It's 1984, game four, Cubs-Padres, Jack Murphy, Chicago on the verge of going to its first World Series in three million years. Lee Smith facing Steve Garvey. It's high, it's far, it's . . . gone.

Bert Blyleven: When you pitch for twenty years and take the hill every five days, you're going to have a lot of wins. Blyleven had 287. He also had 250 losses. Won 20 games only once. And he lost 17 games that year. He had just two great seasons. He was 19–7 for the Indians in 1984 and 17–5 with the '89 Angels. That's it. I always thought that Bert was a guy who, if his curveball wasn't working—and that was 50-50—then you could hit him.

Terry Pendleton: He gets way too much credit for the intangibles. Pendleton, the MVP in '91? An MVP with 22 homers and 86 RBIs? What a joke. He's a light-hitting third baseman, a guy with a .270 career average and 140 home runs. And he's Lonnie Smith in reverse. He played in five World Series for the Cardinals and the Braves and never won a championship. And those were close series—all six or seven games, too. A homer at the right time from Mr. Pendleton—he hit two in 27 World Series games—and maybe things are different.

And a few current players who get more attention than they deserve.

Jason Kendall: He's a light-hitting catcher who can run a little bit. The thing that most people remember him for was the stomach-churning replay of that terrible ankle injury running to first. And yet the Pirates gave him all that money. I don't understand it.

Raul Mondesi: He's got a lot of things that you like—some power, great throwing arm, he can run. But look at his numbers. He's never knocked in 100 runs or scored 100. And he makes almost $12 million a year. I'm sorry, but Raul Mondesi is not a big-time baseball player, and we in New York learned that the past couple of years.

Manny Ramirez: Sure, he's an RBI machine, but I wouldn't want him anywhere near my team. He's moody, he never plays hurt. He's a terrible base runner. You've basically got to coerce him to play left field. He's a manager killer. And he makes a billion dollars. You can keep him.

Bernie Williams: Maybe this is a product of the fact that I have to work with my partner, Mike, the Yankee fan, on the air every day, but I think

Bernie Williams is a bit overrated. Forget those Gold Gloves: He's not a great center fielder. He can't throw. And he's been hurt a lot. He's a terrible base runner. He floats in and out of games. Go look at his numbers in the World Series against quality pitching. He does nothing. Basically, Bernie's a .300 hitter. He'll knock in 90 runs, score 110, and have a good on-base percentage. That's not worth $15 million a year in my book.

Fighting the Irish

Is Notre Dame football awe-inspiring—or just annoying?

Politics. Religion. And Notre Dame. If there's one subject in the world of sports on which there's no middle ground, it's Fighting Irish football. You either reach for the hankies when Rudy comes on or reach for the remote. Guess where the Under Dog stands on this one?

Notre Dame is like the Yankees, you either love 'em or you hate 'em. And I don't like Notre Dame. I went to the Notre Dame–Florida State game in 1993 when both teams were right up there in the rankings and undefeated. Florida State was the best team in the country, Charlie Ward was their quarterback, but Notre Dame won the game 31-24. I spent a day out there in South Bend. Touchdown Jesus. The great stadium, all the history. The place reeks of it.

As a sports fan, you've got to like that tradition. And yes, they do things right, they don't cheat, they don't fire their coaches, their kids go to class. I think their priorities are in the right place.

But if you're not among the converted, there are plenty of things that bother you. First, they get huge advantages when it comes to the polls and the bowls just because they are Notre Dame. That ticks me off to no end because it's not fair. The kids from another good team get shafted out of going to a good bowl because Notre Dame is in the mix. Even though Notre Dame's got a worse record, the committee will probably take the Irish because they bring people to the bowl—and to the television set. That bothers the hell out of me.

The second thing is the subway alumni. All across the country you've got these fair-weather Notre Dame fans. They're arrogant, they're cocky, but you never hear a word from them when they lose. They are nice and quiet when the Irish are 6–5. But when the team is going good, it produces a bandwagon effect and all of a sudden people you haven't heard from in twenty years love Notre Dame football.

The last thing is that, almost like Augusta in golf, Wimbledon in tennis, and the Yankees in baseball, Notre Dame puts itself on a separate level above the rest of college football. We can have a separate television contract with NBC. We can decide who we're going to play and who we're not. We can decide what bowl we're going to. They almost give you that sense of "We're Notre Dame, and you're not."

A perfect example of this is the demise of the Notre Dame–Miami rivalry. Notre Dame got all bent out of shape when Jimmy Johnson beat Gerry Faust 58-7. And when they didn't like the way they were treated the last time they were in Miami, that was the last straw. But when Notre Dame beat Miami at home a few years earlier and everyone was passing out Catholics vs. Convicts T-shirts, Notre Dame officials didn't have any problem with that. I say, what goes around comes around.

You won't find a better example of the whole phony Notre Dame thing than the movie *Rudy*. It's a nice story, but the kid played in one play. I

ARA'S BAD BREAK

To be fair, I'll give you one time when Notre Dame didn't get a break. Everyone kills Ara Parseghian for playing for a tie in that controversial 10-10 game against Michigan State in 1966. But I think he got a raw deal. He had backup quarterback Coley O'Brien in there because Terry Hanratty was out, and a backup running back because the starter sprained his ankle getting off the team bus. And Notre Dame had another game the following week against USC, while Michigan State did not, so he understood that if he blew out USC, that could win Notre Dame a national championship. People blame Parseghian, but Michigan State coach Duffy Daugherty had the ball late, ran it, and then punted. Notre Dame got it back, threw on first down, and then ran out the clock. And Ara is the only one who gets killed? That's wrong.

mean, give me a break. I'm sure there are a million stories in college football about the walk-on kid who finally gets to play one game. If it's at Alabama or Florida State maybe there's a little story about it in the campus newspaper. If it happens at Notre Dame, all of America has got to sit up and take notice.

All of this makes it hard for me to root for Notre Dame. So a week after my visit in '93, when Notre Dame played Boston College in South Bend and David Gordon made that huge field goal that ultimately cost the Irish the national championship, I was a happy camper because I was a little Notre Damed out. And I can't say I didn't have a secret smile when it came out that George O'Leary fudged his résumé and had to resign. And while there are a lot of sports fans who bleed green, I don't think I'm alone in enjoying seeing Notre Dame get knocked down a peg or two.

Gimme an E, Gimme an S, Gimme a P . . .

What's right—and wrong—with the biggest sports cable network?

Dah duh duh . . . Dah duh duh. *For the true sports fan, playing the* SportsCenter *theme music is like Pavlov ringing the dinner bell. But the* Boys in Bristol aren't infallible. Mad Dog plays TV critic.

I can remember in the early 1980s, when I was right out of college, working the graveyard shift at an Amoco gas station in Syosset, Long Island, trying to get myself a job on the radio. I got there at eleven at night and stayed until seven in the morning, and that was tough. They did have a TV there with cable, and one of the things that got me through the night were the ESPN replays of the previous Saturday's college football games.

The Good . . .

And while there are a lot of things that I don't like about ESPN—and we'll get into that in a minute—they never forget that the main reason for their existence, and why they are successful, is to serve the huge sports fan.

Whether it's ESPNews, whether it's the Deuce, or ESPN Classic, which is one of the greatest things you'll ever see in your life, they have done a tremendous job of making sure the serious sports fan gets what he (or she) wants.

When there's a wild card play-in game in Major League Baseball that the networks don't want, you know ESPN is going to be there. Now that they have the NBA, Utah will be playing the Clippers for the eighth spot in the Western Conference playoffs in the last game of the regular season, and you know ESPN will televise the game for you. You know when there is an impending strike or a tragedy in the sports world, ESPN will get you the people you need to hear from. ESPN Classic and *Sports Century* are both tremendous, making you feel that you're right there for a game that happened twenty-five years ago, or getting to know an athlete who's been retired for half a century. For example, I didn't know much about basketball star Maurice Stokes. I watched his episode on ESPN Classic and it really filled a gap for me. After twenty-five years, ESPN still takes care of the sports junkie, and that's a tremendous achievement. I give them a lot of credit for that.

The Bad . . .

Sometimes ESPN loses its ability to be journalistic. I don't need to see Chris Berman giving Brett Favre a pass for allowing Michael Strahan to set the single-season sack record. Berman's laughing, saying, "Ahhh, that's football. What's wrong with it?" because he doesn't want to upset the football guys who watch the show. Come on, Favre was wrong. If you're doing *NFL Primetime*, you say it—"That was a garbage thing for Favre to do," and if Favre never talks to you again, so be it.

And at the Super Bowl media day, you've got Stuart Scott schmoozing with Ray Lewis and he doesn't even ask him a question about the killings in Atlanta. ESPN wants to make sure that if the Ravens win the Super Bowl, Ray Lewis will put his arm around Scott before *SportsCenter* "Sunday Conversation" and say, "To hell with the rest of the media, let's you and I have some fun." And that's garbage. It's not just ESPN. Ahmad Rashad was always kissing Jordan's fanny, and don't even get me started about FOX Sports's *Best Damn Sports Show Period*. But when these guys who are supposedly journalists try to become too buddy-buddy with the athletes they're supposed to be covering, it drives you crazy.

The Ugly

I'm convinced that ESPN even affects how athletes play the game. Remember that ad campaign where you see Peyton Manning and Nomar Garciaparra sitting in their houses watching *SportsCenter*? I think there's a message in there. I think that with these Boo-Yah signature calls and the Plays of the Week and the Plays of the Day and the Plays of the Minute— ESPN's main objective is to make sure the athletes watch *SportsCenter*.

And you'd be shocked to find out how much these athletes want to see themselves on TV. That's why you'll see guys going for the reverse dunk instead of the layup, trying to hit the 500-foot home run when a sac fly would do, going wild with an in-your-face celebration after a touchdown or a sack. You almost wonder if they don't want to be on Plays of the Week more than they want to win the game.

So ESPN's a mixed bag. For the most part they take care of the serious sports fan, but too many times there's too much schtick and not enough substance. The good news? If you're all ESPNed out—you've got a remote control.

Rage On

Who would win a fantasy fight between Jack Dempsey
and Rocky Marciano?

Is it the sweet science, Muhammad Ali sticking and moving, bobbing and weaving? Or Mike Tyson proposing to drive the nosebone into the brainbone? In choosing up sides for a fantasy matchup, Mad Dog gets to the center of boxing's primal attraction.

When you're thinking about all-time greats in boxing—and which ones you'd like to see face off in a fantasy matchup—to me you're thinking Jack Dempsey, Gene Tunney, Joe Louis, Muhammad Ali, and Rocky Marciano. I'm talking the heavyweight division, so I'm not giving you a fantasy matchup between Roy Jones and a beefed-up Marvin Hagler or a fight with Sugar Ray Robinson in the mix. I'm doing the heavyweight division. There are too many weight classes in the sport now—gain two pounds and you're in a different weight class—but everybody can relate to the heavyweight division.

And I'm not going back to Jess Willard or John L. Sullivan or Gentleman Jim Corbett. Nobody saw those guys fight. Even Jack Johnson in 1915, how many people saw that? But I am going back to Dempsey. If you can put Babe Ruth in this kind of fantasy, you can put Dempsey in there, too.

So if I'm going to pay money to see the ultimate fight, the one I would go see would be Dempsey and Rocky Marciano. The Manassa Mauler against the Brockton Blockbuster. That is pure, unadulterated rage. I'm gonna go after you with everything I've got for as long as you stay standing. That's the matchup that I would love to see.

To me boxing is about fire. Boxing is primitive. Boxing is about knocking out the other guy, giving him a concussion. That's what boxing is about. You may not like it. The American Medical Association certainly doesn't. You may not like the way the sport is run, but boxing brings out an element of rage in all of us. At its best, boxing brings out the dark side of our personality in a funny, and I think healthy, way. For better or for worse, it's two people beating each other up. That's the sport.

To me it's not rope-a-dope. To me it's about two guys going in there and throwing haymakers. It's Apollo Creed and Rocky. There are the boxing aficionados that would argue that the sport is about defense, that dodging punches is just as important as throwing them. That's why this matchup might not impress them.

To me boxing is less about Sugar Ray Leonard–Marvin Hagler and more about Thomas Hearns–Marvin Hagler. Sugar Ray didn't do an awful lot in that Hagler fight. He frustrated him. He danced. He looked pretty. He did a good job. He threw enough punches to make an impression with the judges. He won. But as I said, boxing to me is more about pure, unadulterated rage.

That's why I want to take Dempsey, for his fire and his passion. He was crude. He'd hit you in the groin. He'd step on your toes. He'd pull your hair. He was really a nineteenth-century boxer in the twentieth century. And Marciano was a bull. Relentless. He knocked you out as quickly as he could and quit at the top. He carried Louis, but other than that, didn't care if he blew you away in two or three rounds. Just a brawler.

A Marciano-Dempsey brawl wouldn't go the distance, and it wouldn't be pretty. From what I've read about the both of them, they seem pretty similar. Marciano was a bull who kept on coming after you. Dempsey was an animal. Pure power from both of them.

I think from a matchup standpoint, Dempsey would have a lot more trouble with a guy like Ali than with Marciano, because when Dempsey would see Marciano coming at him, he would see himself. And Dempsey would just throw haymakers. He would get knocked down and get back up again. I don't think that Dempsey would be intimidated by Marciano. Dempsey beat Jess Willard, who was a huge guy, 250 pounds. Dempsey used to fight five or six guys in one night in 1916, 1917 at the old Madison Square Garden. Knock him out. Next guy comes in the ring.

Marciano never faced a guy who could match him in sheer brutality. So I think that Marciano would be a little more taken aback by Dempsey than Dempsey would be by Marciano.

I think they both would knock each other around for a while, but I just think that Dempsey's heart would be enough. So I think that Dempsey would eventually catch him with a good shot and knock him out, probably between rounds eight and ten. But there'd be some scary moments before that.

FLOAT LIKE A BUTTERFLY

The one that boxing people—the Burt Sugars and the Michael Katzes of the world—would want to see is Muhammad Ali and Joe Louis. They'd like to see how Ali would avoid Louis, how would he dance, how would he maneuver, how would he use his footwork. Ali was a tremendous defensive fighter. He had great heart and a great chin. How would he handle Louis in his prime?

Ali, of course, would try to psych Louis out. He'd play mind games with him. He'd call him an Uncle Tom. Ali would try to get Louis off his game and then capitalize on that. This would be a matchup of the minds. Personally, I want fighters who use their fists, so that's why I'm picking Marciano-Dempsey.

Sideline Einsteins

What does it take to succeed as an NFL football coach?

With 310-pound employees who make ten times as much as they do and every decision second-guessed on national television, it's no wonder that NFL head coaches are a little stressed out. Mad Dog tells you what separates the true clipboard visionaries from the Lombardi wannabes.

A lot of football coaches will try to convince you that their job is more complicated than nuclear physics. Don't believe it. Sure, football is a little more complex than baseball or basketball. The defensive schemes are different. The blocking. But I think that football coaches try to make it seem so complicated that nobody can understand it but themselves. I'm sorry, but football is not that complicated. Vince Lombardi was not Albert Einstein. He said, "We're going to run this power sweep until you show that you can stop it." That's not complicated.

The difference between a good head coach in the NFL and being a guy who ends up being someone else's defensive coordinator is the ability to motivate your team. In football you can be a great scheme guy and a lousy coach. A head coach has a million specialty coaches—offensive, defensive, linebacker, secondary, tight end, offensive line—and he has to delegate a lot of the responsibility for teaching and devising a game plan to these guys. But when it comes to motivation, the buck stops with the head coach. Bill Belichick was always a great Xs and Os guy, but until the Patriots won the Super Bowl, the rap on him was that he couldn't relate to his players.

A head coach has a tough selling job. Football is about pain. No two ways around it. A quarterback who stays in the pocket when there's a blitz coming might complete the third-down pass, but he's going to get flattened from behind as soon as he releases the ball. The wideout going over the middle to catch that pass, he's going to get clotheslined. And the safety who makes the tackle is sacrificing his body to make the play, too.

If you are a coach in football, you've got to convince your players that they are going to experience pain, but the pain is going to be worth it.

They need to understand that one way to win football games is to dish out more pain than your opponent—be more physical, tackle harder, block better. If you don't play hard, you're going to get killed. All of this runs against human nature—nobody wants to be hit, but in football that's the game. If you're not going to play hurt, you're not going to play.

Getting a player to play hard for you in football is much harder than it is in baseball or basketball. In baseball and basketball, most players are self-motivated because if they screw up we all see it. They're in the spotlight. They either strike out or hit a line drive. They nail the jumper or it's an air-ball. In football we can't see everything. With an offensive lineman, the average fan is not going to notice whether he had a good game or a bad game. He doesn't have the spotlight on him as much. So a coach has to find different ways of getting his attention. That's why Bill Parcells is so good. He is such a great motivator. He can relate to a twenty-two-year-old African-American player, which isn't easy to do if you're a fifty-five-year-old white guy.

Football is also an adrenaline-rush game, and a good coach will use it. But he also has to realize that adrenaline will get you only so far, that you can't play on pure emotion sixteen times a year. You've got to pick your spots, knowing when to lay off and when to push.

Remember that the football season is much shorter than in baseball. In football each game is like ten baseball games. So there is a lot more emphasis on each individual game. Each game takes on a life of its own. This obviously means that the coaches can't be as loyal. They can't be as patient. They can't wait for a player to get out of a slump. They can't put a guy out there every week if he's not getting the job done. If an offensive lineman has a bad game, okay, you've got to stick with him. If he has a bad two weeks you probably get nervous, but you've got to stick with him. If he has a bad three or four weeks, you get somebody else in. Jason Giambi has a bad month in baseball, what are you going to do? He's going to go out there and play. You hope that he snaps out of it. A baseball season is 162 games. It's a marathon. In football the season is more like a series of wind sprints.

But a football coach has one big weapon. Players in football play for their jobs on a week-to-week basis much more so than basketball and baseball players do. In those two sports, coaches and managers can't cut their regulars, or even discipline them too harshly because most decent players have got long-term guaranteed contracts. So if he plays poorly or he's not hustling, you've still got to leave him in there.

But in the NFL virtually none of the contracts are guaranteed. Maybe you can't bench or waive a quarterback who has a $5 million bonus, because that's $5 million that counts against the salary cap. But a head coach has the hammer over maybe 45 of the guys on his 53-man roster. This gives an NFL coach more freedom to rule with an iron hand. So the football coach can motivate and coach out of fear. When he does cut someone, it gets the whole team's attention. A player says to himself, "Man, that was cold. And if I don't play well he's going to cut me, too." He has the power of dismissal. And when you're trying to convince a guy to forget about what happens when a 310-pound lineman lands on you, that's a great motivating tool.

The Tracks of My Tears

What moments are the biggest tearjerkers in sports history?

Admit it. You get choked up watching Brian's Song *or* The Pride of the Yankees. *And there have been plenty of live sports moments where you're wiping your eyes, and it's not because of allergies. Mad Dog remembers those shining moments that prove that real fans do cry.*

I'm a sentimental guy. There have been some sports moments that personally, for me, brought a lump to my throat and tears down my face. Simple as that. Moments that made you feel really good about what you were watching. Made you glad to be a sports fan. And that's kind of the reason why we watch sports. You wade through a lot of boring events, waiting for that moment that's going to thrill you, that's going to move you.

So when I look back on those moments, I'm looking for events that had a near-universal resonance. You might have been thrilled by Kirk Gibson's World Series home run. But how about if you're an Oakland A's fan? How about if you like Dennis Eckersley? Or you hate the Dodgers? Or Tommy Lasorda, who drove a lot of people crazy? So that's why I didn't put Gibson's homer or something like that up there. Here are some moments that got to me, and that I'll bet got to you, too.

Wade at Wimbledon: When Virginia Wade won Wimbledon in 1977, it was one of those moments when everything came together. It was the one-hundredth anniversary of Wimbledon. It was the Queen's Jubilee. And an English player finally won the tournament for the first time in nine billion years. When Wade was on she was fun to watch, but she had a strange head. She could be up and down. She could blow matches. This is a woman who said, "I'd rather play beautiful tennis than win." Against Betty Stove that day she didn't play particularly beautiful tennis, but she did win. And after the match, with the Queen in the Royal Box and the fans singing "For She's a Jolly Good Fellow," that's a moment I'll never forget. Sure, there were some fans in the Netherlands who were bummed out about Stove losing. But that afternoon just about every other tennis fan in the world was English.

One Shining Moment: I'll give you one that might sound a little crazy, but I love it every year. At the conclusion of the NCAA championship game on Monday night, CBS does a two- or three-minute montage of the highlights of the tournament, set to the song "One Shining Moment." Every year I can't wait to see this. It captures all the emotion, the last-second shots, all the loser-go-home mentality. I almost look forward to it more than the game. I know you're going to say, "Oh, come on, Chris . . ." but I just get goose bumps every time I see the damn thing. Laugh if you want, but it makes the college game feel a little more pure to me.

McGwire's 62nd Home Run: It's lost a little bit of its luster in the last couple of years, with Bonds breaking the record and baseball's steroid controversy, but I'll bet you can remember where you were when Mark McGwire broke the home run record. I do. I watched it with my old man. Against the Cubbies, early September, at Busch Stadium, McGwire running around the bases, Mark Grace giving him a high five, Sammy Sosa coming in from right field. The Maris family in the box by the dugout. How could you not get a tear in your eye?

McGwire handled the pressure beautifully. Maris's record stood for longer than Ruth's—thirty-seven years. And he did a great job with the Maris family. He made Roger Maris come alive again. And it did phenomenal television ratings. It had 21.5 for an otherwise meaningless game in September. I'm a Giants fan, and I still think that moment is far more significant than Bonds's seventy-first homer. Not even close.

BUT WHAT ABOUT THE GAME?

A lot of people, including my radio partner, Mike, got very upset over the fact that the Cubs were out there relishing this moment in a game that they needed to win because they were fighting for the wild card. But, in my opinion, that moment was bigger than Cubs-Cards. That moment was baseball history. And Chicago did win the wildcard.

Ripken's Record: Though I'm not a huge Ripken fan, it was a tremendous moment when Ripken ran around the field high-fiving everyone once the Orioles and the Angels played the top of the fifth inning and made it an official game. The players in both dugouts with their cameras out, all the picture-taking. The big, beautiful sign on the warehouse out in right field. The legacy of Gehrig, with DiMaggio in the building. It was the first huge baseball moment following that terrible strike. And it was fitting that Ripken provided it, because he is the ultimate throwback to purer, simpler, go-out-there-every-day-and-do-your-job times. If Gehrig could have picked somebody to break his record in the next fifty years, the guy he would have picked was Ripken. Now I have some problems with Ripken (see "They Call It The Streak," page 81), but that moment was a classic, tears-running-down-your-face moment. Even my wife got into it. There's no other way around it. That was great for the sport.

Williams's Coronation: Remember that night when Ted Williams went back to Fenway Park for the announcement of the finalists for the All-Century team? The crowd was cheering at Fenway Park as he drove out in his golf cart. He had a love-hate relationship with the Boston fans over the course of his career, but it was unadulterated love that night. DiMaggio had just died that spring and it was like Williams's coronation as the greatest living player. Baseball is the one sport that can do this. In football they bring out the old-time players, you could care less. Frank

Gifford shows up, or they bring out the old '58 Giants, you go get a beer at halftime. They do it in baseball, you pay attention to it. Baseball has nostalgia that no other sport has. Willie Mays and Hank Aaron and all those guys were there, but it was Williams's night. It was great to see the active players, Tony Gwynn especially, hovering near him, almost paying him homage. I'll tell you how I knew that was a great moment. There was a big stink this year about the fact that Williams's son put a stupid cap on him that night, promoting whatever it was he was promoting at the time. I don't even remember that cap. That was another classic baseball tear-jerker.

The Pride of the Yankees Speech: Gehrig's speech is still as powerful today as it was fifty to sixty years ago. The great Iron Horse, who played every day and kept his mouth shut, finally had a great singular moment. "I consider myself the luckiest man on the face of the earth." He can't even lift up the plaque. Ruth coming out. Both teams on the field. It's humbling.

The thing to remember about that speech is that very few people, if any, knew at that time that Gehrig was dying. That day was supposed to be about his retirement. And you'll remember that Mickey Mantle echoed those words when he addressed Yankee fans on Mickey Mantle Day in 1969. It was sixty-five years ago, but it still gives you chills.

Gretzky's Last Game: I wasn't around for Babe Ruth's last game. And Michael Jordan retires every five minutes. So this was a real goose bump night, seeing the best player to ever lace up a pair of skates play his last game in the NHL. Madison Square Garden handled it beautifully, and it was one of those great moments that even a non-hockey fan could get into. On that day you understood that Gretzky *is* hockey.

Making Book

What are the all-time best sports books ever written?

What did they say about Mickey Mantle? He's the only guy to write more books than he's read. But fortunately the world of sports literature doesn't end with The Mick. Here are Mad Dog's picks for the best jock books of all time.

It's tough to sell a sports book to a big-time sports fan. Those quickie books, those recaps of a championship season, or an autobiography of a great thinker like a twenty-seven-year-old Len Dykstra, they're a complete waste of time. It's three-hundred pages of fluff.

Very rarely do I get turned on by even a serious sports book. After I read a sports book, I ask myself one thing: "Did I learn anything?" I'm a tough grader, because it's not going to be easy to tell me something I didn't know. I've done a sports talk show here for five and a half hours a day for fifteen years, and I've interviewed a million people. Not that many things can inspire me. Here are some of the books that contributed to my sports education.

A Season on the Brink by John Feinstein: Feinstein is America's sports author, kind of the John Grisham of the jockstrap set. With *A Season on the Brink,* he had tremendous access and dealt with a very controversial figure fairly. On the one hand Bobby Knight hated the book, and Feinstein and Knight obviously no longer have a relationship. On the other hand, after reading the book, I would have still sent my kid to play basketball for Knight at Indiana or Texas Tech. That, to me, is a perfect happy medium.

Bums by Peter Golenbock: You won't see it on any other list, but I thought *Bums* was a better book than Roger Kahn's *Boys of Summer*. I'm looking for a great sports book to teach me something. And this one told me a million great stories. One of my favorites is about how the Dodgers screwed up the coin flip in the 1951 playoff. In 1946 the Dodgers had won the coin flip for the playoff series against the Cardinals and elected to take the home field. They lost the first game at St. Louis and then had to come all the way back east for game two, and ended up losing. According to Ralph Branca, Dodger ticket manager Jack Collins vowed the team wouldn't make the same mistake again in 1951 and gave the Giants home field advantage in the three-game series, even though there was no travel involved. And if they had played game one in the Polo Grounds and game three in Brooklyn, both of Bobby Thomson's homers would have been just long fly balls. That's the kind of thing that you get in *Bums* that you do not get in *Boys of Summer*.

When Pride Still Mattered by David Maraniss: Maraniss is a great biographer, wrote big books about Clinton and Al Gore, so his take on Lombardi was much anticipated and he had a lot of pressure on him. He spent three or four years on Lombardi and gives you a tremendous football book. Detailed. Specific. He tells you how Lombardi got the Army job by convincing the Army coaching staff that when you snap the ball with the laces a certain way you save an eighth of a second. Maraniss explains Lombardi's offensive strategy in the 1958 championship game when he was a coach with the Giants, punting on fourth and inches late in regulation and how the Colts tied the game and won in overtime. This book is as good as it gets.

Hogan by Curt Sampson: You don't read too many old-time golf books, and it's an era that not a lot is written about, but Sampson's portrayal of Hogan is fascinating. He was a self-made golfer. He worked his butt off, practicing until his hands bled. Nothing but practice, practice, practice. You get his great battles with Sam Snead and Byron Nelson. You get his near-fatal car accident and his tremendous comeback. Sampson did a great job.

Sandy Koufax: A Lefty's Legacy by Jane Leavy: No, this book isn't very critical of Koufax, but it's great with the details. Of course, it's got the perfect game that he pitched against the Cubs in '65. But Leavy also tracked down Bob Henley, the Cubs pitcher who gave up only one hit and lost 1-0. When Henley retired from coaching at a small school in Georgia, Koufax sent him a ball signed, "To Bob, Great game. Your pal, Sandy." You get a little scene of Koufax after he got divorced from Ann Widmark, sitting in some bar in New Hampshire with Andy Etchebarren and telling him that he's going to go to Indonesia for four or five months. It's full of these kinds of nuggets. A tremendous book.

SITTING ON A STORY

Here's my favorite story from *A Lefty's Legacy*: In '65, Sandy told Phil Collier of the *San Diego Union*, "Phil, don't print this, promise me, but next year is my last season." Collier sat on his great story for a year. He wrote it and it sat in his drawer for fourteen months. At noon the day before Koufax was going to announce his retirement after the 1966 season, he called Collier. "Phil, tomorrow I'm announcing my retirement. Anything you need?" Collier did not betray his loyalty to Koufax. And Koufax made sure a year later that he took care of Collier by giving him an exclusive the day before he made his announcement. A great story from a great book.

Honorable Mentions

The Jordan Rules **by Sam Smith:** The Bulls were a fascinating team and they had a rock-and-roll aura about them, and Smith doesn't pull any punches. The fact that Jordan felt he had to write his own book in response is reason enough to read it.

Summer of '49 **by David Halberstam:** A good book with a couple of big negatives. The first is that Halberstam didn't talk to DiMaggio. The second is that he didn't go into nearly enough detail about the actual pennant race. Halberstam wants to write these huge books on the American consciousness. That's fine, but I'm looking for the down-and-dirty strategy, and this book left me wanting for more.

Joe DiMaggio: A Hero's Life **by Richard Ben Cramer:** It is a great *baseball* book. From 1936 to 1951 you get every significant Yankee game in there. His hitting streak, World Series, his relationship with Stengel. This book is very underrated from a baseball standpoint. The problem with the book is that it is too anti-DiMaggio. You know after the first five pages that Cramer doesn't like DiMaggio and that he's going to spend the next five-hundred pages telling you why he doesn't like him. By page ten it's enough already. The tone of the book is just too nasty.

A Flame of Pure Fire by **Roger Kahn:** I like this Jack Dempsey biography a lot, but my knock on it is that it's too pro-Dempsey. It's almost a little hero-worshiping. The balance isn't there as much as you would like.

If Dreams Came True

What would the Dog do if you handed him the ball?

How many times do you sit in your Barcalounger and say to the television, "Hey, I could do that." You've played Little League, Pop Warner, the scramble down at the local club, how much different can it be in the big time? Mad Dog addresses that very question.

If I could trade places for a day and step out from behind the microphone and be an athlete in a big event, what would I like to do? You remember the old saying, "Be careful what you ask for because you might just get it"? Let me tell you first what I *wouldn't* do.

I like team sports and always get a thrill from playing basketball in a three-on-three or four-on-four setting, doing the little things that could contribute to a victory—getting an offensive rebound, making a good pass, slapping the ball away on a fast break. Those are the kinds of plays I could make. I'm not going to make the twenty-foot jump shot. I'm not good enough. So as far as being the hero, basketball's not going to be my game. There's always going to be somebody on the court who is better than I am.

And I love catching passes in football. At Split Rock School across from where I used to live in the mid-'70s, I was a miniature Freddie Biletnikoff catching pass after pass. Of course, I'd have so much stickum on me that my mother would give me a hug when I got home and her apron would stick to me.

But I don't like getting hit, and I can see myself in a big spot as a wide receiver getting thrown off my route by a very big and physical corner-back playing bump-and-run coverage. Plus, I can also see myself getting a little frustrated in the course of the game if I did not get the ball thrown to me all the time, like, say, Terrell Owens.

Could I see myself on the eighteenth hole at the Masters nursing a one-stroke lead? I've always liked playing golf in front of people. It seems to motivate me, and I seem to overachieve a little bit and play better than normal. But if I had a green jacket on the line and was at the eighteenth tee at the Masters facing that narrow shot up the fairway with people lining both sides of the course, I'd be worried about slicing one and plunking some poor person in the head and knocking them out.

Plus, I think the silence and the concentration needed to make a huge putt would overwhelm me. It's one thing to hit a 7-wood from the fairway and surprise people by hitting it straight. It's quite another to sink a six-foot putt for a major championship. I think I would get a little stage fright.

Hockey, game seven, season on the line, I would love being a goaltender. I like the individuality of it, but I think during the dead time, sitting there for three or four minutes while the play is going on at the other end, the anxiety would overwhelm me. Great athletes have an ability to turn their brain off—to react instead of think. I think I would be too conscious of making that mistake, giving up a soft goal that would cost my team a championship. The weight of that would overwhelm me.

If I had a baseball dream, it would be to have the ball in my hands, game seven of a World Series for the Giants. I'd be Livan Hernandez, but hopefully with different results. I understand that in between innings you'd have to sit in the dugout and think about it, but I'd be so absorbed in the game that I don't think it would bother me. But I do I think I would nibble too much. I think I'd be afraid to throw the ball over the plate, thinking of how I could give up the big home run and end up being the goat, a poor man's Calvin Schiraldi. If you're a pitcher and you fail in a postseason spot, that would haunt you through the whole winter. So it wouldn't be baseball.

So I guess if I had a fantasy, it would be in a Wimbledon final. The idea that I'd be on the pristine grass courts wearing all white on a late Sunday afternoon bowing to the Royal Box. I think that out of all the sports, the one I could see myself having some success in would be tennis. It's individual. If I choke it's only me. If I lose the Wimbledon final, I'll go play at the Kremlin Cup. And the play is continuous, so you don't have a lot of time to fret over a poor shot. It's on to the next one.

Besides, the accent at Wimbledon normally is on the person who wins and not on the person who loses. If I lost to Sampras three straight sets 6-1, 6-1, 6-1 in one hour, twelve minutes, that would not overwhelm me. Okay, I gave the fans a lousy final, but I would sit there next to the umpire's chair clapping away and watch Pete go greet his mom and dad and his wife and newborn child. So serve 'em up.

Monster on the Campus

What can be done to clean up college sports?

The best college football player in the country gets his picture on the cover of Sports Illustrated. *The best physics student? He's not famous in his own dorm. Mad Dog explains how to realign the priorities in college sports.*

We've created a monster in big-time college sports. There's too much pressure on the coaches to win. Too much pressure on college presidents to put athletics ahead of academics. Too much fudging. Too much cheating. Too many people who don't have their eyes on the prize of getting these student-athletes an education.

Let's first put the blame where it ought to be. The first culprit is the alumni. They want to win and that's pretty much all they care about. It's about the forty-five-year-old guy who wants to brag to his buddies how good his alma mater's basketball team is. Or he wants to go out and tailgate on Saturday, and maybe plan his vacation around a trip to the Rose Bowl. He derives his self-worth from his university's success.

These alumni are the two-thousand-pound gorillas of college sports. They donate a lot of money. But only when the team's winning. It's a kind of subtle blackmail: win games or else. That puts an undue pressure on the kids, the administration, and the coaching staff.

And then there are boosters who take it a step further. They get so wrapped up in a college's athletic program that they get involved with the athletes directly and do things that are detrimental to the school, things that are against the rules. And in many situations the school looks the other way—at least until they get caught—because these guys are also such big financial contributors. You want that new music hall built? Then go win some football games.

The second problem is TV. Television is the engine that drives these tendencies in football and basketball. Look at all the money that CBS pays for the rights to broadcast the NCAA tournament. Not millions. *Billions.* TV has made The Big Dance so important in college basketball that for a lot of programs not making the Sweet Sixteen is a disaster. If your team doesn't have that little shining moment during March Madness and loses in the first round, or, God forbid, has to take an NIT bid, you've had a bad year.

Same thing in college football. You'd better be good enough to go to a bowl game, and a good bowl, too. Got to play New Year's Day. Got to get on TV. Got to get on ESPN, at least. When there's that much money floating around, that's where a school's priorities get all fouled up. They look at a player and say, "Who cares whether he can pass his chemistry class as long as he can catch a pass on Saturday afternoon." It gets to the point where a university would rather have the guy be a lousy student and a great athlete instead of the other way around. We'll get a tutor for him. We'll fudge the grades. We'll cheat.

And a college president needs a coach who can win, first and foremost. A couple of 11–18 seasons in college basketball and this guy is gone. Forget his graduation rate. Couple of 3–9 or 3–8 seasons and the football coach is history. And if a guy wins, he can get away with almost anything. Do you think that a math professor would be able to get away with acting the way Woody Hayes did?

That said, what could colleges do to make this a little better? Here are a few modest proposals.

Sit the Freshmen: First of all, freshmen should not be eligible. It's tough enough making the transition from high school to college without putting pressure on a kid to be a huge star in a sport. It's hard to make that adjustment of living away from home, managing your own time, the distractions of girls and parties. Just doing your own laundry is a culture shock.

Think about what it's like for the kid at a big football program. He's been pampered through high school and he gets thrown right into the mix of the football grind in August. He has football practice before he cracks open a textbook. He plays a game before he even walks into a classroom. That's a problem. Freshmen should not be eligible. Period.

Institute Graduation Incentives: I want to base scholarships on graduation rates. Your kids don't graduate, you lose some scholarships. Sure, there are some universities that could take advantage of that and make it super-easy for kids to graduate. But in the long run, hopefully, this will encourage universities to recruit the kid that has some indication that he wants to work, and help the kids once they do get to campus. If they worked half as hard in the classroom as they do in the gym or the practice field or the weight room, any of these athletes should be able to learn a few things, get decent grades, and get a degree. I don't have a problem with cutting athletes a break, giving them another semester or two to finish up their coursework. But before they leave campus, they should have that sheepskin.

Hire a Czar: The NCAA needs a Kenesaw Mountain Landis. Forget Cedric Dempsey or Myles Brand. Bring in a guy with some teeth. We need a real czar to help clean up college sports. Someone who's omnipotent, a commissioner who will dole out punishment in a tough but consistent way. He can put pressure on the programs to do things the right way. "Your kids don't graduate? Then you're going to lose some scholarships. You've got a kid that's flunking out? Then he's not playing. You cheat? Your whole program is on probation." Put some pressure on these colleges. If the level of the play goes down a little bit, so be it.

Don't Pay 'Em: Athletes should not be paid. That's ridiculous. You can't pay them enough to make a difference. What? Giving a guy fifty dollars is going to change the system? If they don't have money, let them go get a job. They get a free education that's worth $150,000. Let them use that education. Work in the summertime. Big athletes at big schools get so many other advantages, why do I have to give them another advantage by paying them?

Nip It in the Bud: While they shoulder a lot of the responsibility, it's hard to put all the blame on the colleges. This emphasis on athletics doesn't start when kids turn eighteen and become college athletes. It's a problem in the tenth grade, the sixth grade, the *fourth* grade. A great athlete in America gets a break his whole life. Certainly more than a great piano player, a gifted artist, a math whiz. The answer is to deemphasize sports from day one. And that's got to start with the parents. They've got to get it through their kid's head that, while sports are fun, the odds of becoming a pro athlete are a million to one. And they've got to give him as much positive reinforcement when he busts his butt writing a term paper as when he scores twenty points.

BLAME ME, TOO

I'm not blameless in all of this. When I do my Friday college picks here on WFAN, do I pick the Princeton-Brown game? No, I don't. I pick the Auburn-Alabama game. I pick the USC-UCLA game. I pick the Nebraska-Oklahoma game. Do I pick some Division 1-AA game? No, they don't give scholarships there. There's no spread. Do I spend time talking about academic all-Americans? No. So I've got to take some of the heat, too.

But the problem is that we've created this vicious cycle. We all love college sports—the big bowls, March Madness—so the monster isn't going to go away. But maybe we can tame it just a little.

Batter Up

Who would prevail in baseball's ultimate fantasy matchup?

The live ball era takes on the dead ball era. Baggy gray flannels versus teal double knits. If you took one of today's best pitchers and let him face a batter from yesteryear—or vice versa—what would happen? Mad Dog gazes into his crystal baseball.

What would you do if you had a baseball time machine? If you could put any pitcher from any era on the mound, and bring up the batter of your choice, who would you pick? It's a tough call. I thought about this long and hard. What about Tony Gwynn against Warren Spahn? Or maybe George Brett trying to dig in against Bob Gibson? Money pitcher against a clutch hitter, it'd be fun to see who blinked first.

But if I've got a wayback machine, I'm going to go waaay back. Here's the first matchup I want to see.

Walter Johnson versus Mickey Mantle: Walter Johnson is the best pitcher of all time. There is no way around it. Go look at his statistics. 417 wins. Dominating earned run averages. Led the league in strikeouts 12 times. 110 shutouts. Mike Francesa told me a story not too long ago about how he had an old baseball coach in high school who played in the majors during the early '20s. In his rookie year he was behind the plate in the second game of a doubleheader that Johnson was pitching. This catcher was a kid right off the farm, he went out to the mound and said, "All right, Walter. What are we going to throw today?" Walter said, "Son, go back down there, put the glove out, and enjoy the afternoon." That's the sort of guy Walter Johnson was.

Johnson was baseball's first great power pitcher. So I want to have somebody to go up against Johnson's power, who if he got hold of one would hit it out of Yankee Stadium, but who would also have a propensity to strike out. When he swung, his hat would be flying. He'd fall on his fanny so the guy who I want to face Walter Johnson is Mickey Mantle (see "Tools of the Game," page 76).

I want to use Mickey from the mid-'50s, the years he won the Triple Crown. For those five or six years he was better than anybody in the second half of the century, better than Aaron, better than Mays. I believe that Mickey was a better left-handed hitter than he was a right-handed hitter. I want to see power against power. Mantle against Johnson.

Now, Johnson is a better pitcher than Mantle is a hitter, so I'm going to give Mickey an advantage and play it in the old Yankee Stadium with that short porch in right. But I'm not putting Mantle in any old bandbox, like Tiger Stadium or the Jake. If Mantle hits the ball 425 feet straightaway center, it's an out.

What would happen? I think Johnson would challenge him and Mickey would come out hacking. On the first pitch he'd almost fall over trying to uncork on a Big Train fastball. On a 1-1 aspirin, Mickey would just miss and foul one right back to the screen. On the next pitch Johnson takes a little bit off, and Mantle gets in front of it and hits a shot way into the upper deck—just foul. But I don't think that the Big Train would back down against The Mick. When he retired, Walter Johnson held the all-time strikeout record. And so did Mantle. So, on a 2-2 count, I think Johnson would get Mickey swinging.

Randy Johnson versus Ted Williams: The second one I'd like to see—pitting a modern pitcher versus a hitter from the past—is Randy Johnson against Ted Williams. Ted Williams was the greatest hitter of all time. Greatest eye. Not afraid of anything. Hit .406. Loved the challenge. But one little gap in his career is that he missed the great lefty power pitchers. Lefty Grove was his teammate when Grove was getting old and Williams was very young. He never faced Sandy Koufax when he was at his best, and of course he never stood in against Steve Carlton. Ted did face Lefty Gomez and Whitey Ford, but they weren't as dominating as these guys.

So The Splendid Splinter is taking his hacks against The Big Unit. Now Randy Johnson is not quite as good as Koufax or Grove. But I don't know if there's ever been a guy who's as intimidating. Even Koufax is a guy who didn't make you take your lefties out of the lineup the way Johnson does. At 6' 10" with that long mane of hair, he's pretty scary even when he doesn't have the ball. With that slingshot delivery it must seem like the ball is coming from out in right field. And he throws 98 miles an hour.

We'll do this at the Kingdome. It gives Johnson a home field advantage, but it's also a hitter's haven, with the balls flying out of there and scooting through on the Astroturf.

And we'll allow the Mariners to put the Lou Boudreau shift on. What Randy is going to try to do is get ahead of the count and then get Ted out with a slider. The key for Williams is distinguishing between Randy's great slider and his fastball, and nobody could distinguish a pitch better than Ted Williams.

What would happen? I think Williams would fall behind in the count. He'd take a strike, maybe even two. He'd get behind 0-2 but he wouldn't fold. With a lot of guys, falling behind 0-2 would mean the end of the at-bat. But not with Teddy Ballgame. Johnson would try to get him to swing at that slider in the dirt, but Ted's not going to bite. When Johnson does come in the strike zone with the high fastball, he'd foul it off, waiting for his pitch. He's going to work the count full, and Johnson's going to come in with a belt-high fastball. Williams swings and he scorches a line drive over the shift. Griffey would be on his horse, but he can't catch it and it's one bounce to the wall for a stand-up double. Johnson glares back at second, and Williams won't even look at him.

Serve 'Em Up

How can you make professional tennis a big-time spectator sport?

Tennis players are remarkable athletes. They've got the hand-to-eye coordination of Barry Bonds, the footspeed of Marshall Faulk, and duke it out mano-a-mano like two heavyweights. But they don't get much respect from the average sports fan. Here's how Mad Dog would make tennis a game everyone could love.

Want to fix tennis? Give me a calendar and the clout. Make me commissioner. Commissioner Mad Dog. If I had David Stern–style power, where I was really bigger than Andre Agassi and Serena Williams, here's how the pro game would change.

Tweak the Calendar: I'll start with a modest proposal. Play the Australian Open a few weeks later. Right now the beginning of the tournament comes just after the holidays in the U.S., and some years the finals are played the same weekend as the Super Bowl. Change the date, and tennis can hit that black hole on the U.S. sports calendar in mid-February between the end of football season and the beginning of spring training.

Next, I'd squeeze a little more space between the French Open and Wimbledon. Why? Well, in boxing, does Lennox Lewis fight Mike Tyson and two weeks later fight Evander Holyfield? No. Well, it's just as ridiculous to finish one major and then start another fifteen days later. So I would push the French Open back to early May and move Wimbledon to early July, which would also move Wimbledon past London's rainy season. That gives tennis fans a chance to recharge their batteries between the two big events.

And the players, too. Under the current schedule it's virtually impossible for a man to win the French and Wimbledon back to back—Björn Borg was the last to do it back in 1980. Nowadays guys don't even *play* Wimbledon. Gustavo Kuerten wins the French and heads out on a surfing vacation. Albert Costa goes off and gets married. If the players had more time to make the transition, to really prepare on the grass, you still won't see Alex Corretja beating Lleyton Hewitt at Wimbledon, but it might give all-court guys like Andre Agassi, Andy Roddick, and Marat Safin a realistic chance to do the double. And maybe even make a real run at a Grand Slam. As Tiger Woods can tell you, that kind of buzz can only help the game.

Go Co-Ed: And speaking of Grand Slams, the men and women play together only a few times a year now. That's not enough. Women's tennis isn't the WNBA or the LPGA. It's big-time, and there are very few sports fans who hate women's tennis and love men's tennis or vice versa. So let's take advantage of that. In a way, the two games complement each other. I have a problem with women's tennis because the first week of a Grand Slam is a total waste of time—38 minutes 6-0, 6-1 see ya. The women get interesting only in the quarterfinals, and sometimes even the semis. On the men's side there are more close matches and big upsets in the early rounds. The problem is that you can get a men's tournament where the semis stink. So to keep the tournament juiced up from beginning to end, get the men and the women together.

Juice Up the Davis Cup: While I'm on a roll, I'm going to pump some life into the Davis Cup, too. Play the darn thing every two years. What's so hard about that? Sports fans love the Ryder Cup, and you could get sports fans just as jazzed about the Davis Cup. When Spain beat Sweden a couple of years ago, they won their first Davis Cup in, as McEnroe said, three-hundred years. And five months later they're playing qualifying matches. That's absurd.

If it's every two years, you build a little anticipation for the fans. Countries would take it more seriously, and more of the top players would play. Get all the countries together and play a Davis Cup round-robin in the defending champion's country for a couple of weeks after the U.S. Open. And women could use the same format for the Federation Cup and play it on the alternate years when they're not playing the Davis Cup.

Have an Off-Season: Which brings me to my biggest change. After the U.S. Open in September, I don't want to see anyone hitting a ball in a tournament until the tune-ups for the Australian Open. Not one. The thing tennis needs most is to create a real off-season. Why do they play all those tournaments between October and December? To decide who's number one? Here's what makes you number one to the fans—winning the Grand Slams, period. Nothing that happens at the Paris Indoors should change that. The only reason they play tennis twelve months a year is because there's a billion dollars out there. But it hurts the game. The fans get burned out and the players get burned out and injured.

What's the best day of the year for a baseball fan? Opening day. Because it's the day when months of waiting and anticipating come to an end and everything starts over with a clean slate. Tennis fans have never had an opening day, a chance to see Ken Rosewall or Boris Becker serve up the ceremonial first ball at the start of a brand, spanking new season. It would be the one time when the words "Ready? Play" really get a fan excited.

The Ultimate Home Run Derby

When you absolutely, positively need a tater,
who do you want at the plate?

*The outlook isn't brilliant for the Mudville Nine today. It's the bottom of the
ninth, down 2-1, two outs. But you've got the deepest bench ever. You can
hand the bat to any slugger in baseball history. Who is the Dog sending up
to pinch hit?*

When you're thinking about a tight game late, the great home run hitter is not going to get many chances to hit a home run. If you're a
reliever with Mark McGwire up there at the plate, and you're up 2-1, two
outs in the ninth, are you going to allow him to hit a fastball out of the
park? No. You're going to pitch around him. And you'll walk him if you
have to, even if that means putting the tying run on base and the winning
run at the plate.

That's why, of all the sluggers I've seen—we'll make it from the mid-
'60s on—I'll take Sammy Sosa in that situation. Is Sosa the best home run
hitter ever? Hardly. McGwire is our generation's Babe Ruth. Barry Bonds
is a far better hitter than Sosa, period.

And if you want to go back in history, there's Mickey Mantle and Babe
Ruth and Willie Mays and Hank Aaron just to name a few.

Here's why Sosa's my guy in that situation. All of those other big home
run guys are very, very disciplined hitters who drew tons of walks. Sosa is a
great *bad ball* hitter. He's much more willing to expand his strike zone. In a
game situation, any pitcher worthy of a spot on a major league roster is going to throw him curveballs down and away, and if he hits the ball to right
field for a base hit, you're going to live with it. Sosa will swing at that breaking ball out of the strike zone and try to hit it to right field for a home run.
McGwire won't do that. Bonds won't do that. But Sammy will. Which is
why I want him up there hacking for me with the game on the line. Of
course, the negative is that he'll often get himself out in that situation, and
won't take the walk where a double by the guy hitting behind him could tie
it up. But if you absolutely need that home run, Sammy's the man.

All for Love

Who would win tennis's Grand Slam face-off?

One guy played for trophies and expense money. The other had a billion TV commercials even before he won anything. So when one of tennis's great masters takes on one of today's most charismatic champions in the ultimate fantasy match, who'll come out on top? Mad Dog's at courtside.

In tennis, it all begins and ends with the four majors—the Australian, the French, Wimbledon, and the U.S. Open. And when you're talking about the Open Era of tennis, believe it or not, there are only two men who won all four in a career. The first is Rod Laver, the great Australian champion who completed a real Grand Slam, winning all four majors in the same calendar year. And he did it not once, but twice. First in 1962, then again in 1969. When you're looking at his career numbers, you've got some asterisks. On the one hand, when he won his first Grand Slam in 1962, there wasn't Open tennis—the Grand Slams were amateur tournaments—so he was playing against a lot of has-beens and never-wases, while the best players in the world, guys like Jack Kramer and Pancho Gonzalez, were off playing on the little barnstorming pro tour. But on the other hand, Laver turned pro, too, right after his Grand Slam. Between 1963 and 1968, Laver was in his prime, so he would have won a bunch of singles titles between 1963 and the beginning of Open tennis in 1968. You have to think he would have won more than eleven majors, and probably would be way ahead of Pete Sampras in that category.

To find a guy in modern tennis who managed to win all the slams, not in a single year but over the course of his career, you've got to fast forward all the way to Andre Agassi. Björn Borg couldn't win the U.S. Open. Jimmy Connors, John McEnroe, Pete Sampras, Boris Becker, and Stefan Edberg couldn't win the French. Ivan Lendl couldn't win Wimbledon. Now, I'll grant you that Agassi got a little lucky the year he won at Wimbledon, getting to play Goran Ivanisevic, who choked the match away in the fifth set. And a lot of these guys—Sampras, for one—could have beaten Agassi on their best days. Just because I'm picking Agassi for this confrontation doesn't mean that I think he's one of the two best players of all time, but he did win all four slams, and I do like the way he matches up with Laver.

Paul Annacone, Pete Sampras's former coach, once told me that Agassi is the best pure striker of the ball in the history of tennis. That's good enough for me. Now I don't love Agassi's mental makeup. There are too many times when he's had these inexplicable moments, and he just loses to guys like Andres Gomez in the French Open final, quits in a match against Michael Chang. And there have been times when he's taken a whole year off, drops to nine thousand on the computer.

So we've got to catch Agassi at the right time. Let's play this in a year when he's in rhythm, in shape, when he's throwing the medicine ball around, and when Steffi Graf, a great champion herself, has rubbed off on him. We'll take Laver in his second Grand Slam year of 1969.

We'd play it on the clay at the French Open. The red dirt of Roland Garros would slow down the game a little, put a little more emphasis on finesse, fitness, and mental toughness, and blunt some of Agassi's sheer power.

Who's going to be holding up the trophy at the end? Well, I think that Agassi would come out smoking, pound returns for winners, move the Rocket around, and take the first set. But then I think that Laver would change his tactics a little bit. He'd pick his spots and come to the net behind his serve. He'd change things up in baseline rallies, hitting some slice, some angles, some drop shots, and take the next two sets. He has more ways to beat you than Agassi does. And when it got to crunch time, 4-5, 15-40 in the fourth, I think Agassi is more likely to get a little tight and dump a forehand into the net. Game, set, and match, Laver.

Jocktown, USA

Which city is America's best sports town?

In some cities, people just naturally turn to the sports section first. Kids learn about the hit-and-run before they learn to read. And winning a championship is more than an excuse to loot stores and overturn cars. Mad Dog goes out on a limb and ranks cities according to their sports quotient.

To be a good sports town, you got to have passion. You're not a great sports town if baseball fans leave in the fifth inning. You're not a great sports town if you don't sell out playoff games. People should live and die by their teams. The whole city is in a bad mood on Monday morning if their football team loses on a Sunday afternoon. Everyone's in a good mood on a Thursday because the baseball team swept a series and moved into first place. There is a little spring in your step when your team is doing well. You are a little depressed when your team is doing badly.

With good sports towns, the love of the game is just part of the fabric of the place, it's passed down from generation to generation, father to son. That makes it tough for a city with an expansion team—Orlando, Tampa, even places like Houston. I hate to say this but the best sports towns are usually those East Coast Rust Belt cities that have had sports teams for seventy, eighty, a hundred years. Boston, Philadelphia, New York, Washington, Chicago, Detroit. I'm sorry, but Ty Cobb did not play for the Colorado Rockies. Ralph Kiner did not play for the San Diego Padres.

And it's strange to say it, but most great sports towns have cold winters. On a Sunday afternoon you don't want to be distracted: Should I go sailing today or should I watch the Jets? Should I play golf today or should I watch the Lions? Look at the ratings on the East Coast for football the first month of the season. They're never very good because people are still outside doing other things. That's one of the reasons why teams like the Dolphins and the Astros and the Braves don't sell out playoff games. Weather is a factor, there's no other way around it.

Here are the other factors that distinguish a good sports town:

Be Cosmopolitan: If the Sacramento Kings are in the Western Conference final—and your hometown team is out of the playoffs—I still want a little juice. I want a little watercooler action: "Boy did you see the Kings last night against the Lakers?" That's the sign of a good sports town. I'm not saying you've got to know who Sacramento's backup two-guard is. But I don't want you to tune out just because your team got knocked out.

Be Media-Savvy: To be a good sports town you've got to have the games covered right. Whether it's a good sports guy on TV, whether it's a good couple of newspapers with some smart columnists, or even a good sports talk radio show, I want some good media people. It helps to hear a lot of different ideas. Did you read what Bob Ryan said? Did you read what Mike Lupica wrote? Did you hear what Mike North said? Did you see Tom Boswell's column this morning? It gets the brain churning a little bit.

Don't Be a One-Team Town: To be a great sports town, I don't think a city can be dominated by one particular team. There are a couple of big sports towns where the fans love one team and treat the others like orphaned children. For instance, the Redskins are so big in Washington, especially before Michael Jordan, that almost nothing else counts. Fans in D.C. talk Redskins twenty-four hours a day, seven days a week, twelve months a year. Same with the Dolphins in Miami. You go to Miami in June and they are talking about the backup offensive guard for the Dolphins. A big-time sports town has got some seasons to it: in the summer they like baseball, in the the winter they like football, in the spring they get into the NBA playoffs.

So without further ado, here are the top five sports cities in America. The envelope please . . .

5. Cleveland: Cleveland is an excellent sports town. Sure, there's a conspicuous lack of championships. The Cavs have had only brief periods of success, the Indians haven't won a championship in three million years. You've got to go back to the Browns in the 1950s really. The town has done a good job with the Indians, building them a new stadium, filling it up pretty regularly while they were good. The knock that you would have on Cleveland if you had one is that they don't have a hockey team.

Second, I know that this annoys the Browns fan to no end, but you can come up with a lot of games in the 1980s and early '90s where Municipal Stadium had sixty-thousand people in it for games with some meaning. I know that Cleveland likes to consider itself the pro football capital of the Midwest, with the Dog Pound and everything else, but I can remember a lot of empty seats for big division games. I think Cleveland's a great town, but this idea that they sold out NFL football games week after week with a waiting list that stretched around Lake Erie is just not true.

4. St. Louis: They don't have an NBA team, but I think St. Louis is the best baseball town in America. Bob Costas can live anywhere, and this is where he wants to be. Great tradition, great stadium, guys like Stan Musial and Ozzie Smith will come back at a moment's notice. You had the great Jack Buck here as a local institution. When a player gets traded here—Mark McGwire, Jim Edmonds, Scott Rolen—the town loves them so much that they immediately sign on for the long term. Actually, it's a little too lovey-dovey. The relationship between the players and the fans can be a little too cozy. St. Louis also has some football history to it, and while the Cardinals left—and we'll blame the owner, not the city for that one—they've done a good job with the Rams.

However, I think the media aspect hurts St. Louis. The sports talk is vanilla, there's one newspaper, and the *Post-Dispatch* is a little too much in bed with the local teams. They're a little homer-ish, which drives you crazy, and a little short on critical analysis.

But it's a great town.

3. New York: New York's got a lot of things going for it. A ton of teams, at least two in almost every sport, and at least one of those teams has a really strong tradition. But some of the buildings aren't as good as they should be. The media is too omnipresent, and beat guys are a little too tabloid oriented, too focused on making that big back-page splash. What hurts New York most, I think, is that it's too much of an event town. There's too much of that corporate clientele filling up the stadiums for big games. You go to the Yankee playoff game and there are businessmen sitting in the front row on their cellphones who haven't been to a baseball game in thirty years. Their clients took them to a ball game and they think it's a big deal so they call their relatives back in Houston: "Hey, guess what? Turn on the TV. I'm at Yankee Stadium." The flip side of that is that when a team stinks, nobody shows up. There were twenty-three thousand people at Yankee Stadium when Roger Maris hit his sixty-first homer, and you could count the crowds in the mid-'60s when the team started going bad even though Mantle was still there. There's too much of a flavor-of-the-month factor in New York.

2. Chicago: The good thing about Chicago is that the fans are as loyal as a golden retriever. And the bad thing about Chicago is that the fans are as loyal as a golden retriever. The fans love their teams here. The Bears get to the Super Bowl or the Cubbies make the playoffs and everyone's going crazy. (Although they did get a little jaded about the Bulls winning so much.) But Chicago fans are too nice. A Cubs fan is happy if it's a sunny day at Wrigley Field and Sammy Sosa hits some home runs. If they win, it's lovely. If they lose it's a shame. The fans never put pressure on the ownership. They never tell the Tribune Company, "We're mad as hell and we're not going to take this anymore." It lets the ownership off the hook. And that's why Chicago has had more than its share of bad teams with rich owners who don't want to spend money.

1. Boston: Boston is the number one sports town in America. The fans love all their teams there, and they know all their teams there. The Red Sox might just be the best franchise in baseball, right there with the Yankees, and in the summer all of New England becomes Red Sox Nation. The Patriots had an unbelievable run, and right now the Patriots and Red Sox are basically neck and neck in the hearts of Bostonians. The Celtics are legendary, and Bruins fans are still carrying the torch for Bobby Orr. The one little negative I have on Boston is that they couldn't draw flies when Russell was winning all those championships in the '60s with his Boston team, and all of a sudden Larry Bird showed up and they were all going to the games. That bothers me, whether it was a by-product of racism or just being jaded by all that Celtic success. Unfortunately it's probably the former.

And the ratings for big games when there isn't a local team in the game are pretty low. But Beantown's got classic franchises in every sport, passionate, knowledgable fans, and exceptional media coverage. That makes Boston the best sports town in America.

Small Markets, Big Hearts

Two cities that deserve a little credit here are Portland and Sacramento. Portland for years and years and years has been a tremendous NBA town. There's been a college atmosphere there. For years at the old Portland Memorial Coliseum they drew 12,888 every single game. That number was etched in stone, the longest sellout streak in NBA history. They had closed-circuit television in downtown Portland. They still cherish the championship they won. I don't have any doubt that if the opportunity came about, Portland could do a great job supporting a hockey team or a baseball team. So even though it's a one-team town, Portland deserves a special mention.

Sacramento does, too. I think Sacramento has got a little bit of an inferiority complex going, which I think helps a sports town. Sacramento feels "We're out in the middle of nowhere, overshadowed by the Bay area and all its teams, but, hey, we're the capital of the state, and we have the Kings." I think Sacramento wants to prove that it belongs on the sports map. Sacramento has produced a lot of great athletes—Dusty Baker, Steve

Sax, Kenny O'Brien. And they have a little Portland thing going with the Kings. They've put 17,317 in the ARCO Arena every single night since the building opened, and those guys are their heroes. If you went on Sacramento radio the day after they lost game seven to the Lakers, with Chris Webber doing nothing, I'm not sure if they would kill Webber, and you want a good sports town to do that. Still, I think Sacramento is another city that under the right scenario would be able to support another team or two. And I think that sooner rather than later both Portland and Sacramento will get that chance.

DOG TO CITY: FILL 'EM UP

Here's the litmus test for a great sports town: I want to see the playoff game sold out. You want to tell me about an NHL first-round game—Panthers and Carolina, you got 2,000 empty seats, okay I can live with it. You want to tell me that the Cavs have 3,000 empty seats for game one of a five-game series against the Hawks, that's not the end of the world. But I don't want to hear about a baseball playoff game with empty seats. I don't want to see the NFL have to walk in and buy the 3,000 seats left on Thursday so the game can be seen in your local market. I don't want to see a conference final in the NBA that has only 18,000 seats filled. If that happens too many times, I don't want to hear about you being such a great sports town. There's no excuse for not selling out playoff games.

Fantasy Foursome

Which partners would you pick to play the ultimate round of golf?

Filling out a golf foursome is not something to be undertaken lightly. Choose the wrong guys and your dream turns into a five-hour-long nightmare. Mad Dog tells us who he'd take to the first tee and why.

Let's say I give a million dollars to my favorite charity, and in return I can pick three golfers from any time in history to play eighteen holes with me, any golf course in the world.

I'm going to be a populist and play the round at a public course. I'm going to put it at Bethpage Black, the Monday after the U.S. Open is played there. Not in the middle of the summertime after they've had two hundred thousand rounds and the course is a little beaten up. Let me play it when the course is at its best, the first day it's open to the public. I'll wait in line, I'll sleep in the car at two o'clock in the morning, and I'll get my bracelets and bring some donuts from the Ritz Bakery in New Canaan for the other guys. I'll do that.

But I'm playing from the white tees, where I could shoot 100 if I have a huge day and make a couple of putts. I can't hit the ball 265 yards off the tee with my little 5-wood and clear all that fescue. I'm not good enough to beat the course, but I don't want to get bloodied to the point where I've got to quit after the fifth hole.

I want my playing partners playing from the tips. Let me see them hit the ball in the rough occasionally. Let me see a double bogey on 15. I don't care what you say, when you are having a bad day on a golf course with three pretty good players, when they miss a couple of shots it makes you feel a little better.

When you're choosing up the foursome, personality has to enter into the equation. I don't want to spend a million dollars and play golf with a bunch of stiffs. So that eliminates a guy like Ben Hogan, who won't even shake my hand at the first tee.

The first guy I want out there is Arnold Palmer. Arnie will sign my golf ball, he will be a regular guy. He'll be fun. We'll have a gallery, have Arnie's whole army follow us.

And we'll have a couple of beers. We could have some laughs with Arnie. Remember that famous Jimmy Durante line? At a tournament in the early '60s at Pebble Beach, Palmer hits one onto the beach: "It's Arnie on the rocks." Bada-boom. With Arnold Palmer you can just grip it and rip it.

The second guy is Tiger. I've got to have some seriousness here. He doesn't know how to relax on a golf course, and that's what makes Tiger Tiger. I want Tiger with me because Tiger gives us credibility. He's the best player in the world. I want his game face on. I want him to wear his red shirt. And if Tiger doesn't want to join Arnie and me for that Pabst Blue Ribbon, fine. I can live with that.

Rounding out the foursome, I want a little class here. I want a guy who can give me a little history of golf. I know we are going to have to get a cart for him, but I want Byron Nelson out there with me. The guy was a great player, but more to the point he's a great historian, a great storyteller. He played with Bobby Jones, Ben Hogan, Sam Snead. And his mind is still sharp as a tack. Byron Nelson was once on WFAN with Bill Mazer, and Bill asked him how many holes-in-one he had. Told you right away: I had six holes-in-one. I want to hear the stuff that doesn't make it into the golf books. Why did Hogan and Snead hate each other? I want to hear the story about the time when they both landed in Dallas to go play an event and Ben wouldn't give Sam a ride to the tournament. And I wanna know why.

It'd be a perfect foursome. So whadya say, guys, two weeks from Monday? I'll buy the donuts.

A LESSON? NO THANKS

I thought about a guy like Butch Harmon, Tiger Woods's coach, but when I'm out there I don't want a lesson on a golf course. Whenever I played that Seniors Pro-Am in Upper Montclair, N.J., I was always scared to death I would be stuck with Lee Trevino. Lee wants to give you a lesson on the golf course. I stink as it is, I don't need a lesson on the fifth tee. When I hit a bad shot, let me go roll up my pants, wade in there with the ticks and the mosquitoes, get out my 5-iron, and hit it again. I want to play golf. I don't want a clinic. No, no, no.

Good Top, Bad Top

What makes a good owner—and what makes a tyrant?

A lot of sports fans would give up the chance to vote for mayor if they could vote for the owner of their favorite team instead. Get a quality owner and you're halfway to a championship. A bad one, and it's the express elevator to the basement. Dog explains the difference between the two.

What kind of owner do you want for your pro sports team? Do you want an owner who is just going to go out there and spend, spend, spend, and if he doesn't get the desired results, he is going to fire, fire,

fire? Do you want an owner who thinks he's the GM? Do you want an owner who's got an ego the size of the Superdome? No, you don't. I'll give you some characteristics of what I think make a good owner for a twenty-first-century sports team.

Not a Miser: First of all, you want an owner who's going to spend some money. You can't win in sports today unless you have that. Mike Brown, who owns the Bengals, throws money out there like it's manhole covers, not even spending money on scouts, and it shows in the team's record. If you want to win a championship, that means that you've got to spend some money on stars, and if sometimes you have to overpay for those stars, then so be it.

I understand that a team is a business. I understand that you just can't throw money away. And I'm not asking an owner to take money from his personal fortune and throw it into the franchise. I'm not saying you can't make a profit. I *am* asking an owner to use the revenue he gets from the team and put some of it back in the club. There's a certain amount of public trust in owning a sports franchise. And too many owners abuse that.

Stay Off the Sidelines: I want an owner out there who has enough self-esteem that he doesn't need to hog the limelight. Just because you spent a fortune on a ball club doesn't mean that all of a sudden you become an expert. These guys didn't become billionaires by knowing sports. So I don't want a Daniel Snyder type, or a Jerry Jones type. Or even a George Steinbrenner type before he changed his ways.

A good owner hires smart people that he trusts and then stays out of the way and lets them do their job. It doesn't mean you can't be apprised of what is going on, that you can't ask certain questions of your general manager or your head coach. But the guy who says, "It's my money. So I'll decide who's our first-round draft pick. I'll decide who's playing third base." Him, I don't want.

Keep an Even Keel: I don't want a guy who's going to overreact over a six-game losing streak. If his team loses a football game in the last minute, I don't want to see the owner going crazy, stomping up and down and making a scene in the luxury box and being a distraction. You've got to realize that you are not going to win every game or be great every season. These guys aren't robots, these athletes, they are human beings. You are going to have years when the ball doesn't bounce your way or you have some injuries, or good players just have bad years. So I want a guy who realizes that.

Look Long Term: An owner has to have a willingness to see the big picture, to understand that the team is going to be around here for forty, fifty, eighty years and it is going to go through one generation of fans to the next. Planning for the long term means building a good farm system, drafting well, having guys in reserve, being willing sometimes to take a short-term hit for a long-term gain. If you are floundering in the pennant race in July but you still have an outside chance at the wild card, you don't go and sacrifice your best young player in the minor leagues for the borderline starter who might—or might not—help you salvage that season. Stability. That's the word.

Keep Your Eyes on the Prize: But if I'm an owner, I want to win a championship. I want to have them spray me with cheap champagne, plan the parade, read that *Sports Illustrated* special edition about my team. That has got to be the goal. You have little goals below that, but ultimately you should be working toward winning it all.

You've got to be able to read the situation, to recognize the window of opportunity.

That's when you might be willing to make a little less money and add a little more payroll. You might sacrifice that minor league player, or make that salary cap move in the NBA and bring in the veteran. After all, it's all about winning.

Don't Gouge the Fan: When you do win a championship or have a good run, don't take advantage of the fan. Don't say, "Aha! We're winning. I'm going to triple the prices for my season tickets." In certain situations I understand raising ticket prices. You've put together a competitive team; you've done some nice things, you need to adjust for inflation, to get your ticket base in line with the rest of the league. But too many owners have that one decent season after twenty years and all of sudden they look to make a bundle, like the Nets did after they made it to the finals, raising some tickets from $80 to $125. The Nets have one good season and it costs an arm and a leg to go to a game? That's not right. And of course, if you've had a lousy year you shouldn't raise ticket prices either. I like what the Atlanta Falcons did a couple of years ago. They acknowledged that they were rebuilding, so they slashed ticket prices across the board to get people in the stadium.

Be a Good Citizen: A quality owner puts the good of the league over the interests of his individual team. New York Giants owner Wellington Mara shared his television revenue so that teams like the Packers could compete. Good for him. In sports you need to be a capitalist to own a team, but to have a successful league you need a little bit of socialism: from each according to his abilities, to each according to his needs. Sure, you want to win, but you need opponents.

Here are some of the worst owners in sports.

Al Davis: Nobody wants to win more than he does. But he thinks he's still coaching, and because of that he lost quality people like Mike Shanahan and Jon Gruden. And he could care less about the league or the fans. Al Davis had a phenomenal situation in Oakland in the 1970s and he got greedy and bailed out of the city. Bad job.

The Tribune Company: I've always thought the Tribune Company is just happy with looking at the Cubs' bottom line. "Okay, we sold out Wrigley Field again. The ratings are good on the TV superstation. Things are fine." How about winning? The Cubs haven't won in fifty years.

Donald Sterling: The Clippers owner is a joke. He's cheap. All he cares about is being seen. And he doesn't care if he's 30–52 every year. He's got a good young team now, and somehow or another he'll find a way to screw it up.

Jerry Jones: Part of me likes Jerry Jones. He's aggressive, knows how to make money. But his ego gets in the way. He tries to run the Cowboys himself, but he doesn't know a heckuva lot about football. He can get off this list if he can peacefully coexist with Bill Parcells three or four years.

Art Modell: What he did to Cleveland was a disgrace, bailing out of a great football town. It bothered me to no end that he won the Super Bowl a couple of years ago. He's really hard to root for. Ditto for Bill Bidwell, the Cardinals owner.

MR. GOOD EXAMPLE: OWNERS WHO DO IT RIGHT

Peter Magowan: I hate to bring him up because everybody knows I'm a Giants fan. He kept the team in San Francisco when they were about to go to Tampa in the early '90s. He built that stadium without asking for a dime from the taxpayers. He doesn't gouge the fans. He spends money and tries to win— although he should have tried harder to keep manager Dusty Baker. And he stays out of the way. He's a good owner.

Jerry Colangelo: He's a good NBA owner. He's handled the Suns well. He lets his coaches coach and he deals decisively with problems, like the drug scenario with Walter Davis, or even the situation with Jason Kidd. But with the Diamondbacks, he paid a fortune to get guys like Todd Stottlemyre and Jay Bell, tapping his bank account so deep that he has to borrow money from Major League Baseball. And then he wins the World Series.

Jerry Buss: He's had two dynasties with the Lakers, and his team's success has been good for the league. He found smart guys to run the team—Jerry West, Pat Riley, Phil Jackson—and he stayed out of the way. He's had great players— Magic, Kareem, Worthy, Kobe, Shaq—and kept them around. You can't argue with his success.

William DeWitt: Following in the footsteps of the Busch family, DeWitt has done a great job with the Cardinals. He's got baseball in his blood—he was the batboy who gave midget pinch hitter Eddie Gaedel his uniform and his father worked for Bill Veeck. The Cards have a loyal fan base and he doesn't abuse them.

(continued)

139

(continued from previous page)

And he respects the team's great tradition. Guys like Bob Gibson and Ozzie Smith and Mark McGwire, and even Joe Torre, think of themselves as Cardinals. That's a good sign.

Snap Decisions

Who's the greatest NFL quarterback ever?

While there's no consensus of opinion as to what makes a great gridiron leader, four out of five experts agree that it's about more than just throwing the football. Mad Dog rates the NFL's best field generals.

What is it that makes a truly great quarterback? Is it being able to throw the ball 60 yards in the air and hit that open receiver on the go route? Is it being able to thread the needle and hit that third and eight pass over the middle? Is it being willing to stand in the pocket when an outside linebacker is about to flatten you like a crepe? Is it being able to stay calm in the huddle when you're down by six, you've got 82 yards to go, 1:13 on the clock, and one time-out?

Well, it's all of those things. But with a couple of exceptions, I rate quarterbacks by their ability to win. Do they get to championship games? And do they win when they get there? Here are my top ten quarterbacks, guys who can run my offense any day.

10. Sammy Baugh: Although he also played some at tailback, Baugh was the first real modern quarterback. He was also one of the great all-time punters. He won two championships with the Redskins, including one his rookie year.

9. Otto Graham: Graham was great on those classic Paul Brown teams, winning seven championships in ten years, four of them in the AAFC. He's also got a couple of MVP awards and was All-Pro five times.

8. Bobby Layne: Lane wasn't much of a passer—his balls looked like wounded ducks. But he was a tough SOB and a fantastic leader, the kind of guy who cusses at you in the huddle and then buys you a beer—or ten—after the game. He beat the Browns for the title three times in the 1950s. I'll be the first to admit that while the consensus is that these three guys were all great quarterbacks and deserve to be included in any top ten, I never saw them play. So I'll defer to any old-timers as to how you rank them.

7. Dan Fouts: I love Fouts. He had a great arm and put up phenomenal numbers. But I can't put him any higher for two reasons. He was 3-4 in the postseason and never even made it to the Super Bowl. That 17-14 playoff loss at home to Houston with Gifford Nielson at quarterback really sticks out. One of those years he should have found a way to get the San Diego Chargers to the Big Game. And maybe if it wasn't fifty-five below that day in Cincinnati, he would have. Still, his career wasn't very long. He only had six or seven great seasons, whereas the guys ahead of him played for ten, twelve, thirteen years.

6. John Elway: People forget that Elway was bad in the first three Super Bowls that Denver lost. And in that first one that he won against Green Bay, he was not a factor. It was all Terrell Davis, who ran for 157 yards and 3 TDs. Elway made one big play and that was running the ball. One of the reasons why people think highly of Elway is that he went out on top. He had a good game in the Super Bowl against Atlanta and then he retired, kind of like John Wayne walking off into the sunset. He doesn't crack my top five.

5. Bret Favre: Elway and Favre are pretty close, they are both extremely durable, both great out of the pocket, both good in bad weather. I like Favre more than I like Elway. I know that Elway has two Super Bowls compared to Favre's one. Favre also had a little gap in his career after Mike Holmgren left, but still I like Bret better. They both were swashbucklers, go-for-broke guys, so they are very similar, but I think that Favre was a little more central to his team's success than Elway was. If I have a game to win, I am taking Favre over Elway.

4. Terry Bradshaw: It's amazing that a guy could win four Super Bowls and be underrated, but Bradshaw is. People remember Chuck Noll experimenting with Joe Gilliam at quarterback. People think that because the Steelers had such a great defense and such a great running game, that Terry Hanratty or Mike Kruczek could have won the four Super Bowls with that team. No. No. No.

The bottom line is that Bradshaw is 4–0 in the Super Bowl. Bradshaw was a great bad weather quarterback, and he was tough as nails. In that first Super Bowl against Dallas he got knocked out throwing a touchdown pass to Lynn Swann to clinch the game. Bradshaw also won that last Super Bowl by himself against the Rams with that long touchdown pass to John Stallworth. Those were great teams, but Bradshaw never had a bad day in a big spot.

3. Dan Marino: He's my exception-that-proves-the-rule guy. Marino is probably the best pure passer that the game has ever seen. But while he was there Miami never had the great defense, never had the great running back. And never won a championship. No, he didn't play great the one time he did make the Super Bowl, and he lost a couple of championship games at home, but to me Marino is the third best quarterback of all time. If you put Marino on the Denver Broncos, I'll guarantee you that he'll win the two championships that Elway won, and maybe a couple more to boot.

2. Johnny Unitas: I did not see Unitas in his prime, but I did catch the tail end of his career. Unitas was a phenomenal quarterback, a great thrower, a great leader. He threw a touchdown pass in a record 47 consecutive games. He won back-to-back championships with the Colts in the late '50s. If you want to summarize his greatness, just look at the end of the classic 1958 championship game. That team was down 17-14, he brought them down the field twice, once to tie in the fourth quarter, another time to win in the overtime. On that drive Unitas had the guts to throw an eight-yard pass down to the one when the Colts were already in field goal range. He was the hero of one of the most important games in the history of the NFL. One knock on Unitas, he had a terrible championship game in Cleveland in 1964, passing for only 95 yards and two interceptions.

1. Joe Montana: Before the 2002 football season, Phil Simms said that Elway was his pick for the best quarterback of all time. He argues that Montana was helped out big-time by the West Coast offense. Phil knows his football, but I totally disagree with him. Montana won four championships in four tries. He was the MVP of every darn Super Bowl he was ever in. He got to a championship game while playing for Kansas City. Even in games he lost in the playoffs he was phenomenal. He won with a rotating cast in San Francisco. He won with Freddy Solomon. He won with Jerry Rice. He won with Roger Craig. He won with Wendell Tyler. In the ten years since he left, San Francisco has won only one championship, not four, not five. And of course Montana was Mr. Intangible. Remember that great 92-yard drive against Cincinnati? Montana's so cool that he looks over at the sideline and tells the other guys in the huddle, "Hey look, it's John Candy." If I had a game to win or a drive where I need to score, I'm picking Joe Montana.

BUT WHAT ABOUT . . .

Roger Staubach: He won only one Super Bowl, lost to Pittsburgh twice, and was a little erratic throwing the ball. But boy was he fun to watch.

Bart Starr: A great player but he was overshadowed by Lombardi's system. The Packers won with defense and the power sweep.

Joe Namath: If you were picking a quarterback for one game, Namath would be right there. But he had only four or five years where he was really great, and the guys in the top ten were dominant for a decade.

Hearing Is Believing

What does it take to be a great baseball play-by-play man?

If there's a rite of passage for a sports fan, it might just be hiding under the covers with a transistor radio, listening to a baseball game. What is it that makes video-free baseball so special? Mad Dog weighs in.

B aseball is the one sport that plays on radio. Basketball and hockey move too fast to be really great on radio, and the regular season doesn't have all that much drama anyway. And NFL football happens once a week, so most big fans are going to be sitting in front of their televisions on Sunday afternoon.

But baseball on radio is a magical thing. The season is 162 games, and you can listen to the game while you're driving to the beach. You can listen to the game while you rake the lawn or clean out the garage or wash your car. You can sit out here on the patio in the middle of July with a glass of lemonade, listening to a ball game and taking a nap between innings.

And unlike the TV guys who don't do every game—one game's on cable, one game's on free TV, one game's on Fox, one game's on ESPN—a radio play-by-play guy is there every day. You build a relationship with him. He's almost like a member of your family. Radio play-by-play guys are the gym rats of Major League Baseball. So many of these guys, Ernie Harwell, Bob Murphy, Vin Scully, even Bob Uecker, kept doing games when they could have retired because it's so much in their blood.

So what does it take to be a good radio play-by-play man? First and foremost, you need a good voice. You cannot be a good radio baseball play-by-play guy with a lousy voice. All the greats have a sound, a tone, something that's ear-catching. I think it's something that you're born with. I don't care how many scotches you drink, you're not gonna get more baritonish. And you can't be phony—that Biff Barf in Columbus, Ohio, schtick wears thin in a New York minute. The best way to explain it: You need a voice that cuts through.

Two: You need good cadence. The game has to flow, it has to sound smooth, not choppy. You've got to know when to talk and when to shut up. You've got to know when to be a wordsmith and when to let the game speak for itself. And how to keep the game moving, without rushing it. Pacing baseball play-by-play is a knack, and I don't think it's something that you can teach.

And you've got to be able to paint pictures with words. You've got to know the game, understand what just happened, that's a given. But you've also got to make the listener think they were there watching it with their own two eyes. Every play-by-play guy has got to remember that there's a shut-in somewhere who lives and dies by his descriptions, somebody who's blind who's hanging on every word. The night watchman and the guy pumping gas on the graveyard shift. Don't let 'em down.

Finally, you need to be a good storyteller. Baseball is a slow game. You got 162 games at three-plus hours a night. That's bare minimum 486 hours. Think about it. That's over twenty solid days and nights. So you need to have some great stories from five or twenty or fifty years ago to fill out those dead innings.

A BARBER POLL

One guy who I've always felt is a little overrated is Red Barber. Now you'll say, "Hold on, Chris. That's Red Barber. He's the dean." Well, to me Barber was too aloof, too removed. I don't want my radio play-by-play guys to be homers, but I do want some passion shown during both good times and bad. I want to sense a little frustration coming out of the broadcast booth, when things are going badly, and I want to sense a little happiness coming out of the broadcast booth when things are going well. Objective is one thing, but dispassionate is another. Wear your emotion on your sleeve a little bit. Barber never did that. Barber never liked Russ Hodges's call of Bobby Thomson's home run—"The Giants win the pennant! The Giants win the pennant!" He thought it was a disgrace. Give me a break—it's the greatest pennant race of all time, one of the greatest moments in the history of the sport, and Red Barber didn't like the fact that Russ Hodges was too enthusiastic about it. Here's my problem with Red Barber: Barber could have done any team. Give Barber a Yomiyuri Giants game and he'd go do it. I want an announcer to feel the same way about the team that I do.

And if you do all those things, you might get lucky enough to have a few moments where your career intertwines with the fortunes of the team. Bob Murphy blurting out at the end of one of those wee-hour, seesaw marathons, "The Mets win the damn thing, 10-9." John Sterling getting to say, "Theeeeeeeeeeeee Yankees win," after the last out of the World Series.

That said, I think that ranking the great play-by-play guys is very, very subjective. I think Vin Scully's number one, no contest. He's Michael Jordan and everybody else is trying to get up there to that level.

After Scully, who's next? I think it all depends on who you used to listen to on your old radio going to bed at night when you were a fifteen-year-old. I think it comes down to that. The guy I love more than anybody else is Marty Brennamann. I used to go to bed at night trying to flip around looking for Giants-Reds games, and I could pull in WLW in Cincinnati, 700 on your AM dial. Brennamann was a tremendous baseball guy. He took over for Al Michaels in the '70s and that's a tall order in itself, but Brennamann did himself proud.

Some of the other guys I love: Harry Kallas and that great baritone voice of his: "2-2 to Michael Jack Schmidt." Bob Prince calling Roberto Clemente "Bobby." How could you forget Milo Hamilton, who described Hank Aaron as "Sitting on 714"? That's a great line. I was fortunate enough to be able to get WBAL in Baltimore and hear Chuck Thompson, who did those great Orioles teams of the 1960s and '70s. And of course there's the late great Jack Buck, Harry Caray, Gary Cohen. I'll listen to these guys any day. Even when the game is on television.

MY FAVORITE SCULLY STORY

Vin Scully used to tell this story all the time and I love it. The Dodgers wanted to play a gag on home plate umpire Frank Pulli in a game that Jerry Reuss was pitching. Pulli and manager Tommy Lasorda had a huge fight in the 1978 World Series between the Yankees and Dodgers over the ball that hit Reggie Jackson in the hip, a play that really changed the momentum of that Series. After that there was a love-hate relationship between Pulli and Lasorda. So before the game, Reuss wrote on a ball, "Dear Frank, Love you always, Tommy," and slipped it in the umpire's ball bag. So the game is being played, Reuss is pitching, it's the middle innings, Pulli throws him a ball, and lo and behold, there's the ball. "Dear Frank . . ." Reuss is cracking up on the mound. He throws it and the batter hits a foul ball into the crowd. The fan at Dodgers Stadium who caught the ball, do you know what his name was? Frank. That's being a storyteller, ladies and gentlemen.

What a Waste

Which players got the least out of their talent?

"For of all sad words of tongue or pen, the saddest are these, 'It might have been.'" John Greenleaf Whittier probably wasn't a sports fan, but he should have been. Mad Dog lists the sports world's greatest underachievers.

The sports world is just filled with guys who are supremely blessed athletically, but for a variety of reasons didn't fulfill their potential. Guys who had Hall of Fame talent but not Hall of Fame careers. Maybe they had a few brief, shining moments to tease you into thinking they had turned a corner. But when you think about them, your first thoughts are about how much better they should have been.

Not every player who underachieves is going to make this list—Mickey Mantle should have been better than he was, but he hit 536 home runs and he's in the Hall of Fame. He could have been supergreat, but he still was great. And I'm not going to get into guys who were highly touted prospects who just didn't pan out—a Todd Van Poppel or a Clint Hurdle.

And when I think about the guys on this list, I'm of two minds. First, I feel a little angry—they cheated me out of some great moments—and then I feel a little sad—they cheated themselves. Most of these guys didn't just screw up their games, they also screwed up their lives—with drugs, drinking, hanging around with the wrong people. And that's the biggest waste of all.

Mike Tyson: A no-brainer. Tyson is a guy who was groomed to be a great boxer. Cus D'Amato and Jimmy Jacobs worked him superbly, getting him out of Bedford-Stuyvesant, bringing him up to the Catskills, making him a heavyweight. He was the ultimate intimidator, relentless, a tremendous puncher. A bull in a china shop. A lot of writers go revisionist on Tyson. Today they say, "Tyson was never a great fighter." Well, look at the columns after Tyson knocked out Michael Spinks in ninety-one seconds in 1988. They wrote tremendous stories about the greatness of Mike Tyson. People forget this, but Tyson was a good history guy, too. He loved talking about other great fighters.

But once D'Amato died and then Jacobs got sick with leukemia, that was the beginning of the end. Robin Givens came into the picture and then the rape case with Desiree Washington, and Tyson ended up going to jail. Bottom line is that Tyson was a thug. D'Amato and Jacobs knew they had a guy who's a caged animal, but they were able to focus his rage by making him fight every five weeks. They knew that if he got off that routine, as he eventually did, he would dissipate all his ability. Once he lost his mentors, he just became a bully, in and out of the ring.

Ilie Nastase: There was never a tennis player with more pure talent than Ilie Nastase. He was a magician. He could do anything with the racket. He could belt huge serves and then follow it up with the most delicate drop volley. Against guys like Jimmy Connors and Arthur Ashe, he'd just tease them, using their own power against them, changing spin, changing pace, then ripping a winner. And he could run like the wind. He was an artist on the tennis court.

But the problem was his head. He'd get a bad call and he'd explode. But when John McEnroe exploded, he'd concentrate more. Nastase exploded and then he started to feel bad about the way he acted and his game would go right down the tubes. Sometimes he'd be charming, joking and clowning around with the crowd. Sometimes he'd be just a nasty SOB, cursing out linesmen, spitting on the umpire, calling his opponent a Nazi. But whatever his mood, he always seemed more interested in being a playboy than being a tennis player.

John Daly: He has tremendous distance off the tee, nice touch around the greens, and he's a great putter. He's won the British Open and the PGA.

He's also a nut case. He drinks too much—too much Diet Pepsi, too. He's been in and out of rehab. He's been married four times. And you can never tell what Daly's going to do on a golf course. If John Daly has got his swing down that particular week, he's in great shape. When it gets a little off-kilter, then he starts playing stupid golf. He uses a driver on holes where he should hit a 3-iron. He'll shoot 16 on a hole and just walk off the course in the middle of a round.

John Daly, for whatever the reason, doesn't really have the mental toughness to hang in there on a bad day. And if you cannot hang in there on a bad day in a major, your 73, which keeps you in the tournament, becomes an 85.

How much talent does John Daly have? Put Vijay Singh's head on his shoulders, he could play with Tiger Woods shot for shot. This is a guy who should have won a lot more than two majors.

Ryan Leaf: The skinny on Leaf: great size, great arm; terrible work ethic, no desire. You knew you were in trouble with Ryan Leaf when after his senior year at Washington State, between the Rose Bowl and draft day, he gained sixty pounds. This was a guy who everyone knew would be one of the top two picks in the draft, and he can't push himself away from the buffet table. The San Diego Chargers give up two first-round picks, a second-round pick, and former Pro Bowler Eric Metcalf so they can trade up to get him. They anoint him as their savior, and he totally blows it. He doesn't put any effort in, goes back to Washington State, gets into a major fight. In three years he starts 18 games and goes 4–14. It set the Chargers back three or four years.

And now, believe it or not, Ryan Leaf is out of football. At twenty-six years old. He had chances with the Cowboys and the Bucks and the Seahawks and couldn't do anything in these places either. In a league where if you can throw the ball ten feet in a straight line they give you a guaranteed contract, this guy is off sitting on the beach somewhere. Pathetic.

Benoit Benjamin: He had a great NBA body at 7' 2" close to 300 pounds. He had excellent athletic ability, good moves, great shot-blocking ability. And he had Willis Reed coaching him at Creighton. This is a guy who had the perfect pedigree to be a great NBA center. But he didn't have the killer instinct. He didn't have the hunger. Didn't have the drive, the ambition. He was a complete bust in the NBA, the Stanley Roberts of his day. And the worst part is that he was a tease. He'd be going along in a regular season, scoring his 11 points, getting his 5 rebounds, a couple of shots blocked, playing his 25 minutes. And then he'd have a little stretch, for a week, ten days, where he'd have 25 points, 15 rebounds, and 6 blocked shots. So you knew he had it in him. You knew down deep somewhere there was this great player. But you'd never see it for more than a couple games at a time.

Darryl Strawberry: When Darryl Strawberry came up in the mid-1980s, he had Hall of Fame written all over him. In high school they were comparing him to Ted Williams.

Nobody would have been too surprised if he had the kind of career that Barry Bonds did. Darryl had a great throwing arm, was a pretty good outfielder, a lot better than a lot of people thought out there in right, and just incredible power. With that great looping uppercut swing, he'd scare the living daylights out of a pitcher.

And Strawberry had some good moments. He hit 39 home runs with the Mets. He hit some big postseason homers for the 1996 Yankees and won three rings with them.

But even in the years in which he was good, he wasn't good enough. When he hit 35 home runs and knocked in 105, you always thought that Darryl could have done a little better. The 35 homers should have been 45. The 105 RBIs should have been 125. You always thought that if he came to play every single day that the sky was the limit.

As it was he put up the first half of a Hall of Fame career. If he had been able to keep his nose clean—in more ways than one—he could have easily put up Reggie Jackson–type numbers: .280 lifetime, 550 home runs, 1,400 or 1,500 RBIs. But Strawberry fouled up his life. His decision to go to L.A. in 1990 was a disaster, with all the pressure, and all the bad influences he had from high school. He had drug and drinking problems, problems with money, problems with his wife. Injuries. Colon cancer. He had a lot of bad things happen to him, and when bad things happen to weak people, it's a terrible, terrible combination.

Kings of Diamonds

Which is the greatest baseball team ever?

It's the granddaddy of all sports arguments. What's the best baseball team of all time? Back when Grover Cleveland was president, fans were hashing out the relative merits of the 1871 Boston Red Stockings versus the 1884 St. Louis Maroons. But who sits on the top of the heap today? Mad Dog tells all.

B race yourselves, Yankee haters. As much as it pains me to say it, four of my top six baseball teams of all time wear the pinstripes. There's no way around it though.

Still, this argument highlights one of the great things about baseball. The game has changed, but not so much that you can't compare a team from the 1920s with a team from the 1990s. And ranking them is tough. Here are a few of the factors we'll take into consideration. How many Hall of Famers are there on each roster? How good is the balance between pitching and hitting? How did they do in the postseason? Did they blow people away or did they have to struggle? And how good was the competition? The teams they beat in the postseason or regular season, were they great teams? Were they one-year wonders or did they win a couple in a row? That's how you separate these great, classic clubs. Here are my top six.

6. The 1975 Cincinnati Reds: This just might be the greatest hitting team of all time, but I can't put them higher than sixth. The Big Red Machine had four Hall of Famers—Joe Morgan, Johnny Bench, Tony Perez, and even though he's not in Cooperstown, Pete Rose. George Foster was certainly playing like a Hall of Famer back then. But the balance wasn't there. The starting pitching doesn't blow you away. The starters are Gary Nolan, Jack Billingham, Fred Norman, Don Gullett. That's not a big-time staff. They did have a nice bullpen with Pedro Borbon and Rawley Eastwick, Clay Carroll and Will McEnaney. But those starters . . .

The Reds won 108 games, and won the West by 20 games. But in the postseason they were lucky to win a tough seven-game Series against a very good Red Sox team that had Carlton Fisk, Carl Yastrzemski, Luis Tiant, Dwight Evans, Fred Lynn, and Jim Rice. The two big knocks against the Reds are the starting pitching and the fact that they barely survived against the Red Sox. That's why the Reds are sixth.

5. The 1998 Yankees: I'm putting the turn-of-the-millennium Yankees as number five. Now, they won the most games of any team on this list—114 in the regular season, 125 including the playoffs—but they've got only two future Hall of Famers on the team: Derek Jeter and Mariano Rivera. Roger Clemens wasn't there yet. David Wells and David Cone are not Hall of Famers. Bernie Williams? No. Paul O'Neill? Very good player, not a Hall of Famer. This team's strength was its great balance. However, their competition wasn't great. The San Diego Padres are not an all-time great team. Still, I put them ahead of the Reds because they won more games, three championships in a row and not two, and they dominated the postseason, winning an extra round against Texas and sweeping the World Series.

4. 1961 Yankees: The Kennedy-era bombers hit an incredible amount of home runs and won 109 games. They won their pennant by eight and Detroit was pretty good with Al Kaline, Frank Lary, Jim Bunning, and Norm Cash. The '61 Yankees had three Hall of Famers: Mickey Mantle, Yogi Berra, and Whitey Ford. Of course, Roger Maris was having a Hall of Fame–type year as well. Still, the Yankees had only two guys with 100 RBIs. And they lost a game in the World Series to a decent but not great Cincinnati Reds team. If you divorce these Mantle-Maris Yankees from the dynasty of the 1950s, you'll note that between 1960 and 1964, New York lost three of the five World Series the team played in, and their postseason record was a less-than-impressive 14–16.

3. 1939 Yankees: A lot of people think the '39 Yankees are the greatest team ever. The Yankee team of '39 had three Hall of Famers—Joe DiMaggio, Bill Dickey, and Lefty Gomez. They won 106 games, and won the pennant by 17 games. That year in the World Series they beat a decent Reds team in four straight, and in 1938 they swept, too. In fact, those Yankee teams between '36 and '40 were 16–3 in the World Series. A really great team.

2. 1929 Philadelphia A's: How close is it between my top two teams? This close: If the A's had polished off St. Louis in 1931—a year in which they won 107 in the regular season—instead of losing in seven games, I would rank them number one of all time. Both the '31 A's and the '27 Yankees won two in a row. And the Cardinals were the spoilers. St. Louis beat the Yankees in 1926. The A's lost to St. Louis to end their streak.

1. 1927 Yankees: I'm going to put the Murderer's Row Yankees number one and the A's number two. Here's why I like the '27 Yankees. Lefty Grove was a great pitcher for the A's, one of the best ever, but the Yankees had two Hall of Famers in Herb Pennock and Waite Hoyt.

The Yankees everyday lineup had four Hall of Famers in Babe Ruth, Lou Gehrig, Tony Lazzeri, and Earle Combs. The A's had three in Jimmie Foxx, Al Simmons, and Mickey Cochrane. Foxx and Simmons are great. But Ruth and Gehrig are better.

Plus, the Yankees did not lose a World Series game, while the A's lost three World Series games in their run. And the Yankees were a little better in the regular season. The A's won 104 in '29 and 102 in '30. The Yankees of '27 won 110, and they won 101 in 1928.

Two great teams, the two greatest teams. But the Yankees get the edge, just barely.

A'S AREN'T ENOUGH

Even though they three-peated, I'm not putting the 1972–74 A's in here. They had three Hall of Famers in Reggie Jackson, Rollie Fingers, and Catfish Hunter, but they didn't have enough wins. They were never that dominant in the regular season. The other teams on this list won 105, even 110 games. The A's won 91 or 92 games. That's why they don't make the cut.

Braves New World

Are the Atlanta Braves baseball's ultimate underachievers?

Through the last dozen summers, the Braves have been hotter than the Fourth of July. But come October, things tend to cool off in Hotlanta. Is this glass half empty or half full? Mad Dog weighs the evidence.

How do you evaluate the Atlanta Braves from 1991 through 2002? They won the division eleven consecutive times. I mean, that is unmatched in sports. On the other hand, they're one for five in the World Series. Do you give them credit for their incredible consistency in the regular season? Or do you smack them around because they have lost a lot of terrible games in the postseason? It's an interesting debate. Here's a question. Off the top of your head, what do you think Atlanta's postseason record is in the NL playoffs not including the World Series? 5–8? 6–8 maybe? Take a deep breath: 11 and 6 in the National League playoffs. That's pretty surprising considering all the disappointments.

The Mets over that same period have won three playoff series. The Giants have won two. The San Diego Padres have won two. The Astros haven't won any. The Yankees in this same period are 10 and 3 in the American League. Braves are 11 and 6. Doesn't sound so bad, does it?

The difference is that the Yankees have won four out of their five World Series. And the Braves are one for five. Since game six of the 1996 World Series, the Braves are 2 and 7 in elimination games. And they're 0 and 6 at home in elimination games.

Let's take it year by year.

1991: They beat the Pirates in seven games in a classic Series. In that memorable World Series they lost game seven to the Twins 1-0 on a sac fly in the tenth inning, with Jack Morris outlasting John Smoltz. That is not a big deal. Both teams went from worst to first. That was a victory for baseball, not a loss for the Braves.

1992: Again they beat the Pirates in seven games in the NLCS, this time on the great play by Sid Bream on the base hit by Francisco Cabrera. But then they lost to the Blue Jays in six, even though they outscored Toronto 20-17. This one bothers you if you're a Braves fan because Atlanta won the first game behind Tom Glavine, and in the second game Ed Sprague hit that big homer off Jeff Reardon in the ninth to get the Blue Jays the road split. The bullpen collapsed, and that's a theme with Atlanta. Toronto won three of the next four games, all by one run. That 1992 World Series you're a little annoyed about.

1993: This year is weird. How do you evaluate the '93 Braves? They won 104 games. They won one of the classic pennant races coming back from eight and a half games out in August to catch the Giants. They played great down the stretch, went 104 and 58, and then somehow lost to the Phillies in six games, dropping two out of three at home. That's a bad loss. Another theme with the Braves. Every year they lost a World Series or a playoff, they always did something dramatic in the same year.

It's a little bit like the '86 Red Sox, who were a strike away from losing to the Angels in the ALCS and then they lose to the Mets in the same spot two weeks later.

1996: See the accompanying "A Schuerholz Thing."

1997: This was another bad one. It's two games to two, and Livan Hernandez beats them in game five, striking out fifteen guys because home plate umpire Eric Gregg gave him a strike zone as big as he was. The Braves lose in six games. Which brings up the question of why Tom Glavine and Greg Maddux have been so disappointing in the postseason. Their ERAs have not been terrible, but their record isn't as good as it is in the regular season. I think it's because, unlike Smoltz, they work on the fringes of the plate. Lots of times the good hitters on the good teams don't swing at those pitches and, with the exception of guys like Gregg, the umpires in the postseason call a tighter, more consistent strike zone.

1998: They were down 3–0 to San Diego, won two dramatic games, and lost game six back in their building. You think that the Braves might just be the first baseball team to come back from 3–0 down, and then they run into Sterling Hitchcock.

1999: The playoffs were typically dramatic. They beat the Astros in part due to Walt Weiss's great play with the bases loaded in game three. And they beat the Mets on their walk in the eleventh inning of game six of a roller-coaster series. But this dramatic win was followed by a crushing fall—they got swept in the World Series by the Yankees. Sure, they were kind of banged up, but they should at least win a game there.

2000: They were embarrassed by St. Louis. They lost the last game of the regular season when John Rocker gave up a big home run and blew a ninth inning lead against the Rockies, which cost them home field advantage. They had to go straight to St. Louis and got swept. No excuses. That's a bad one.

2001: Again they were all banged up. They won a playoff series against the Astros again, but lost to Randy Johnson and Curt Schilling in the NLCS. You can live with that.

2002: This one should stick in their craw. They had a two games to one lead against the Giants and left twelve guys on in game five.

A SCHUERHOLZ THING

I place a lot of the blame for the Braves' postseason failures on GM John Schuerholz. He didn't have a bull pen there for most of the run. He hung in there with guys like Jeff Reardon and Alejandro Peña and Mark Wholers and Kerry Ligtenberg and John Rocker, which is a total mistake. He should have traded Denny Neagle for a lights-out closer. You don't need a fourth starter in the postseason. Look at the 1996 Yankees with Kenny Rogers.

He never built up the bench, either. In '96, when he won the pennant by a bunch of games and the Yankees were adding guys like Cecil Fielder and Charlie Hayes, he sat back and did nothing. In the tenth inning of game four, down two

---

games to one, the Yankees had Wade Boggs, a .328 lifetime hitter and a Hall of Famer, pinch hitting. Who made the last out for the Braves in game five the next night? Luis Polonia. Think about that for a minute. There's no excuse for that.

Remember, Bobby Cox was the GM there in the late 1980s when they brought all those pitchers in, Glavine and Smoltz and Steve Avery. So for the Braves, pitching was more put together by Cox than Schuerholz. So what I'm telling you is that Atlanta's GM is overrated.

So how will history judge the Braves? You can't call them the baseball version of the Buffalo Bills. That's totally unfair. They won a World Series by beating a Cleveland Indians team that won 100 games in a shortened season. The Bills did not.

When you make the playoffs eleven consecutive years, should you have more than one World Series? Probably. But baseball is a regular season sport. This is not the NBA or the NHL. It's not easy to make the playoffs in baseball. They won eleven straight division titles and twelve postseason series, an average of better than one a year. And they had their share of improbable victories to balance out the disappointing defeats. That's got to be weighed in their favor.

The Unwatchables

Which sporting events aren't worth flipping the channel for?

Don't want to watch the Yankees and the Red Sox? You can always switch to the World Lumberjack Championships or maybe some ladies' bowling. Mad Dog comes clean about the sporting events you couldn't bribe him to watch.

Now I'm a big sports guy. I love watching sports on TV. But I won't watch just anything. Here are five sporting events I wouldn't watch if you put me on a desert island with a broken satellite dish that got only one channel. I would read a Marvin Miller book on baseball labor before I'd watch some of these events. And I've covered a couple of these, but there's no way I'd watch if I weren't getting paid for it.

The WNBA: David Stern, commissioner of the NBA, keeps trying to get me to one of these games. My wife or my daughter had better be involved if you think you're going to get me to a WNBA game. I might watch Sue Bird play a little bit in college for U. Conn, but the last thing I'm going to do is watch Sue Bird play for the Seattle Storm. What a total waste of time. We've just watched eight months of the NBA. We've watched Shaq and Kobe and Vince Carter, and we're supposed to get pepped up to watch Theresa Witherspoon and Rebecca Lobo after that? Imagine if you got into baseball for nine months, lived and died with it on an everyday basis, watched the World Series, and they put together a women's baseball league to keep you going through December, January, and February. Would you watch that? Enough basketball. Give me a break with it. Let's face it, if the NBA weren't behind the WNBA, it would fold in about a week.

Did you ever look at the ratings? They can't even draw flies.

Track and Field: Outside of the Olympics, would I watch track and field? No way. A race lasts nine seconds and these guys are still pulling hamstrings. The problem with any kind of world track and field championships, or even a world record, is that it's superseded by the Olympics, and that hurts the credibility of the sport. Your memories are made in the Olympics—Lasse Viren, Bruce Jenner, Carl Lewis, Michael Johnson. Who holds the world record in the 100-meter dash? I have no idea. None. Zero. Edwin Moses's streak? Who cares? It's about gold medals.

The LPGA: Who watches the LPGA? Outside of seeing Babe Didrikson on ESPN *Sports Century*, who cares about women's golf? I didn't know Nancy Lopez was retiring until about six months after she quit. And did you ever notice the crowds they get at these things? There's nobody there. A great finish to a major championship and you've got five people following Annika Sorenstam on the last day. The women hit the ball 235 yards. I just can't get into it. I've been doing sports talk for fourteen years and I've never once taken a call about women's golf. They could play a tournament in my backyard—I'll make them a beautiful par three—but I'm going to draw the blinds.

NASCAR: You sit there for three and a half hours watching them go around a stupid oval, and the announcers are talking about drafting like it's rocket science. "Gee, you can use the back of one car to catapult yourself past the other car into first place." But the whole thing comes down to the last two or three laps anyway. Go down to the infield and all anyone's doing is drinking. It does nothing for me. To me NASCAR is a Southeastern, rural sport. No, I won't call it a sport. A Southeastern rural *event*. It was born in these places you wouldn't want to find yourself in under any circumstances. Talladega, Alabama. Darlington, South Carolina, Bristol, Tennessee. You're in Talladega for the race and you go down to the grocery store and buy the local papers and try to get the baseball scores. You can't find them. But you get twenty pages on the race. It's a waste of time.

The Tour de France: You know what drives me crazy is when I'm watching a ball game and at the bottom of the hour they give the Tour de France results. Although I love Europe, you couldn't get me to watch the Tour de France under any circumstances. What a complete waste of time watching Greg LeMond ride a bicycle up a couple of mountains. Who gives a damn? You can't understand how the team aspect works. Up a mountain, down a mountain, it's riding a bicycle for goodness' sake. We made such a big deal about this. I know Lance Armstrong is a nice man and he battled cancer. And LeMond got shot, that's bad, too. But you couldn't get me to watch it on ABC. I don't care if Jerry Lewis is on the lead bike riding down the Champs-Élysées. Who cares? I went down in the subway the year that Greg LeMond won *Sports Illustrated*'s Sportsman of the Year and asked people what they thought about it. Nobody had ever *heard* of him.

Get Backs

Who should your QB be handing off to?

Taking handoffs in pro football is a dirty business, but somebody's got to do it. But who? Mad Dog explains that it's not always about the yardage.

Who's the best running back? I have to look at that as a two-part question. The first question is "Which guy, week in and week out, is going to get me the most yardage?" If that's the yardstick, the best guy I ever saw was Walter Payton. Payton was an absolute workhorse. He never got hurt. You couldn't bring him down. You could put seven or eight guys at the line of scrimmage and Payton is still going to get four or five yards a carry. Remember that 275-yard game against Minnesota? That's classic Payton.

He was a great all-around back. He could dance through a hole or he could pound for those tough yards between the tackles. He could catch some passes out of the backfield. He was willing to block. He was also a great guy, a good teammate.

Who were the other guys I thought of here? I think that O. J. Simpson might be the best pure runner that I ever saw. Barry Sanders was fantastic, too. You could put Eric Dickerson on the short list, too, at least until you remember that he fumbled three times in the 1985 NFC championship game against the Bears. I didn't see Jim Brown, and the consensus is that he's the best back ever, period, no argument. He wouldn't block and he wasn't Mr. Personality, but he was a great, great runner. I didn't see Gale Sayers, although he was more of a finesse back, and like Terrell Davis he had a short career.

Notice one thing in common with all of those guys? They played on pretty bad teams for most of their careers. Sayers never won a championship, and neither did O.J. or Sanders. Brown won just one title with the Browns. Payton was on the downside of his career when the Bears finally won a Super Bowl.

Here's my theory: When you've got a superstar back like Walter Payton or Barry Sanders, you have to give him the ball thirty-five to forty times a game. And that restricts what you can do with the rest of your offense.

So here's the second question: Which back do you want if you're starting a franchise?

I think you're better off with a blend-in guy. What do I mean by that? I'm talking about a guy who can carry the ball eighteen to twenty times a game, run for 90 yards, get his first downs, catch five or six balls out of the backfield, and have his impact on the game that way. Some days you'll go to him more, but most of the time he's going to be just one facet of your attack.

That's why I'd start my franchise with Emmitt Smith. I love Emmitt because he is a classic blend-in back. He was part of a great offense. You didn't have to give him the ball thirty times a game, and on days when he wasn't the man, the Cowboys would still usually win the game. Marshall Faulk is the same kind of back. Franco Harris was, too. Even a guy like Roger Craig for the 49ers.

Walter Payton was a great running back. But I'm not sure that I would take Payton over Emmitt because I think if you gave the ball to Payton only twelve or thirteen times a game you probably wouldn't win. So if I just want to watch a guy run roughshod over a defense, just for the pure pleasure of it, Payton is the guy among the backs that I've seen. But if I want to win, I'm going to take Emmitt.

THE RUN AROUND

Who are the NFL's best pure running backs ever? Here's my list.

1. **Jim Brown:** An incredible combination of power and speed.
2. **Walter Payton:** More versatile than Brown, and played forever.
3. **Barry Sanders:** He did everything but win a championship.
4. **O. J. Simpson:** Owned both the single season and single game rushing records.
5. **Gale Sayers:** Electrifiying to watch, but a short career.
6. **Emmitt Smith:** The consummate blend-in back sticks around long enough to capture the all-time rushing crown.
7. **Franco Harris:** Another great blender.
8. **Earl Campbell:** A dominant power back, run into the ground by the Oilers.
9. **Jim Taylor:** Raised the power sweep to an art form and won the MVP in 1962, while Brown was still in the league.
10. **Marshall Faulk:** The best out-of-the-backfield receiver ever.

Goal Oriented

Who would prevail in the NHL's ultimate penalty shot?

It's tantalizingly simple. One shot. Either it's a goal or a save. That's the al-lure of the penalty shot, a mano-a-mano match in the middle of the ulti-mate team game. Mad Dog selects a shooter, picks a goalie, and tells you what happened.

The penalty shot, with that one-on-one confrontation between the great skater and the great goalie, is one of the most exciting things in sports. The puck's at center ice, the offensive player circling like a vulture waiting for the whistle to blow, the goalie is getting his gear together, fiddling with his pads and his stick, and then the puck drops. And here comes the skater down the ice with the puck. A goal. Or a huge save.

A penalty shot in hockey isn't like soccer, where you score four times out of five.

In hockey it's roughly a 50-50 proposition. That's why you like the penalty shot so much, because there's an even chance of failure or success.

When you're trying to create a fantasy penalty shot, you've got to remember that it's kind of an art unto itself. So you just can't pick the two best players and have them go head-to-head. A lot of guys who are great players aren't great on penalty shots. Gretzky's a perfect case in point. Never great on breakaways. One great player who was great at penalty shots: Mario Lemieux. He's the all-time leader in penalty shot goals and percentage.

And who's Mario shooting against? Billy Smith of the Islanders. He was two for two in stopping penalty shots in the playoffs. Billy Smith won't give an inch. He's a cantankerous SOB, so he won't be intimidated by Lemieux's speed or size. And he's a stand-up goalie—not a Tony Esposito–type who's going to flop. Which makes him tougher on a penalty shot. And he's got that perfect cocky gunslinger attitude. He's not going to get rattled even if Mario does score.

So here's the setup: It's the early 1980s Islanders versus the early '90s Penguins. The Islanders are on the power play, and Lemieux steals the puck from Bryan Trottier and heads into the neutral zone for a short-handed solo breakaway. Just as he's about to take aim on Smith, Denis Potvin hooks Lemieux with his stick and pulls him down from behind. The ref whistles a breakaway penalty.

Now the fun begins. A penalty shot is a huge mind game. If you're the offensive player, you need to make sure the goalie makes the first move. But Smith is very smart, and he knows how to get in your head and under your skin. He knows what Lemieux is thinking, so he's not going to commit one way or the other. And Lemieux knows that Smith knows. He's ticked off about getting robbed of a goal, but he understands that on the penalty shot he's going to have to create an opportunity on his own in the span of two seconds. He knows that it's going to take two moves on his part to score, one move to fake Smith out, the second to put the puck in the net.

So Lemieux moves in quickly, waits until he gets to the right side face-off circle to make his first move. He dekes and Smith bites but not all the way. Lemieux shifts the puck to his backhand and tries to go low on Smith. He shoots. Smitty sprawls and just deflects the puck with his skate. *Clank!* It hits the post. A moral victory for Lemieux, but this round goes to Billy Smith.

THE GAME CHANGER

In a close game, a penalty shot always means a big momentum swing. And one of the two penalty shot scenarios that I think about a lot has Pavel Bure going against Mike Richter in the 1994 Stanley Cup final between the Rangers and the Canucks. Richter made the save and the Rangers won the game and eventually the series.

The other penalty shot moment that I think about had Canada versus Czechoslovakia in the Olympic semifinal game in Nagano in '98. In the penalty shot tiebreaker that followed regulation and overtime, Marc Crawford, the Canadian coach, opted not to use Wayne Gretzky against Dominik Hasek. Hasek stonewalled five consecutive shooters for the win. A great hockey moment. Even if it happened at 3 A.M., Eastern Standard Time.

Start Me Up

Who are baseball's ultimate aces?

No, Yogi Berra didn't say it, but you know that you're sitting pretty when your starter is a stopper. As in stopping every losing streak at three games. Mad Dog reveals who he'd choose as the ace of the ultimate rotation.

When you're talking starting pitchers, you've got to look at the question two ways. Do I want a guy for one game, a pennant clincher, or maybe the seventh game of the World Series? Or do I want a guy for the long haul, twenty years?

If you want a guy for one game—or even one season—you're looking at a lot of one-season wonders. You've got to think about Vida Blue in 1971. Or Ron Guidry in 1978. Maybe Dwight Gooden in 1985. Or any number of seasons from Pedro Martinez or Roger Clemens. All of those guys were great, almost unhittable for a season or a two.

But if I'm managing the game, I'm picking one guy: Sanford Koufax. He didn't have a long career, but for five years in his prime Sandy Koufax was the most dominant pitcher in the history of the game. He had an unhittable lefty fastball and the King Charles of curveballs. From 1963 to 1966 he went 97–27—that's a .782 winning percentage, sports fans. His *highest* ERA over that period was 2.04. Koufax struck out 1,228 batters in 1,192 innings and held hitters to an average of under .200. He *averaged* a no-hitter a year for four years.

But there was also the Koufax aura. Whenever he went out, you mentally chalked up a win for the Dodgers. It wasn't only that teams didn't beat him, they didn't even *score* against him. My partner, Mike Francesa, says that when you were at the game on a night when Koufax was pitching, and they put up the out-of-town scores and the Phillies or the Cardinals would score a run or two against him, there'd be this buzz of disbelief in the ballpark.

And Koufax was tough. His World Series ERA was 0.95, and in the 1965 Fall Classic he pitched two consecutive shutouts, winning game seven 2-0 on the road against the Twins on two days' rest. If I need to win a game, I'm giving the ball to Koufax.

But if I'm starting a franchise, and I can hand the guy the ball every fifth day for twenty years, I'm going a different route. There are lots of guys who would fall into this category—Warren Spahn had only a few seasons where he was super dominant, but 363 wins is 363 wins. Tom Seaver, Steve Carlton, or Lefty Grove didn't rack up quite as many wins as Spahn, but when they were good, they were *very, very* good. And before it's all said and done, Roger Clemens or Greg Maddux could easily fit into this mix.

But there's one guy who lets me have my cake and eat it too: Walter Johnson. He was simply the best pitcher of all time (see "Batter Up," page 120). The Big Train was baseball's first great power pitcher. He did for the strikeout what Ruth did for the home run—leading the league in Ks twelve times in 15 years. He led the league in wins six times, and ERA five times. The bottom line—Johnson won 417 games. That's pretty amazing. Now I realize that Johnson pitched in a different time. In the dead ball era he didn't have to worry so much about the home run, so he didn't have to throw as hard, go all out with every batter. And in his prime he pitched in 47, 48 games a year, which he couldn't do today. But Johnson was really the first modern pitcher, and I think he would have made the adjustment. Would he win 417 games if he pitched today? No. But I wouldn't bet against him winning 317.

Dreams of Fields

How can having the right stadium save a franchise?

The lush green grass. The perfectly manicured mound. The foul lines that stretch to infinity. The money rolling in. Mad Dog explains that it may be a stadium to you, but to your team, it's a cash machine.

Call it the Camden Yards factor. When you think about baseball economics over the last fifteen years, so many of the story lines come back to that jewel in downtown Baltimore. When that stadium opened in

1992, some teams discovered a whole new way to make money. And other teams were left out in the cold.

Let's start with a quick history lesson. In the early 1970s the birth of the multipurpose Astroturf cookie-cutter stadium—Veterans Stadium, Three Rivers, and Riverfront—set the stadium deal back about three thousand years. They were too big for baseball, the sight lines were bad, and they were in the middle of nowhere.

And in a lot of cases, these parks were built to replace the downtown parks from the turn of the century: Philadelphia's Shibe Park, Connie Mack Stadium, Cincinnati's Crosley Field, Pittsburgh's Forbes Field, St. Louis's Sportsmans Park. In one way Camden Yards turned back the clock. It looked like a turn-of-the-century park. It was cozy, built right in the city with that old warehouse out in right field. You can walk there from your office or hotel.

But it was modern in one very important way: The stadium itself became part of the attraction of going to a game. The Orioles realized that the days of bringing your two kids to Yankee Stadium and sitting out in the bleachers for eight innings to watch Joe DiMaggio play were long gone. People have shorter attention spans. Now people want to watch a game the way they do on television, catch the first couple of innings and the last couple of innings. At Camden Yards if you get bored with the game, you can walk over to Boog Powell's barbecue, or you can get yourself a crab cake, and then go and buy some souvenirs at any one of a dozen shops. If you have kids you can check out the pop-a-shot or the radar gun pitching cages. All of these things brought people to the park. And all of these things put money in the team's coffers above and beyond the price of admission.

And Camden Yards has plenty of luxury boxes. And teams, although they like the everyday fans spending their $25 a ticket to sit down the left field line, they also know that those fans might come to five or six games a year. But those corporations who buy those luxury boxes, they buy them for eighty-one games a year. If it's half a million a year to buy a luxury box, that adds up quickly. Two more factors: While day-of-game sales are just that, a team gets the money for a luxury box well before the season even starts, which helps the cash flow. And all those seats are presold. If the team stinks, or if it rains for a week, the walk-up customer will stay home. The guy who owns the luxury box will hand the tickets to the guy who works in the mail room. But they're already bought and paid for.

All of these things conspired to make Camden Yards a cash cow for Baltimore and almost instantly turned the Orioles into a high-revenue team. And while every team can't sign a big cable deal like the Yankees, every team saw the chance to get its own Camden Yards. Cleveland got one, and Colorado got one, and Seattle got one. Houston. Atlanta. A lot of teams got those kinds of parks. And the teams that got those kinds of parks had a revenue stream that other teams did not have. A new park provided a kind of cushion. If you have a brand-new park that people like to go to, you're going to draw two million a year no matter how bad the team is. If you're in a lousy ballpark, even with a decent team you're in trouble.

It became a have and have-not situation. The haves had a shiny new park. The have-not's didn't. The Twins won the World Series in 1991 and

---

THE CONTRACTION CONNECTION

How do you get a new ballpark? Well, until recently you got your new ballpark by threatening the local government. "Mr. Mayor, this team can't survive unless we have a new stadium. If you don't help us pay for one, we're going to have to leave and go to a city that will." The owners were banking on the fact that no mayor wants to be remembered as the guy who let their baseball team leave town.

But that isn't working anymore. After a couple of rounds of expansion during the '90s, there aren't a bunch of places clamoring for teams anymore. In fact, that's part of what was driving Bud Selig's contraction plans. Why can't you just move the Montreal Expos and the Minnesota Twins, you ask? If you move them, that takes away leverage from the other owners who are angling for a new stadium.

And more to the point, cities now see that the owners are bluffing. No baseball team has moved in thirty years. Compare that to football, where you've had plenty of teams move out of good football markets in a heartbeat: L.A., Baltimore, Houston, Cleveland. That's why, even though there are only eight home games in football a year compared to eighty-one in baseball, it's almost easier to get a football stadium built today.

IT'S OUTTA HERE

The new stadiums are also one of the biggest factors in the hitting explosion of the last few years. The owners figured out that fans want to see home runs. They want to see home runs that splash down in the bay. They want to see home runs that bounce off a warehouse. They want to see home runs that land in a pool in centerfield. Watching a great pitcher like Tom Glavine is an acquired taste. But everyone can see how far Larry Walker hit the ball. So most of the new parks—Camden Yards, The Jake, Coors Field, the BOB—are havens for home run hitters.

An interesting exception: Safeco Field. Seattle built a new ballpark that's tough for home run hitters. So the two big boppers—Griffey and A-Rod—leave. They also lose Randy Johnson. And what happens? Far from folding, the Mariners won 116 games and made it to the ALCS two years in a row. Why? Because those ballparks help pitchers. And pitching wins.

The same with the San Francisco Giants. Pac Bell Park is a great pitcher's park, the team has a tremendous record at home, and the Giants went to the World Series. It's not a coincidence.

drew almost 2.5 million people. Two years later the Metrodome was obsolete. The White Sox had rebuilt Comiskey along the old cookie-cutter model, and they were out of luck. Fans in Montreal and Oakland were stuck with their outdated stadiums. And cash-strapped teams.

So the stadium issue is very complicated. And there's no guarantee that just because you have that spanking-new ballpark, you're going to have a $100 million payroll and be able to compete with the Yankees. The attendance in Pittsburgh and Milwaukee dropped—not to mention in Cleveland and even Baltimore—because the teams weren't winning. But if you want to be competitive, having your own little Camden Yards is five steps in the right direction.

No Guts, No Glory

What are the gutsiest coaching calls of all time?

Normally coaches and managers are more like financial analysts than high rollers in Vegas. They weigh the odds, they sample public opinion, and then they make the most conservative choice. But not always. Mad Dog remembers some of the big gambles in sports history.

There are good reasons why coaches play by the book. First off, the book is usually the percentage play. And second, if you play it by the book and lose, at least you don't get second-guessed. But what makes games memorable is when a coach says, "Aw heck," tosses the book out the window, and plays it by the seat of his pants. Here are some really gutsy calls that paid off big-time.

1984 Orange Bowl: Sure everyone remembers Tom Osborne going for a two-point conversion to win the game when kicking the extra point for a tie would have won Nebraska the national championship. The call I remember is the one that set that one up. It was fourth and eight, late in the game, 48 seconds left, and Nebraska was down 31-24. Mike Rozier, their Heisman Trophy–winning running back, was out with a sprained ankle, but Osborne stayed with his bread and butter. He didn't chuck a Hail Mary pass into the end zone. On Nebraska's fourth and eight he ran the option, with quarterback Turner Gill tossing to Jeff Smith, who rambled for a 24-yard touchdown run. That's got to be one of the gutsiest calls I've ever seen in all my life.

1967 NFL Championship Game: Another last-second play. You've got to give Vince Lombardi credit for going for it on third and one with sixteen seconds left and no time-outs against Dallas in the 1967 Ice Bowl. It's 17-14, so the Packers can tie it with a field goal and go to overtime. Now, it is 80 below zero, the field is frozen solid, and there are a million things that could go wrong on that quarterback sneak. Trouble with the snap. Bart Starr could slip going behind Jerry Kramer. He could miss his block.

Today every coach in the NFL would kick the field goal in that spot in a championship game. Because if they don't score they're going to get killed by the second-guess. Lombardi always said that he went for it to get people out of the cold. Enough already when it's 35 below. Who knows? Having the guts to make that call is one of the reasons why Lombardi won five championships.

2001 World Series: Diamondback manager Bob Brenly deserves a lot of credit for pitching Schilling on three days' rest. We all killed him about it at the time. In the fourth game, Brenly had to take Schilling out after seven innings because he ran out of gas, and the Yankees came back in the dramatic ninth inning, winning it in the tenth. He took a lot of grief for that.

At the time I thought it was a mistake because Arizona had won the first two games at home and really only had to win one game at Yankee Stadium. And if Schilling had pitched game five on four days' rest, he probably could have gone all the way and the bullpen wouldn't have had a chance to collapse.

But even though it backfired in the short run, it paid off when they got back to Arizona. It gave him the chance at having Randy Johnson and Curt Schilling back-to-back in games six and seven, and of course they won both games. Brenly rolled the dice and it worked.

The Warner Call: This wasn't a game decision, but I really admire what Dick Vermeil did in 1999 after Trent Green got hurt. The Rams had built their whole offense around Green and he got hurt in an exhibition game, out for the whole year. Vermeil could have easily gotten a veteran quarterback to fill in for the year. But he went with Kurt Warner, a guy who played in the Arena Football League. And he won the Super Bowl. And you remember, Vermeil was on thin ice at the beginning of that year, and still he made the unorthodox move. That took a lot of guts.

Heimlich Time

What are the worst choke jobs of all time?

There should be a gag rule in sports. Players can choke if they want to, but we shouldn't have to watch it. Mad Dog takes you through some of the most cringeworthy moments in athletic history.

Athletes choke. We don't like to talk about it, but it happens. They get to the fourth quarter, the eighteenth green, the deciding set, the ninth inning, and their chest gets tight, their palms get sweaty, and their games go straight to hell. They grasp defeat from the jaws of victory. They're human.

It's tough to watch, and everyone—fans, the media—are pretty quick to give athletes a pass on it. A guy who's an also-ran—Jean Van de Velde at the British Open a couple of years ago—we don't go too hard on him because we never really expected him to win. At the same time we'll give John McEnroe a little pass for blowing a two-set lead in the French Open final against Ivan Lendl because he won so many times before. So you'll notice that this list is full of players and teams that have the curse of being "very good." But not quite great. It's a tricky spot to be in.

Greg Norman: Yes, he won two British Opens, but there were too many big events where he just bit the big one. He's the only golfer to lose all playoffs in all four of the majors. In 1986 he led four of the majors after three rounds—a Saturday Slam—and won only the British. The Masters in '96 was a disgrace. That is a choke, there is no other way to explain it. In some of these other tournaments he was unlucky—Larry Mize hits a miracle chip shot. But in 1996 he blew a huge lead, he collapsed before our very eyes on the back nine, with three bogeys followed by a double bogey. Nick Faldo, who was the perfect player to take advantage of Norman's choke job, was way behind coming into the final round, but they were in the same pairing. They went eyeball to eyeball and Norman blinked. A supreme choke job. On the seventeenth hole he says to his caddy, Bruce Edwards, "I guess it's better to be lucky than good." And his own caddy says to him, "I want to caddy for someone who has heart."

JEANNY BE BAD

What about Van de Velde, who lost the 1999 British Open? He only choked, really, on one hole. He needed a six on 18 and he triple-bogeyed it, 'cause he made dumb decisions. Norman choked the whole back nine, choked the whole round. Van de Velde unraveled for five minutes, Norman unraveled for five hours.

The '51 Dodgers: Now, this team later won a championship, but still when you blow a thirteen-and-a-half-game lead in August and then blow a three-run ninth inning lead in the last game of the playoff, that's a choke job. Now I know it's hard to say it about great players like Duke Snider, Gil Hodges, Jackie Robinson, and Roy Campanella, but they choked twice. I know the Giants went 39–8 down the stretch, which is incredible, but the Dodgers were 26–24 in the last fifty games. Yes, the Dodgers had to win the last game of the year just to get into the playoffs, but there's no two ways around it: The '51 Dodgers choked twice. They choked during the last six weeks of the season where they should have been able to figure out a way to win another game or two and hold a thirteen-and-a-half-game lead. And once they got to the playoff, they should have been able to figure out a way to hold a three-run lead in the deciding game. You're up 4-1, bottom of the ninth inning, you've got to win the game. That's brutal.

SOX SAGA

Now, I don't consider the 1978 Red Sox chokers because they were actually three-and-a-half games behind the Yankees and had to win eight in a row to force a playoff. And in the playoff game, I know it was 2-0 top of the seventh, but that's not 4-1 bottom nine.

The Portland Trailblazers: It's really easy to forget just how bad this was. Remember, the 2000 Lakers hadn't yet won a championship and Kobe's still a baby. The Lakers were the ones who had a history of coming up short in the playoffs. There is no way the Portland Trailblazers should blow a fifteen-point lead in the fourth quarter of game seven of the NBA Western Conference finals. And for all intents and purposes the NBA championship. Give the Lakers credit because they made some shots, but all the Trailblazers had to do in that period was make a couple of baskets, and they gagged. Remember, they had Scottie Pippen, a guy with six rings. Now Pippen never could make big shots in the fourth quarter, that was a huge flaw in his game. When he had to take charge in game seven against the Lakers, he couldn't do it. He did a terrible job and Rasheed Wallace missed shots and Bonzi Wells missed shots, too. Portland, again, was near great, but when you are near great and you blow it, you get double the hammer job.

Michelle Kwan: I hate to say it, but she choked at the 2002 Olympics. Sarah Hughes came out of nowhere and performed superbly, give her credit. But Kwan was an athlete who loved the cameras, ate up the publicity she got. That's fine, but you better win. And she didn't. It was hers to lose. All she had to do was perform solidly, and she couldn't. She fell right on her fanny. That's choking. No way around it. You'll remember that she also came up short in 1998, losing the gold to Tara Lipinski. I'm gonna give her a break on the first one. There is no excuse for Kwan losing the second one.

Jana Novotna: This one was hard to watch. Novotna absolutely choked against Steffi Graf in the 1993 Wimbledon final. She was up 4-1, love-40 in the third set. Four points away. You've got to win the match. She just unraveled in front of our very eyes. It was a tough sight to see. Novotna was a very good player, she was athletic, she was an excellent serve-and-volleyer, she got around the court well, she had beautiful strokes, but when push came to shove and she was about to grab the championship trophy, she gagged. There is no other way around it. She choked. In the 1997 Wimbledon final, Novotna plays Martina Hingis, wins the first set 6-2, then has a point to go up 3-0 in the third set and loses again.

But Novotna's story has a happy ending. Remember her crying on the Duchess of Kent's shoulder and the Duchess saying, "Don't worry about it, you'll be back." Well, in her third final, she beat Natalie Tauziat. She was fortunate. She played the right opponent in the final, kind of like Virginia Wade getting Betty Stove in the 1977 final. But Jana did manage to win finally.

RIDING THE GIFT HORSE

What do you do when you're on the other end of a choke? After Novotna handed her that 1993 Wimbledon final, Steffi Graf felt so unsatisfied that she went straight to the practice courts and hit for two solid hours. Isn't that amazing?

The 2002 New York Giants: What can you say when you blow a 38-14 lead in a playoff game. That's a big-time choke job. I don't care if the game was played on the moon, you can't blow a 38-14 lead late third quarter in a playoff game. Everything went wrong. The defense just imploded as the 49ers scored on four straight possessions and converted on two consecutive two-point conversions. No pass rush (a no-show from All-Pro Michael Strahan). Awful coverage in the secondary. Just awful. Plus the coaching decisions by Jim Fassel left plenty to be desired. Attempting a 42-yard field goal on their second-to-last possession instead of going for it on fourth and a yard and a half. Doing a poor job with clock management on the Giants' last drive. Everything broke down, including the officiating on the last play of the game. That gave the Giants fans something to cry about for weeks. But the Giants should never have been in that position to begin with. Just one big play on defense, even drawing a holding penalty, would have given the Giants the win.

Remember that when you put yourself in a position to lose, sometimes you are going to. It's hard to imagine, but this one was even worse than the Oilers blowing that 35-3 lead early third quarter that playoff game in Buffalo in the early '90s.

One footnote: Wellington Mara said after the debacle that this was bad but we've had worse. Boy, if that's true, I don't understand why he didn't sell the team a long time ago.

The 1980 Russian Olympic Hockey Team: I know everyone wants to feel good about the United States team, but that 1980 Russian hockey team choked. They had NHL-caliber players on that team. They beat the U.S. 10-3 at Madison Square Garden before the Olympics. Killed them. They should never have lost that game. In that semifinal game against the U.S., the great Vladislav Tretiak allowed a freak goal to Mark Johnson with one second left in the first period to tie the game. Russian coach Viktor Tikhonov panicked and pulled Tretiak out of the game. When defenseman Slava Fetisov was asked about it after he was in the NHL, he just shrugged and said, "Coach crazy." I know this is heresy, but the Soviets absolutely gagged.

Ronnie Franklin on Spectacular Bid: He was a young jockey, only a teenager, going for the Triple Crown in 1979. Spectacular Bid was far and away the best horse, a 1-5 favorite. I know that before the race the horse stepped on a safety pin that was used to secure a bandage, but the pressure got to Franklin. And during the race he pushed too hard too early. Anyone you talk to in horse racing circles will tell you that that was a terrible ride that Franklin gave Spectacular Bid.

The Other Football

Why can't soccer make it in the U.S.?

It's the world game. But since when is the United States part of the world? Mad Dog explains why soccer in America will remain the province of nine-year-olds running around on Saturday morning.

For the last twenty-five years we've been hearing about the generation of young kids who play soccer on Saturday mornings, and how this is going to lead to a soccer explosion in America. And it's true that the U.S. World Cup team has gotten better and soccer has become a little more mainstream in the American consciousness.

But will soccer ever become a huge deal in American sports? I was asked that by a lot of people after the U.S. performance in the 2002 World Cup. I reminded them that we all thought that there would be a huge hockey explosion after the 1980 gold medal in Lake Placid and that tremendous win against Russia. We're still waiting for it.

Sure, it would've been fun if the U.S. had made the semis or the finals of the World Cup. We all would've watched the last couple of games, gotten into Landon Donovan for a week. But I don't think you would have seen the whole country start watching soccer because of a couple of wins, any more than everyone did after the American women won the World Cup.

And I say this as one of those kids on the front line of that soccer revolution. I played soccer as a kid and in high school. I was a good goalie, and we were in a good league, and we even played in a small–school state tournament. Soccer is a great game. But I don't watch it.

Let's face it. Soccer is not in our blood. Baseball is our game. Football, too. Soccer is competing with too many sports that have real tradition in America. Soccer's tradition is in Europe, it's in South America. And I think it's almost impossible to bring another country's tradition into your country and have it become a national sport. If we put baseball leagues in England and Spain and Italy, nobody is going to watch. The World League of American Football didn't exactly set the world on fire. Soccer is not our game and nothing you are going to do is going to change that.

Major League Soccer, the U.S. pro league, has a lot to overcome. First off, there's not enough offense. It's too difficult to score goals. The field is too big, there is a lot of standing around at midfield. There's also no natural season. They play in the fall, they're up against college and pro football. They play in the spring and they're up against baseball. Either way they're dead.

The biggest problem with the pro leagues in the U.S. is, if you ask the best young American player where he would like to play, he'll tell you he wants to play for Real Madrid or somewhere in the Premier League in England. He's not going to play for the Columbus Crew. And why should he? He wants to play against the best in the world and get paid for it. That's not going to happen in the MLS. And fans know that, too. We know that when the Red Wings win the Stanley Cup, or the Lakers win the NBA championship, they're truly world champions. But if the Columbus Crew won the MLS, even the casual soccer fan understands that they'd get murdered if they played another team from Europe.

In a funny way the old North American Soccer League back in the 1970s hit on a good formula. They brought in these great legendary players like Pele, and Franz Beckenbauer, and Georgie Best. Americans weren't sophisticated enough to realize that a lot of these guys were on the downside of their careers, but the star power was enough to draw seventy thousand a game to the Meadowlands, for a while at least.

It's unfortunate for the one or two hundred world-class American players that they don't really have a world-class league in the U.S. But you can't bring in another country's game, plop it into your country, and expect the fans to get into it. Soccer can be a national pastime. Just not ours.

Know the Code

Should pitchers be allowed to throw inside?

Chin music. The purpose pitch. The brushback. If Major League Baseball has its way, they'll go the way of Astroturf and bullpen carts. Mad Dog argues in favor of letting ballplayers settle their own differences.

We've turned back the clock in so many ways in Major League Baseball. Old-style parks. Retro uniforms. 1930s-style hitting. So let's go back to the good old days in one more way: Let's bring back the Code.

Baseball players have always had a way of policing themselves and the game, and I think when you get the umpires and the commissioner's office involved too much, it only makes matters worse.

Let me start from this premise: Pitchers should be allowed to throw inside. It's part of the game. The inside part of the plate is neutral ground, the hitter doesn't own it and the pitcher doesn't own it, and every at-bat is a battle for that eight inches of real estate.

Of course, there's an intimidation factor involved. If a batter digs in and crowds the plate, he's got to expect that he's going to get dusted a few times. Mickey Mantle and Hank Aaron and Willie Mays didn't have a problem with guys pitching inside, so why should A-Rod and Barry Bonds? You have to wonder what today's players would do if they had to face Carl Hubbell or Sal Maglie or Bob Gibson or Don Drysdale. They'd probably wear armor head to toe—and, by the way, I think that elbow pads belong in hockey, not baseball—and charge the mound twice a game.

That said, there's a fine line between pitching aggressively and head-hunting. You can throw inside without endangering someone's life. It's one thing to throw a fastball that sails past a guy's ribs, and it's another to try to put one in his ear. If a guy can throw a 3-2 slider on the black, he should have enough command to avoid hitting the batter in the head. Shoulders, yes. Beanballs, no. It's only a matter of time before someone gets seriously hurt.

And then there's the question of motivation. You want to back a guy off the plate, that's fine. But when Gibson or Drysdale—or more recently Roger Clemens and Armando Benitez—hit a guy just because he hit a home run his last time up, that's going too far. If you want revenge, strike him out.

If a pitcher crosses the line, the other team's pitcher should have a chance to settle the score. Dust the pitcher when he comes up to bat, or send a message to his team's best player. Make your point and get on with the game. When you have umpires issuing warnings every time someone gets hit, it gets to be a joke. Because then you are asking the umpire to judge when a pitcher is trying to throw at somebody and when the ball just got away. The umpire has too much discretion in deciding what's a brushback pitch and what isn't. If an umpire ejects a pitcher, he's affecting the outcome of the game with one judgment call.

The current system almost encourages pitchers to make the first move. The first time a pitcher hits a guy in a game, he's not going to get tossed. Clemens didn't get tossed for beaning Piazza. But after that first hit batsman, the umpire will usually warn both benches. So in that example, there was really no downside for Clemens. Piazza was out of the game. Clemens got to stay in the game. And after the warnings, as angry as the Mets were, they didn't plunk Bernie Williams. Sure, Clemens couldn't be as aggressive, but neither could the Mets pitchers, because they knew that if one got away, it's an instant ejection and possibly a suspension. It was like giving Clemens a freebie. Where's the deterrent factor? When this happens it creates bad blood between the two teams. The Mets were still ticked at Clemens two years later. If they had been able to plunk Derek Jeter in the next inning—send him sprawling on the ground, not to the hospital—that would have been the end of it. It's this kind of simmering resentment that leads to hitters charging the mound and bench-clearing brawls and other stuff that baseball really doesn't need.

Pitchers have been throwing inside pitches for a hundred years. You're not going to stop it. It's just part of the game. But when somebody does get plunked, let's let the players settle these things instead of the umpires.

THOU SHALT NOT STEAL . . . WITH AN EIGHT-RUN LEAD

The Code has a flip side, too. You can't show up the other team by running up the score. But what constitutes running up the score? Today the ballparks are small, everybody scores a ton of runs, and the pitching is so bad at times that no lead is safe. Cleveland came from twelve runs down in a game against Seattle a couple of years ago. And Pittsburgh scored seven with two outs in the bottom of the ninth against Houston in the first year of PNC Park. So if you're up 8-0 in the third at Coors Field or 6-1 in the fifth, you'd better be playing for every run. But if it's the top of the ninth and you're up by eight runs, and the game's really over, you don't need to be swinging 3-0. You don't need to be stealing bases. You don't need to make that big takeout slide into second base.

And I think that a lot of times it's not that a player is trying to show up the other team. A lot of the same players who don't know who Jackie Robinson is genuinely don't know the Code. Or in the same way that they'll brainlessly swing at the first pitch down 2-0 in the ninth, they just go up there hacking no matter how big the lead is, and no matter how much it will tick off the other team. The problem, of course, is that the next time you come to town, you're likely to see a 99-mph fastball aimed at your head.

Give 'Em the Booth

What are the greatest television sports teams of all time?

You can see the action. You know the score. So what does a great television team add to a game? A lot. Mad Dog chooses up his broadcast booth dream teams and reveals what makes them great.

Here's a rule of thumb: A broadcaster, no matter how good, can never make an ordinary game into a classic. But there are some bad ones—Dick Vitale, Bill Walton, Gary Bender—who can ruin even a great game. But that said, I'm pretty picky about what kind of announcing team I want to have calling my games. I want guys who know the game, first off. And I want guys who respect the game, too. That means that they understand when they should talk, and when they should keep quiet and let the game breathe. Chemistry is important, too. You need guys who can work together without stepping on each other's toes. It's a lot easier to like a pair of announcers if they like each other. So here are my top television teams in each of the major sports:

NFL: "Chris, you're in Alaska in the wintertime, you're stuck in an igloo—an igloo with a satellite dish—and you've got an AFC championship game to watch. Who do you want calling that game?" I'm going to tell you, it's got to be Curt Gowdy and Al DeRogatis. Why? Blame it on my upbringing. In the late 1960s and early 1970s when I was growing up, it seemed that all the big teams and the big games were in the AFC: the great Larry Csonka Dolphin teams, the Frenchy Fuqua and Franco Harris Steelers, the Ken Stabler Raiders, the Bert Jones Colts, even Joe Namath's Jets. And Gowdy and DeRogatis did those games. And did them beautifully. That's all there is to it. I'm a big fan of Dick Enberg, I think he is a great announcer, but I don't think his partner, Merlin Olsen, was as good as DeRogatis. I love John Madden and Pat Summerall, too, such a great combination of professionalism and enthusiasm. Ray Scott with the Packers also gets an honorable mention. He lets the game be the story, almost like a BBC broadcaster. He didn't overwhelm you. And I'm not picking a

Monday Night Football team because Howard Cosell drove me nuts. He wasn't a sports guy. I always felt that if you went to Cosell's house on a Sunday afternoon and he wasn't doing homework for a game that week, he wouldn't have the Rams-Colts game on.

NBA: Is Marv Albert my basketball guy? Yesssss! Marv is the quintessential NBA play-by-play man. And I'd pair him up with Doug Collins. They didn't work together very long, but they had a really good chemistry. Collins is a tremendous analyst. Succinct, knew how to say things in ten, twelve seconds, to get in and out.

College Basketball: It's got to be Dick Enberg, Al McGuire, and Billy Packer: The way those three played off each other was phenomenal. They had fun. Enberg was a great traffic cop and each of the two color guys had different styles. Packer is sort of the Xs and Os guy while McGuire trusted his gut. McGuire didn't take himself too seriously and Packer liked to make fun of him. Enberg, you could tell, was great friends with both of them. Remember that Packer worked with Enberg long before McGuire came on the scene, so Packer had to give McGuire some room. Give Billy a lot of credit for that.

NHL: My hockey team is John Davidson and Doc Emrick. Emrick is the sort of guy—and this is the highest compliment I can give—that will make the average sports fan watch an NHL game. That's how good Emrick is. You can't say anything more than that. JD can call a hockey game better than anybody. JD won't be critical, which is a knock on him. As part of the NHL brethren, if a team is going bad, he won't get on them. But as far as actually calling a game and recognizing what he sees, JD's magnificent. He's got a great voice, he enjoys what he is doing, you can tell it means something to him.

College Football: I've got to pick Keith Jackson as my play-by-play guy. He's been part of college football for so long, has a great voice, and a great way with words: "Whoa, Nellie, it's a barnburner!" Don't forget they moved him off *Monday Night Football* to do college football, and it's the best thing that ever happened to Keith Jackson. I've got to say, based on his performance in the 2002 Ohio State–Miami championship game, Jackson should retire. I'll tell you the team I used to love. Keith Jackson and Frank Broyles. Broyles was the Arkansas athletic director but he was also a great analyst. So Keith and Frank Broyles are my college football announcing team. I'll also give an honorable mention to Lee Grosscup. He's very underrated, and had a great, great voice.

Baseball: I think Al Michaels is the best baseball broadcaster I've heard. When Michaels wants to be, he is the consummate team player, the kind of announcer who makes a booth click. And that Michaels team of Jim Palmer and Tim McCarver was magnificent. You had the pitcher and the

---

CALL ME

How do you know when something is a great call? When you remember it fifteen, twenty years later. Now, these aren't really famous calls, just ones that have stuck with me over the years.

In 1986, Dave Henderson got dealt at the trading deadline from the woeful Seattle Mariners to the first-place Red Sox. In game five of the ALCS, the Red Sox were down 5-4 and Henderson hit a two-run homer off Donnie Moore to give them the lead 6-5. And Michaels, when the ball went over the left fielder's head in Anaheim, said, "Dave Henderson, it's a long way from Seattle." And for me, that summed it up perfectly.

In 1989, Calgary and Vancouver played a classic game seven that went to overtime. Vancouver was going for a huge upset and Stan Smyl knocked what would have been a game-winning shot right off Mike Vernon's face mask. Calgary came back to win the game and the Stanley Cup. And Doc Emrick summed it up like this. "Folks, sometime in mid-July, take this game out and plug it back in your VCR when you miss the NHL. This is an absolute classic." Love that call.

Here's another one: I love Don Criqui as a football announcer and he did that topsy-turvy 1982 Miami–San Diego playoff game in which Rolf Benirschke made the field goal to win it 41-38. And Criqui's call of a big Tony Nathan play just before halftime is one of the great ones you're ever going to hear. "Hook and lateral, there goes Nathan! Can you believe this! Touchdown!" That's another one that sticks in my mind.

catcher in the booth, each lending his own perspective to the game. If it's game seven of the World Series, I want those three guys calling it.

There are, of course, a huge number of great baseball broadcasters I'm leaving out. I'm a huge Bob Costas fan. Sean McDonough and Joe Buck also deserve a mention here although Buck tries a little too hard to be witty. I also know I'm leaving Vin Scully out. By himself, Scully is phenomenal. The problem with Scully is that he dominates the game so much that his analyst has trouble blending in.

Ice Ageless

Which are hockey's greatest dynasties?

Skating around the ice with the Stanley Cup. It's a once in a lifetime thrill. Unless you played on one of hockey's great dynasties, where waltzing with Lord Stanley became an annual occurrence. Mad Dog ranks hockey's greatest runs.

Hockey has always been a game of dynasties. There are a couple of reasons for that. There's never been a lot of free agency or player movement. Players are good when they're young, and when you get a player you keep him for a while. The prospect of a devastating injury isn't nearly as big as, say, in football. And when you get a great goalie, who's one of the most important pieces of a championship team, he's usually good for a long period of time. That's why all the teams on my list of the best teams of all time have been big-time dominant—four or more championships.

5. 1949-55 Red Wings: They won four Cups in six seasons and finished first in points every year. They had a bunch of legit no-doubt-about-it Hall of Famers in Gordie Howe, Sid Abel, Ted Lindsay, Red Kelly on defense, Terry Sawchuk in goal. That's damn good and that's why the Red Wings crack my top five.

4. 1979-83 New York Islanders: I put them ahead of the Red Wings because they won four Stanley Cups in a row and made the final in the fifth year. My problem with the Islanders is that in two of the years when they won the Cup they weren't first overall in points. The Red Wings were first four straight times. In 1979–80 when they won their first Cup, the Islanders were second in the regular season by 25 points and they had only one player in the top ten in scoring. But four in a row is four in a row. Plus the Islanders won nineteen straight playoff series. They are a better-balanced team than Detroit, with tremendous depth, but the Islanders did not have as many great individual players. Sawchuk was better than Billy Smith. Gordie Howe was better than either Mike Bossy or Bryan Trottier, and Red Kelly was at least as good as Denis Potvin.

3. 1975-79 Canadiens: This was an awesome, dominant team. They won four consecutive Stanley Cups and won regular season titles by a bunch of points. They were 60–8–12 in 1976–77 and lost one playoff game. They were 59–10–11 in '77–'78 and lost three playoff games. They had it all, with snipers like Steve Shutt and Guy Lafleur, Larry Robinson on defense, Ken Dryden in goal. They were a fantastic hockey team. So of the dynasties that won *four* Cups, they're the best.

2. 1983-90 Edmonton Oilers: The sandwich group here is the Edmonton team that won five Cups in seven seasons. These Oilers were tremendous offensively. They had four players with 40 or more goals in '83–'84. They had two with 50 in '84–'85. This team had an unbelievable number of Hall of Famers who had a lot of success in other places. Mark Messier and Glenn Anderson won a Cup for the Rangers. Paul Coffey won a Cup with Pittsburgh. Wayne Gretzky and Jari Kurri were great with the Kings. But a couple of things keep this team from the top spot. For the fifth Cup, Gretzky wasn't there, so it was kind of a different team. And they lost that heartbreaker to Calgary in game seven in 1985–86, when the game-winning goal went in off Steve Smith's skate. If they win that game, they probably win five in a row and get the top spot. As it is, they're the second-best dynasty of all time.

1. 1955-60 Canadiens: No, they didn't have the same kind of unbelievable regular seasons that the Canadiens teams did in the 1970s, and they probably couldn't have beaten the Oilers, but they did win five Cups in a row. That makes them number one. In four of the five years they were first in the league in points. They were 40–9 in the playoffs during the great run. In ten series they lost nine games. That's pretty darn good. Do I have to name all the great players? Jacques Plante, probably the second greatest goalie of all time. Jean Beliveau. Maurice "The Rocket" Richard and his brother Henri. Doug Harvey. They had an incredible hockey team.

THE RIGHT VINTAGE

Here are the best *single-season* teams in NHL history.

5. 1951-52 Red Wings: They were 44–14–12. They scored 215 goals and allowed 133. That's a heck of a goal differential. They won the regular season by 22 points. And they were 8–0 in the postseason.

4. 1981-82 Islanders: The best Islander team of all was in their third Stanley Cup–winning season. They were 54–16–10 for 118 points, winning their division by 26 points. They scored 385 goals and gave up 250. They swept the Canucks in the finals. This was the best year by their frontline scorers. Bossy had 64 goals and Trottier had 50 and was runner-up for the Hart Trophy behind Gretzky.

3. 1955-56 Canadiens: The first team in that five-Cup run was the best. They had 45 wins and won the regular season by 24 points, but most important, they beat the Red Wings in five games in the finals, ending Detroit's run.

2. 1983-84 Oilers: Again, the dynasty's first team was the best. They beat an Islander team that had won four Cups in a row, and in the last three games outscored them 19–6. Of course, Gretzky was great with 87 goals and 118 assists, but I'm especially impressed with the supporting cast. Coffey had 40 goals, Kurri had 52, Glenn Anderson had 55.

1. 1976-77 Canadiens: 60–8–12. That's what you've got to know about this team. They set the all-time record for points. They lost only two playoff games, sweeping the Bruins in the finals. Tremendous offense—Shutt had 60 goals and Lafleur had 56. This is the best hockey team of all time, sports fans.

Punched Out

What's wrong with boxing?

The Fight Game today is neither sweet (just think about some of the pro-moters) nor scientific (the difference between junior featherweight and bantamweight is about two overstuffed sandwiches). Mad Dog wades into the quagmire that is professional boxing.

B oxing is a mess, a disaster. Let's face it. When the most important people in the sport are Bob Arum, Don King, and Rock Newman, you know you're in big trouble.

It's amazing that a sport can be so screwed up that fighters get concussions routinely and even have been killed in the ring, and yet this is almost like a side issue for most people. A lot of times you almost wonder if you wouldn't be better off watching the WWF—at least it's free and it's on at a decent hour. Naming all of boxing's problems could fill a whole book, but here are the biggest ones.

No Trust: You can't trust the sport. What do I mean by that? You prop up your eyelids with toothpicks to watch a fight to its conclusion—until two o'clock in the morning on the East Coast. And then you see the judges' decisions, and you realize that they didn't see the same fight you saw. What were they thinking? Evander Holyfield and Lennox Lewis when they fought to a draw, a total joke. Oscar De La Hoya against Felix Trinidad. Axel Schulz and George Foreman. Julio Cesar Chavez against Pernell Whitaker. Do I have to go on? There are so many horrendous decisions in this sport you can hardly keep track of them all.

No Momentum: Second problem is, there's too much of a gap between fights, so there's no way to build momentum in this sport. You get a pretty good fight, and then the guy doesn't fight again for a year. That's why there are only four or five fights a year that mean something.

No Depth: To be a great champion you have to have some great challengers. Dempsey-Tunney. Ali-Frazier. Duran-Leonard. But the heavyweight division has been a joke for as long as I can remember. Roy Jones hasn't been challenged in a million years, except maybe on the basketball court. There's nobody for a great fighter to go out there and compete against. What's the point of watching these guys fight tomato cans?

No Logic: The weight classes confuse you. I can never figure out who's the champion of what. You gain one pound and you're in a different weight class. At 147 you're a great champion. 149 and you're an also-ran. And there are a billion sanctioning bodies. Do we have three different world champions in baseball from MLB, the MLF, and the MLC? Even huge boxing fans can't tell you who holds what belt. That's a huge problem.

No Integrity: Bob Arum, Don King, and the rest of the promoters are a disgrace. They act like buffoons. They think they're more important than the athletes—and, honestly, they probably are. I'm not paying to watch Don King fight, yet he's got more power than any fighter, which is crazy. And you wonder what goes on behind closed doors with these guys. Half the time you wonder if the fight is fixed.

No Effort: When they ask you to plunk down your credit card for a pay-per-view fight, you never know what you're going to get. You can't expect that the boxers are going to give you even a halfway decent effort. How about Buster Douglas, the time he came out after he won a championship and he weighed five-thousand pounds? They're in it for the payday and that's it. Sometimes the prefight shenanigans take longer than the fight itself. Two guys step into the ring, one guy throws two combinations, thirty-five seconds and the fight is over. Michael Spinks and Mike Tyson is a good case in point. It's crazy.

No Free TV: If boxing wanted to start rebuilding its fan base, it should put some big fights on network television. Remember all those great *Wide World of Sports* fights from the 1970s? The fact that everything is on pay-per-view is wrong. A lot of people can't or won't buy these fights at $55 a pop.

And having said all this, why do I even think about boxing? Because when boxing has a night, it's quite a night. Bowe-Holyfield. Hagler-Hearns. It was only three rounds, but they were the greatest three rounds I've ever seen. I saw Alexis Arguello and Aaron Pryor in Miami, Orange Bowl. What a fight. Fifteen rounds. So when boxing has its moments, there's nothing else like it.

So when there's a big fight coming up, I listen to King and Arum trying to hype it, listen to the trash talk between the competitors, and I get pretty disgusted. But then I think, this might be the one time in five that we get a classic fight instead of a one-round destruction. I don't want to miss it. So I'm a sap. I'll plunk my $55 down and turn the TV on. And hold my nose while I'm doing it.

Russo's Must-Read

Is *Sports Illustrated* really indispensable for the sports fan?

From its guided tours down memory lane to cover stories that shake up the world, Sports Illustrated *has been one of the quiet mainstays of the sports world. Mad Dog tells you why* Sports Illustrated *isn't just for dentists' offices.*

L et me tell you a story. In 1995, I went on vacation with my wife to the south of France and Portofino, Italy, for twenty-six days. I'm married five months, a newlywed. What did I do before I left? I got out my itinerary, realized I'd be gone for three weeks, and called up *Sports Illustrated*. I knew guys over there and asked them to FedEx the magazine every Thursday to where I was going to be. I'm on the French Riviera. With my wife. No kids yet. And my life's not complete until I read that new issue. That's how much I like *Sports Illustrated*. It's always been very important to me to have that magazine.

SI has a little bit in there for everybody. You like auto racing, they're going to cover auto racing. You like tennis, golf, cycling, swimming, track and field, you'll get it. They go crazy with the Olympics, we know that. But they do a big job with the big events, the World Series, the Super Bowl, the NBA Finals. But if you want the little sport covered, whatever that might be, they will cover that for you.

They do a nice job of thinking like a sports fan. They say, "You know what, here's a guy most people don't know too much about, but he's got a great story so let's do a feature on him." They match up a writer to the athlete, so there is a good mix and chemistry going.

And they know that sports fans don't disappear during the off-season. In the middle of January you might have a story in there on Jeff Kent. In the middle of June you might have a story on Kordell Stewart. In the middle of August you might have a story in there on Pat Riley. And they're not all feel-good stories. On the anniversary of the Munich Olympics they did a tremendous story on the terrorist massacre of the Israeli athletes.

And even with twenty-four-hour sports networks, a thousand daily sports sections, and a million websites, *Sports Illustrated* still manages to make news. Let's face it folks, the reason there's a steroid policy in Major League Baseball is because of *SI*. There's no other way around it. *Sports Illustrated* wrote that cover story where Ken Caminiti said that he did

---

THE SPORTS FAN'S SURVIVAL KIT

ESPN and *SI* are the two must-haves for any sports fan. Here are two more:

DirectTV: You need it for the NFL Sunday Ticket package, so you don't have to rely on CBS and FOX getting you the right games. You need it for out-of-town baseball if your favorite baseball team plays in another market. And you need it for the NCAA tournament. That's it. How many movies can you watch?

The Sunday *New York Times*: If you read one sports section a week, make it the late edition of the Sunday *New York Times*. They cover everything under the sun. If there's a Brazil-Russia Davis Cup final, they'll send a writer there.

steroids, and that 85 percent of players in Major League Baseball do the same. Drug testing—even the lame version they adopted—became an issue in the last collective bargaining agreement. Jose Canseco said it before, but nobody took him seriously. But when it was in *SI*, it became an issue.

Sports Illustrated still gives you stories that you don't get anywhere else. When I'm reading the *Sporting News* I feel like it's almost a recap of what I've been reading all week anyway. I don't read *ESPN Magazine* because it's aimed at the twenty-two-year-old who has a short attention span. *ESPN Magazine* wants to appeal to the Randy Mosses and Jason Williamses of the world. I don't care about Randy Moss.

Sure, *Sports Illustrated* spends some space on things you're not interested in. But every week you can find something to read in the magazine. For Christopler Russo, it's a must-read.

Down to the Wire

What are the greatest pennant races of all time?

When six months of nip and tuck baseball comes down to one game, even one inning, there's nothing better in sports. Mad Dog ranks the game's classic pennant races.

Bob Costas is right about one thing. The wild card has all but eliminated the great pennant race. Now a really strong second-place club, like the Angels or the A's, has a fallback position. And if you get two or three clubs fighting for the wild card, it's just not the same in my opinion. So when you talk about the great pennant races of all time you have to go back to 1995, before the wild card. Here are a half dozen all-time nail-biters in reverse order.

6. 1949 Yankees–Red Sox: You had two great teams—the Yankees won 97 and the Red Sox 96—and you had all the Hall of Famers involved, a faceoff between Ted Williams and Joe DiMaggio. And it concluded with a great head-to-head matchup. The Red Sox went to Yankee Stadium up by half a game with two to play and lost both games. Phil Rizzuto told me many times that this was his most enjoyable year in baseball. Phil wasn't a Red Sox fan.

5. 1967 Red Sox-Twins-Tigers-White Sox: This was great because it involved more than two teams. It also involved Yastrzemski's magical triple crown year. Dick Williams took a Red Sox team that nobody thought would do anything—in 1966 they were 72–90 with three different managers—and led them to 92 wins and the pennant. The last weekend of the season the Red Sox beat the Twins in Fenway with Yaz getting big hit after big hit. The Twins and Tigers won 91 each and the White Sox had 89 in fourth. The one big negative is that the other teams on this list won 100 or close to it; finishing second with 91 wins isn't such a heartbreaker.

4. 1962 Dodgers-Giants: Gotta put 1962 on your list. The Giants were four out with seven left to play, and two games out coming into the last weekend. No team made up that kind of ground that close to the wire until the Mets did it in 1999—but that was for the wild card. The Giants and Dodgers played another classic three-game playoff. The Giants beat Sandy Koufax in game one, but then blew a 5-0 lead in game two and lost 7-5. In game three the Giants were down 4-2 in the top of the ninth, and they scored four runs on a million walks to clinch the pennant. Mays scorched the big single that inspired that great line: "If that ball didn't hit the pitcher's mound, it would have left the park." Talk about comebacks.

3. 1993 Giants-Braves: Why is this a great pennant race? One number: 207. That's how many games those two teams won. The Giants were great all season long, and they had an eight-and-a-half-game lead in August. The Braves made a great trade for Fred McGriff at the deadline, fleecing Padre GM Randy Smith, which really helped their offense, and they played 51–17 over the last sixty-eight games. In September the Giants were three-and-a-half games back, but they won 14 of the last 16 and tied the Braves on the last weekend of the season. One unique aspect of the Giants and Braves pennant race is that both teams were tied after 161 games. The Yankees and Red Sox in '78 weren't tied after 161 games. The Dodgers spoiled the party for the Giants on the last day of the season and prevented the one thing that this great pennant raced lacked: a Monday playoff.

2. 1951 Giants-Dodgers: When a season ends on one swing of the bat you've got to put it on this list. But there is one thing I don't like about

1951, and that's the fact that the Dodgers played lousy baseball the last two months of the season. The Dodgers won that wild game the last day in Philadelphia, when Jackie Robinson made all those great plays and hit a home run, but the Dodgers were 26–24 in their last fifty games. But what a playoff they had. The Giants were down by three runs in the bottom of the inning and Mr. Branca delivers to Mr. Thomson and . . . "The Giants win the pennant! The Giants win the pennant!" Baseball fans have been dissecting that ninth inning for more than half a century (see "The Classic Second-Guess," page 247).

1. 1978 Yankees-Red Sox: This one had a little bit of everything. In this topsy-turvy race, the Red Sox had a huge lead, the Yankees came from thirteen-and-a-half games behind and blew past the Red Sox to take a three-and-a-half-game lead. And then the Red Sox won their last eight games to force the tie. Then of course they lost the playoff on the home run by Bucky "Freakin" Dent. Lou Piniella loses that fly ball in the sun and, miraculously, it bounces into his glove. And Yaz was up with the game on the line, two on and two out in the ninth. There was more drama in this pennant race than in a whole semester of Shakespeare.

Next on WDOG

How would Mad Dog change sports on television?

When they interrupt a World Series game to do a promo for that show with Kiefer Sutherland, do you ever feel like that guy in Network*? Mad as hell and you're not going to take it anymore? Mad Dog does, and he's got a five-point plan for fixing TV sports.*

When you think about it, a lot of the problems in big-time sports in the last fifteen years can be traced back to television. Astronomical salaries. Fiscal irresponsibility. Blowing off the average fan. The television money is a cushion that allows owners to be arrogant and cover up their own mistakes.

But the networks aren't giving the leagues money for nothing. They want to be partners. They have a say about what days the games are going to be played, what time the games are going to be played, what arenas they're going to be played in, who is going to do the announcing, how many commercials are going to run, and how long halftime is going to be.

That's why you've got playoff games starting at 8:40 in Major League Baseball, 9:12 in the NBA, and the Super Bowl has become an all-day affair. These decisions aren't made by the sports guys who are trying to get the best contest for the serious fan. They're being made by the programming gurus, who are more worried about the HUT level—Houses Using Television—than whether their decision is going to stink up the game. That's a major problem in professional sports today. And you have to blame the owners for forfeiting that control in exchange for taking every last penny from the networks.

You'd like to turn the clock back fifteen, twenty years and make it a simpler time, when games started at a decent hour and the whole telecast wasn't designed to lure the eighteen-year-old off his skateboard and in front of the television. Sports has become all about attracting the casual viewer. Networks do all sorts of sound effects and loud music and computer graphics to get you all jazzed up even when there's nothing happening. They're going to get some hip announcers—are you listening, Dennis Miller? They're going to show you Kobe and Shaq for the tenth time this year in a meaningless regular season game instead of a Houston-Utah game that will decide the last playoff spot in the West. Why can't I get Houston-Utah? Because NBC gave the NBA a $9 billion television package, so they've got to maximize their ratings. And Shaq and Kobe will do a 4.0 rating while Houston-Utah will do a 3.5.

Television takes the hard-core sports fan for granted. Christopher Russo is just going to have to sit through all the junk because I want to see the good stuff. I've got to see the game. And that's where the Dick Ebersols, the Sean McManuses know they have you. They know that Chris Russo is such a big sports fan that he's going to watch anyway. And until I start shutting off my television set, that's the way it's going to be. So what would I do if I ran a network? Here's the way it would be on WDOG.

Go Live: In a perfect world, if I were Dick Ebersol, the first thing I'm going to do is put on every big event live. I'm not going to tape-delay the French Open women's finals so that I don't have to preempt the Saturday morning *Today* show and cut a couple of hours of kiddie cartoons. I'm not tape-delaying the Olympics as he does time and time again. If Sarah Hughes skates at four o'clock in the afternoon, I'm going to put it on at four o'clock in the afternoon. None of this plausibly live stuff. With the Internet and all the news channels, you're not fooling anyone. People know what happened before the prime-time broadcast. If you need to run a replay in prime time, go right ahead. But give the real fan the option of seeing the drama unfold in real time.

Keep It Early: There's a happy medium on starting times for big games. There's no reason why you can't start NBA playoff games or World Series games at seven o'clock on the East Coast. Then kids and people who have to go to work the next day have a fighting chance of being awake to see the end of the game. If that means that a guy on the West Coast has to get home at four-thirty, that's a fair tradeoff. Instead of the people on the East Coast missing the end of the game, why not have the people on the West Coast miss a little of the beginning?

Let There Be Light: I want to see some day games in the World Series. What's wrong with a Saturday afternoon day game? Mickey Mantle never played a World Series night game. Start it at three o'clock and fans on the East and West Coast can both watch it at a reasonable hour.

And the NFL has issues in this regard, too. They're scheduling playoff games in January in northern cities at night so they can get a prime-time hit. New England-Oakland in 2002 is a perfect example. That's really sticking it to the fans at the stadium who have to endure the weather in Chicago or Green Bay at eleven at night when it's 25 below zero. Does somebody have to die of hypothermia before we change this?

Cut the Chatter: At the NBA finals we have three guys in the booth. We have two guys on the sidelines. We have three guys at halftime. Minimum. Do I need Peter Vecsey, Hannah Storm, Tom Tolbert, Steve Jones, Bill Walton, Marv Albert, Lewis Johnson, and Jim Gray? Do I need eight people telling me about a game? Eight? I understand we're giving these people employment, but this is going too far. After all, Vin Scully does the Dodger games by himself.

Don't Screw with the Schedule: Nothing drives me crazier in the post-season in basketball or hockey than teams having to play games on consecutive days just to satisfy TV. It just makes for sloppy, tired play and really cheats the home team, which worked all season to make the playoffs. And then they have to play two home games in twenty-four hours. Wrong.

Then at other times the NBA will also stretch a five-game series to infinity. In 2001, San Antonio and Seattle started their series on a Saturday afternoon at five-thirty in San Antonio. The next game was Monday night in San Antonio. Game three was the following Saturday. And game four was the following Wednesday in Seattle. Think about it. From Monday at nine to the following Wednesday at midnight—nine days—they played two games. All for TV.

SLAYING THE GOLDEN GOOSE

Don't be surprised if some of this ends soon. You're already beginning to see networks balk at the prices they have to pay to put games on the air. One of the reasons why networks like sports is because it's cheap programming. Well, they're finding out that there are even cheaper ways to fill their airtime—*Joe Millionaire*, *Survivor*, nine different editions of *20/20*. So I think you're going to see a lot of these networks bail out of televising leagues. There was a heavy rumor going around the industry in 2001 that ABC was going to sell its big, new *Monday Night Football* package to CBS at a loss because they were bleeding so much money. Right now the NBA, outside of ten games on ABC, doesn't really have a national television contract over the air. The conference finals are on ESPN and TNT. The silver lining is that owners will be less accountable to television and maybe, just maybe, they'll pay more attention to their hard-core fans.

The Ultimate NBA Draft

Who would you pick to start your team with?

Hi, there, Mr. GM. You're in charge of the NBA's newest expansion team, the Montreal Le Bounds. But with the league's new, improved superexpansion draft, you get to choose one player—any player, from any team, any time. Who are you going to pick?

In basketball more than any other sport, having that one great player makes a huge difference. If you can snag the best player in the game, it guarantees you more than success. It all but guarantees you a championship. If you blow it? Remember that Sam Bowie was drafted ahead of Michael Jordan. So with the pressure on, here are my top five picks in reverse order.

5. Oscar Robertson: You hear it every day, people getting all juiced up when Jason Kidd or Antoine Walker gets a triple double. Oscar *averaged* a triple double for five seasons: 30 points, 10 rebounds, 11 assists. A lot of people will tell you that, in his own way, Oscar was every bit as good as Jordan. The problem is that he never had the supporting cast to show how great he was, and those Milwaukee Buck teams at the end of his career were really Lew Alcindor's teams, not his. Oscar is a guy who had to have the ball to dominate the game, and that's another reason why he's not my number one pick

4. Larry Bird: Let's get this straight. For a period in his career, Bird was a better player than Magic. Go back to the 1984 championship series— Celtics-Lakers. Similar teams. Anybody could have won. In that series Bird won because Magic choked. No other way around it (see "Do You Believe in Magic?," page 270). The moment of that series overcame Magic; Bird never had a bad moment like that in a championship series. He was a tremendous winner, and he was the centerpiece of maybe the best team I ever saw, the '86 Celtics. I know he wasn't a great defender, but he made big shots, and made the other people around him better. How great was he? The year he got hurt, the Celtics with Robert Parish and Kevin McHale barely made the playoffs. To me, he's the greatest forward I ever saw.

3. Michael Jordan: Remember, we're not talking about who's the greatest player of all time. In that category, Jordan's number one. He's the best individual player. Shooting, scoring, rebounding, defense, defying gravity, selling tickets, he's got it all. And he's a tremendous competitor. But we're building a team here. And the one knock on Jordan is that even with those Bulls championship teams, when it came to the fourth quarter, everyone stood around and watched Jordan score. That's why, if I'm starting a team, and my number one guy wasn't on the board, I'd probably pick . . .

2. Magic Johnson: I know this is controversial, but if I'm drafting a team, I'd draft Magic number two ahead of Jordan. He's 6' 8", and he can run your team, play a couple of different positions if you need him to. But there's one reason why I'd pick him over Jordan. He makes the marginal player better. Here's my example: If I were in a pickup game on West Fourth Street in the Village—the game's to seven, you lose you sit for three hours—I would want Magic on my team. If you want to stay out there all day and you don't care if you never get the ball, then you'd be happy to play with Jordan, because he'd score every big basket. But if I wanted to feel part of a team, if I wanted to feel I was making a contribution, I want Magic running my team. He makes other people better. He's going to get me layups, wide open jumpers. He's the guy who can help me play better than I think I'm capable of playing. By being the consummate team player, he can dominate a game by scoring six points. Jordan can't really do that.

I. Bill Russell: He's the ultimate winner, the best of all time at that. Think about this. He won eleven championships in thirteen years. He won two championships in college, he won the Olympic gold medal. He never lost a game seven in his life. Russell did every little thing he had to do to win a game. He scored, he blocked shots, he played defense like nobody ever played it before. He was a master psychologist. He changed the game. I know he played with a bunch of Hall of Famers, he played with better players than, say, Wilt Chamberlain or even Jordan. But Russell was another consummate team player. Like Magic, he could dominate a game scoring by six points. And his unselfishness will make it easier to find that second great player you need to win a title. That's why he's my pick.

The Second Five

10. Elgin Baylor: The first pro to play in midair, Elgin was good for 30 points and 20 rebounds in the mid-'60s, and dropped 61 on the Celtics in the finals.

9. Jerry West: There's a reason why he's the poster boy on the NBA logo. Probably, the best pure shooter of all time.

8. Kareem Abdul-Jabbar: Played on two different championship teams, won six titles, and was the feature player in every game he played. An unstoppable offensive force.

7. Bob Pettit: The best pure power forward ever. Right with Wilt and Elgin at the top of the scoring and rebounding tables.

6. Wilt Chamberlain: See below.

■ ■ ■

WHERE'S WILT?

The big omission from my top five is Wilt Chamberlain. Sure, he was a dominant player. But he had too many moments in the big spot where he came up short. He blew a 3–1 lead against Russell's Celtics. In the '67–'68 Eastern Conference Finals, and in game seven of that series, he didn't take a shot in the fourth quarter. That game seven against the Knicks in 1970, he's asking "Is Willis playing tonight?" If you're Wilt Chamberlain, what the hell do you care about Willis Reed? There are too many things like that in his career. I'm a big Wilt fan, but I've got to pick these other guys ahead of him.

Two active players who could sneak onto the list: Shaquille O'Neal (see "Love Shaq?," page 84) and Kobe Bryant, who already has three titles at age twenty-four.

Willie, Mickey, and the Dog

Who's better, Mays or Mantle?

It's the middle of February, the slowest day of the year at WFAN. Nobody cares about St. John's and Villanova, the Knicks and the Cavs. But Mad Dog's got five and a half hours to kill. "What are we going to do to get people into it?" he wonders. "Baseball . . . old-time baseball." And when it's time to talk old-time baseball, there's one discussion that comes up first. . . .

The absolute all-time classic argument in New York sports radio is Mickey Mantle versus Willie Mays. Fans have been kicking this one around for fifty years, and they'll be kicking it around for another fifty. And why not? These two players are a perfectly matched set. They're the same age. They played the same position. They played at the same time—they broke into the majors within five weeks of each other. And they both played in New York, just a subway ride away from each other, for a good chunk of their careers. Who was better? Here are the arguments for each side.

The Case for Mr. Mantle

In his prime, Mantle was the better hitter. There's no argument there. In 1956 he led not only the American League, but the majors in the Triple Crown categories—52 homers, 130 RBIs, and a .353 average. Mays never did that. The next year he hit .365 with 146 walks—he reached base in more than 51 percent of his plate appearances—and those are numbers that Mays never approached. The best Willie ever hit was .345.

Mantle was also a better home run hitter. Between 1955 and 1960 he won four home run titles, and in 1961 he hit a career-best 54 when he finished second to Maris. He wasn't only taking advantage of that short porch either. Nobody's ever hit a ball out of Yankee Stadium, but they're still talking about the shot that Mantle bounced off the upper deck facade (see "Tools of the Game," page 76). That's power.

You want to know how good a player Mantle was at his peak? Here's the ultimate Mantle trivia question. How many intentional walks did Roger Maris draw in 1961 when he broke the home run record? None, because teams knew that if they walked Maris, they'd have to pitch to Mantle.

And playing in all those World Series with the Yankees made Mantle baseball's first television star. Don't discount that. My father's a huge Joe DiMaggio fan, but how many times did he get to see Joe D play in person in his whole career? A couple dozen times. Maybe. With the advent of TV, every baseball fan in America saw Mantle play sixty-five World Series games between 1951 and 1964. Those big strong arms, that blond hair, that goofy smile, that made an impression on people. Most Octobers he was on television more than *I Love Lucy*.

And unlike Mays, he got more popular as he got older. Early in his career the fans, mostly older fans, were down on him for following DiMaggio, in the same way that they were down on DiMaggio at first for following Ruth and Gehrig.

But after Maris came along to take some of the heat, everything was forgiven. Mantle captured the imagination of a whole younger group of fans. Guys who were born in the late 1940s and early '50s, like my partner, Billy Crystal, and Bob Costas, they were Mantle guys. Mantle's teammates loved him, too. Whitey Ford, Moose Skowron, Bob Cerv, Billy Martin. I don't get the same impression with the Mays teammates, that go-through-a-brick-wall mentality, Mantle always had a little of that "Aw shucks, I'm one of the guys" demeanor, and Mays didn't have that. Even opponents had a certain affection for Mantle. Remember the way Denny McLain grooved him a batting practice fastball so he could pass Jimmie Foxx on the career home run list?

And while earlier in his career Mickey was a little grumpy with the fans, later on people sensed a real vulnerability with him. At the end of his life, they saw him going on the air with Costas talking about how he didn't treat people right, about the personal tragedy in his own life with his son. He admitted he drank too much and went to Betty Ford. People saw that and said, "Look at that, he's fallible." That made people love him even more.

You want the proof? On the day of Mantle's funeral, I was flying to France, I remember it distinctly. While I was at the gate—Delta waiting to fly to Nice—there were a hundred people gathered around watching CNN, like it was a president who had died. If Mays died, as great a player as he was, that wouldn't be the case.

MY FAVORITE MANTLE-MAYS STORY

In 1961, Mickey Mantle and Whitey Ford went to San Francisco for the All-Star Game, and they wanted to play a little golf before the game. They went to Giants owner Horace Stoneham, and they asked, "Can we use your club to play a little golf?"

Stoneham said, "Sure, here's my card, go to Olympic and play as much as you want." And so they did. They bought sweaters and balls and windbreakers—five, six hundred dollars' worth—and signed everything to Horace Stoneham.

They saw Stoneham at Toots Shor's restaurant that night, and Mickey peels off $300 and begrudgingly gives it to Whitey to give to Stoneham.

Horace Stoneham says to Whitey. "I'll make a bet with you, if you strike out Mays the first time he gets up, you don't owe me anything. If he gets a hit, you owe me double." Whitey takes the deal back to Mickey. Mantle says, "Geez, I don't know." But then he throws a couple of scotches in him and Mickey, half in the bag, says, "Oh go ahead."

The next day in the game, in the bottom of the first, Clemente doubles off the right field wall. Two out. Mays is up. Whitey gets ahead of him 0-2.

He looks in. He remembers the bet and he loads up the biggest spitball he can. He throws a pitch that looks like it's heading for Willie's head. Mays ducks out of the way and falls on his fanny. And the pitch breaks over for a strike.

Willie gets up and looks at Whitey incredulously. "What, are you throwing me this pitch in an All-Star Game?"

And then Whitey looks out at center field, and there's Mantle jumping up and down, laughing his butt off, because he saved the $600.

The Case for Mr. Mays

In a lot of ways, Mays gets the short end of the stick. During the early part of his career, the Giants played in the Polo Grounds and drew 500,000 fans. In Mays's last few years in New York—'55, '56, '57—they were a terrible baseball team. For the second half of his career, Mays was stuck in

Candlestick Park freezing his fanny off in a park that probably robbed him of a bunch of home runs. That kills Mays.

And whereas fans kind of gradually warmed up to Mickey throughout his career, the really big Mays moments—the Say Hey Kid stuff that sticks with you—came early on in Willie's career. The hat flying off in the outfield. The basket catches. Playing stickball in the street with the kids on the way to the Polo Grounds. He really seemed like he loved baseball. And when he grew out of that a little—grew up, really—that rubbed some people the wrong way.

Mays may not have been quite the hitter, at his peak, that Mantle was, but he wasn't that far behind. If Mantle was the best hitter in baseball, then Mays was probably a close second most of the time. As far as overall ability, Mays could beat you in so many ways that Mantle couldn't. We'll never know what Mickey Mantle might have been if he hadn't hurt his knee on that drainpipe in the '51 World Series, but he wasn't nearly the complete player that Mays was.

Mantle was a decent outfielder, but Willie was one of the greatest of all time, if not the greatest. The Catch in the '54 Series? Mantle couldn't make that kind of play. And it wasn't just that once. Remember the famous line by Dodger manager Chuck Dressen? He made a diving catch to save a game against the Dodgers, and he said, "Let me see him do that again tomorrow." People expected those kinds of plays from Willie.

Mantle was a decent baserunner. Mays led the league in steals four times in a row, and in his career, he had 185 more steals than Mantle. And it wasn't just the steals. Put him on base and Mays was like a man possessed. He'd be on third base, bottom of the ninth, tie game. On a short sac fly he'd tag, go three quarters down the line, make the guy throw the ball to the plate, get caught in a pickle, beat the pickle, and score the game-winning run. Those are the things that Mays could do for you.

The other big factor in Mays's favor is longevity. In 1965, Mantle was all but done. Mays? He hit .317 with 52 homers and 112 RBIs. And Willie had several productive years after Mantle retired. And that makes a huge difference in the career numbers. And while some of the reason that Mantle's career was shorter was because of the knee injury, a lot of it had to do with the way he took care of himself—or didn't. While they both probably hung on a little too long, I'd have to say that Mays definitely got more out of his talent than Mantle did. When he retired, Mays was second on the home run list, top five in runs, top ten in hits and RBIs. That's pretty good company.

Dog's Pick?

This is a tough decision and it's a pretty nice one for any GM to have to make, but if you're looking long term, rather than say, one game, one series, or even one season, I've got to pick Mays. First off, I'm going to throw out the off-the-field stuff. That affects the way that people remember them, but it doesn't change what they were going to do for your team.

Here are my reasons. Mays wasn't quite the slugger that Mantle was—although if they played in the same park, I think the gap would be narrower—but he did a lot more things in the field and on the bases.

And while he wasn't quite as good when they both were at their peaks, Mays had a much better overall career. Look at the bottom line: Mays hit 124 more home runs, had 868 more hits, drove in 394 more runs. Those numbers would make a decent career for some guys. Or to look at it another way, it's like having a Hall of Famer in centerfield for four extra seasons. That's why I'm going with Willie.

Live or Memorex?

Are sports really better in person?

Okay, it's a couple of days before the big game. One of your buddies calls. He's got a friend who's got a cousin who knows a guy who might have a couple of extra tickets. They're not going to come cheap, so what do you do? Pay your money, or camp out in front of the Trinitron? Here's the Dog's take on whether you've really got to be there.

Okay, this may sound a little crazy, but I'm going to tell you something. A lot of times for the big games, I'd rather watch at home on television. Really.

I'm not going to deny that there's something special about being at the stadium, where the action is. About being crammed in with fifty thousand people, the place packed to the gills. About feeling the upper deck shake like it's 3.0 on the Richter scale when the home team scores. About breathing the same air as Barry Bonds or Michael Jordan. But, if you're a serious sports fan, there are plenty of good reasons why the tube beats being there during the really big game.

The Cost Factor: This is kind of a no-brainer. Today the average fan's ability to score tickets to the big event—the Super Bowl, the World Series, the NBA Finals—without a hassle is next to nil. To even have a shot, you've got to be willing to call in every favor anybody ever owed you, take a second mortgage on your house, or camp outside the stadium for two nights in a row. And even then, it's going to be tough to get the kind of seats you want.

WATCHING THE GAME, DOGGIE STYLE

Here's what I need when I'm watching a big game—a playoff game, a finals match in tennis—at home.

Peace and Quiet: I need to watch the game without being distracted. By the phone. By two kids running around. By thirty people screaming and yelling, so you can't hear the announcer. That's why, for a big game, you'll probably find me upstairs in the small spare bedroom where I've got a TV and a dish. That's all I need. I don't even have a chair. I'm lying on the carpet, but I'm all set. My wife? She's not a sports fan, but she knows when she has to take the kids to leave me alone.

The Right Company: I don't have to have that male bonding thing, going to the game with my buddies, When I watch, I want to watch it in my own head. That's why I can't watch at a bar. You're talking to the guy next to you. Drinking beer. Spilling beer. It doesn't mean I can't have anybody over, but if I'm watching with somebody, he's got to be just as into the game as I am.

No Remote: I'm not flipping channels, using the clicker to go somewhere else during a time-out. During game seven of the 2001 World Series, the Jets-Saints game was on at the same time. I didn't go to the Jets game, not once.

The Scheduling Factor: The schedules are a joke. They started World Series games between the Mets and the Yankees at 8:30 so that some guy in San Diego can watch the game at a reasonable hour. The NFL will schedule a Giants-Eagles Monday night game with a 9:07 kickoff. NBA playoffs, same 9:07 tip.

You're watching one of these games, you know going in that you're probably not going to get to bed until two o'clock, by the time you watch the postgame and wind down a little. And I don't know about you, but my kids aren't going to give me a break and wake up at nine. They're still going to wake up at sixty-thirty.

The Scenemaker Factor: Look behind home plate at a World Series game and tell me who the legitimate baseball fans are. All the good seats are going to corporations and that actress from *Ally McBeal*. And it's obvious when you watch the game. You'll see Bernie Williams hit a weak fly ball, the outfielder is coming in, and the crowd's going nuts thinking it's a three-run homer. The lack of sophistication scares you. Are these the people you want to be sitting with when the season's on the line?

The Rude Guy Factor: It's bad if you've got some corporate suit and his wife who's never been to a game before sitting next to you. But they're probably going to leave at halftime. What's worse is when you've got the fat guy who did take out the second mortgage, and he's got the face paint, the foam finger, and a beer in each hand. You're trying to pay attention to

THE POSTUREPEDIC FACTOR

I'll admit it. Sometimes at the end of the game—not a big game, mind you—you won't find me in front of the tube. Or at the game. You'll find me in bed.

There was a Monday night game, Ravens and Titans—13-10 early fourth quarter. My wife says, "Chris, you've got to go to bed." It's after midnight and I felt that the game was pretty much in hand. I went to bed. As it turned out I missed a wild conclusion in the last hour, the extra play that the Titans got at the goal line. Now I'll stay up until 4 A.M. to watch a big Giants game when they're in the pennant race, but there are some things you have to sacrifice, to get some sleep. Remember the Jets' Monday night comeback against Miami? Didn't see it. Beddie-bye.

what's going on, stay ahead of the action a little bit, but he's yelling like Tarzan, slapping you on the back, spilling beer all over your new jacket.

The See-the-Play Factor: And since Ivana Trump is sitting in the good seats, you're not. Sure, there are pluses to being inside the stadium, even if your seats are marginal. You don't have to depend on the television producer—you can focus your attention wherever you want. So you can see all the little things that the camera is missing—the way the batter warming up in the on-deck circle is trying to time Curt Schilling's slider, or the way Kurt Warner's huddling up with his offensive coordinator. You don't have to wait for Tim McCarver to tell you—or not tell you—that they're playing the infield at double play–depth.

But by the same token, you've got only one seat. And the odds are that when that crucial play happens, you're not going to be in the right spot to see it. A TV crew? They've got twenty cameras. If a big play happens, they're going to get it one way or another.

Let me give you an example. At game three of the 2001 ALCS, from where I was sitting behind home plate, I couldn't see if Yankee left fielder Chuck Knoblauch caught Bret Boone's ball. Biggest play of the game, and I missed it. If I'm at home, I've got the play—and five different replays—right in front of me.

The Unhappy Recap Factor: If your team wins, you're going to be okay with all of this. But what if they lose? Don't laugh. It could happen. Then you're with fifty thousand people acting like their dog just got run over. They say that misery loves company. Don't believe it.

The worst-case scenario? You're on the road, and your team loses. Then everybody's celebrating. Except you. During the division series games against the Mets in 2000, I had great seats, second row behind the Giants dugout. But when Benny Agbayani hits that home run in extra innings, and the Big Apple's blowing up in center field and everyone's yelling and screaming and high-fiving, at that moment I'm thinking, I'd really rather be at home. Really. And the best decision I ever made? Not traveling from San Francisco to Anaheim for games six and seven of the 2002 World Series.

Oops, I Did It Again

What are the greatest vapor locks in sports history?

We all have senior moments. But what about when you take a mental vacation in the middle of a championship game? Mad Dog replays some classic dazed and confused sports moments.

What's a vapor lock anyway? I see it as some kind of momentary mental breakdown. You just forget about something small but crucial for a split second and it comes back to bite you. That's different than a choke, where the pressure just makes your game fall apart.

A classic choke is a process. A choke usually takes nine holes, a set, a ninth inning. It's a different situation. Vapor lock is like a lightning bolt. It comes out of nowhere.

A vapor lock isn't so much about playing badly, it's a fluke where you lose track of the situation for a split second or forget something in the rules.

Here's the other way to look at it. Watching an athlete choke is hard. You cringe and say, "I don't want to watch this anymore." Your reaction to a vapor lock is just stunned disbelief. "Oh my God. Why did he do that? What happened?" You might even laugh. And you certainly want to see it again, because you could hardly believe your eyes the first time. Here are a few freaky moments I'd watch again anytime.

Webber's Time-Out: The first one that anybody is going to think about is Chris Webber's phantom time-out in the 1993 championship game against North Carolina. Michigan's down by two with eleven seconds to go. In the previous time-out, Steve Fisher told everybody they were out of time-outs. Michigan rebounded a missed North Carolina free throw, Webber gets trapped in the corner and he calls a time-out that they didn't have. Technical foul. There goes the national championship. In some cases—like in that Phoenix-Celtics playoff game (see "VCR Classics," page 261) the ref won't acknowledge the time-out request in that situation, but the official was an inch away from Webber so he had no choice.

Knoblauch's Argument: Another famous one. Travis Fryman of the Indians is called safe on a slow roller in the 1998 ALCS. The throw bounces off Fryman into short right field, but instead of chasing it, Chuck Knoblauch stops to argue with the ump. Enrique Wilson comes around to score. This kind of brain freeze happens every now and then, even to guys who we think of as clutch players—David Cone and Scott Spiezio did almost the same thing. And while it's easy to cite this as the start of Knoblauch's defensive problems, let's also give him his due. In the seventh game of the 1991 World Series he made one of the clutch defensive plays of all time, deking Lonnie Smith on a fake relay throw that ultimately saved the game.

Magic's Clock Management: It's game four of the 1984 NBA Finals. Lakers-Celtics, tie game, Laker ball. Magic Johnson has the ball with plenty of time on the clock, and he essentially dribbles away the possession. He holds the ball and holds the ball and finally passes the ball to Kareem too late to get the shot off. The game goes into overtime, the Celtics win and go on to take the title in seven games.

Thurman's Helmet: Here's kind of a funny one. Before the 1992 Super Bowl against the Redskins, Thurman Thomas does an absolutely great dance coming out of the tunnel. He got nice and low, bent down like a crab. It was funny and very good.

Then when the Bills get the ball, he realizes something. He forgot his helmet. His backup, Kenneth Davis, had to take the first couple of hand-offs while they went searching for his helmet. Now it didn't affect the outcome of the game—the Redskins were the better team—but it kind of showed you something about the Bills team. They had been in the Super Bowl the year before—Thomas was great against the Giants—but they seemed really distracted, and maybe a little cocky all week leading up to the game. And played like it.

Willie's Missing Furlong: Here's a legendary one from horse racing I've heard about involving one of the greatest jockeys of all time. In the home stretch of the 1957 Kentucky Derby, Willie Shoemaker was cruising toward the finish aboard Gallant Man. Thinking he had crossed the line, he stood up in the saddle. Only one problem. The line he crossed was the one-sixteenth marker, not the finish line. Iron Liege sweeps past for the win. And it wasn't like this was a rookie mistake—Shoemaker had won the Derby two years before.

Roberto's Scorecard: And way back in the 1968 Masters this forty-five-year-old guy from Argentina, Roberto De Vicenzo, has the tournament of

---

WHOSE VAPOR LOCK?

It's funny, players see vapor locks differently than fans do. In an early December Jets-Patriots game the year New England won the Super Bowl, Tom Brady mounts a big comeback and puts the Pats in the lead in the fourth quarter. The Jets have the ball and they've got a third and goal with time running out and no time-outs. Vinny Testaverde throws a pass to Curtis Martin at the five-yard line. He's tackled, time expires, the Jets lose. My first reaction? "Think, Vinny, think!" That's vapor lock. When I talked to former QB Boomer Esiason, he said, "Yeah, that's a bone-head play." But he put some of the blame on Curtis Martin. He said that Martin's got to drop the football intentionally. He said, "I guarantee you that James Brooks drops that pass if he sees he's not going to score."

his life. He comes into 18 with a one-shot lead and shoots a bogey to drop him back into a tie with Bob Goalby. Or so he thought. Turns out he had signed an incorrect scorecard, which gave him a par instead of a birdie on 17. No playoff. Afterward he said, "All I can think of is what a stupid I am."

This kind of stuff happens a lot because of golf's arcane rules. A few years ago Ian Woosnam lost a chance at a final round comeback in the British Open because he took a penalty for carrying too many clubs. He was trying out drivers on the range and left an extra one in the bag. The caddy didn't count the clubs. Woosnam didn't count the clubs. Vapor lock all around.

Make 'Em Hit

Is the designated hitter bad for baseball?

To DH or not to DH? that is the question. Whether 'tis nobler in the mind to suffer the slings and arrows of outrageous sliders. Or take arms against a sea of fastballs and by opposing end them? Mad Dog weighs this classic issue.

If you think we need the DH in Major League Baseball, you are nuts. DH is an absolute waste of time. There are a million problems with it.

One of the best parts about baseball is decision-making, following along with the manager. When do you bunt? When do you pinch hit? When do you yank a pitcher? Those kinds of things are totally lost with the DH. An American League manager doesn't have a lot to do besides dodge foul balls and pat his players on the butt when they hit a homer. He doesn't have to pinch hit because he's got the DH. He doesn't have to do the double switch. He doesn't have to make the tough decision about when to take out a pitcher or not. It's 2-2 in the bottom of the seventh inning in a big game, a man on second, two outs, and the pitcher is due up. Do you take him out or leave him in? In the American League the manager doesn't have to make that decision. It's crazy.

Then there's the beanball issue (see "Know the Code," page 177). You have more problems in the American League with pitchers throwing at guys because they don't have to get up there and hit. Roger Clemens and Mike Piazza, that happened in Yankee Stadium. Do you think that Clemens is throwing the ball in the general direction of Mike Piazza's head—I don't think he was trying to actually hit Piazza—if he's at Shea and he has to go up there and swing the bat in the next inning? Make that pitcher hit, and you'll make him think twice.

And how about evaluating a player for the Hall of Fame? A lot of these great players in the American League spent a lot of time as a DH. Well, how do you evaluate Edgar Martinez as a Hall of Famer? Jose Canseco? Frank Thomas? Harold Baines? Guys who play DH should have an asterisk next to their names on the Hall of Fame ballot as far as I'm concerned.

All of these problems are most apparent in the World Series. Right now we play a World Series where half the games have a DH and half the games don't. That's stupid. It puts a weird spin on games—who's going to DH for the NL team? Is the DH going to try to play the field for the AL team? It's an unnecessary distraction and it just plays up the silliness of the whole situation.

And major league games take forever. There are too many runs scored, which leads to pitching changes which leads to longer games. One easy way to get things back into balance is to put those three or four automatic outs back into the lineup. You'll have quicker innings and fewer runs and shorter games.

They played baseball from 1870 to 1972 without the DH. Babe Ruth didn't have a DH. Joe DiMaggio didn't have a DH. But now we've got to have a DH for Edgar Martinez? And Walter Johnson pitched to Herb Pennock and Sandy Koufax pitched to Bob Gibson. Why can't Barry Zito pitch to Pedro Martinez?

The V in MVP

What does it take to win an MVP award?

It's the classic off-season dispute. Do you give your MVP vote to the best player in the league? Or do you give it to the guy whose team won a bunch of games? Mad Dog tells you how he'd cast his ballot.

This is an argument that resurfaces almost every season. What exactly does the word valuable mean in Most Valuable Player? Is it the guy who contributed the most to the success of his team? Or is it the guy who performed the best regardless of what happened to the rest of the team? And if you look at MVP balloting, you'll find voters on both sides of the fence.

Personally, I think that winning has got to play a big part of it. For instance, in the NBA two years ago, I don't know how in the world the writers voted Tim Duncan the MVP over New Jersey's Jason Kidd. It was an absolute disgrace as far as I'm concerned. Now I understand that Duncan is a tremendous player and the San Antonio Spurs would be a 25-win team without him. But the bottom line is Jason Kidd came to a team that won 26 games the year before, and when he got there they won 52. That's an MVP performance if I ever saw one.

No, Kidd's stat line wasn't nearly as impressive as Duncan's. Yes, he shot 39 percent from the floor. But Kidd's contributions don't show up on a stat sheet. If you cover the NBA in Salt Lake City and you see Jason Kidd two times a year, you're not going to be all that impressed. I understand that. But Kidd changed the whole chemistry of the team, the players responded to his leadership, and New Jersey went from near the bottom of the Eastern Conference to the top by basically adding one player. Kidd meant far more to his team that particular year than Duncan did.

There's definitely an intangible aspect to an MVP vote, and many times those factors are out of a player's control. I don't think—short of cloning himself—that Duncan could have done enough to deserve the award in my eyes. Duncan's numbers were tremendous, but his numbers have always been tremendous. He did everything he normally does, 25 points, 13 rebounds, shot the ball great, made his free throws. Tim Duncan's team did what Tim Duncan's teams usually do. They won fiftysomething games, won their division, and they finished second in the conference. It wasn't like the Spurs won 70 games or had the best record in the league or even the top seed in the conference. And it wasn't like Duncan averaged 37 points and 22 rebounds a game. He didn't have that extra intangible that could have made this season special.

And I know that it's not completely fair, but if Duncan had missed a whole season or was traded to San Antonio from another team before the season started, and the Spurs went from 22 wins to 55 all of a sudden, you could make a better case for Duncan as MVP.

You see the same kind of thing in the baseball MVP voting. In 2002, Miguel Tejada of the A's won the award, and rightfully so. He had a great year, put up very impressive numbers. But he also had the intangible factor. When Jason Giambi left, everyone thought that the A's would collapse. But they didn't, in part because Tejada stepped up and a) played better than he ever had before, and b) filled the leadership vacuum on the team.

Was he better than Alex Rodriguez, who finished second in the balloting? Not as far as the numbers are concerned. A-Rod hit .300 with 57 homers and 142 RBIs. He won a Gold Glove at short. I think that most people would agree that he was the best player in the league.

But even with A-Rod, the Texas Rangers finished last. And as Branch Rickey said to Ralph Kiner during a contract dispute, "We finished last with you, and can finish last without you." Now, some years you can have an Andre Dawson scenario—he hit 49 homers for the last-place Cubs and barely edged out Ozzie Smith from the first-place Cardinals—in which the great player on the lousy team can sneak in, but that's pretty rare.

It's like Sammy Sosa and Mark McGwire in 1998. McGwire had a better year than Sosa, and he broke a very important record in impressive style. But Sosa hit all his homers in the context of the Cubs making the playoffs, while McGwire was on a team that was nineteen games behind, so Sosa won the MVP, as well he should have.

The flip side is that there's a curse to being on a team that's too good. During their great run, the Yankees didn't have a player that made a serious run at an MVP. I think that most voters realize that Bernie Williams and

Derek Jeter and Alfonso Soriano and Jason Giambi are very good players, but they say, "Well, if he wasn't here, the Yankees would still have won ninety-six games and won the division by nine games instead of thirteen."

When you've got more than one candidate on a team, it creates an interesting scenario. In 1988, when Kevin McReynolds and Darryl Strawberry split the Mets vote, Kirk Gibson snuck in when he drove in 76 runs. And there was a big stink a couple of years ago about the vote between Jeff Kent and Barry Bonds. Bonds had numbers that were slightly better than Kent's—he hit 49 home runs—but as a big Giants fan, I thought Kent deserved the award because Kent made a bigger contribution to the Giants winning that year than Bonds did. He had more timely hits, bigger clutch hits, and he did it earlier in the year when the Giants were hovering around .500. Kent kept San Francisco above water. Bonds did a lot of his damage after the Giants had already won.

So if I had a vote—and I don't—I would vote for the guy who was most valuable to a good team, and that value doesn't always show up in the numbers. I want to pick the guy who was instrumental in getting his club over the top. Winston Churchill would have understood. The V in MVP can also stand for victory.

90 FEET FROM AN MVP

Do you remember Mike Piazza's MVP run in 1997? Piazza that year could have won the MVP, but Larry Walker of the Rockies put up some monster numbers, stats that were inflated by Coors Field. The Dodgers won 88 games and didn't win the division, while Colorado won 86. Late in the season with eleven games to go, the Dodgers were playing San Francisco. If they win the game they go two up with ten to play and probably win the division. In the top of the tenth the Dodgers had men on first and second, nobody out, and Raul Mondesi hit a line drive down the right field line for a base hit. But the third base coach, I think it was Joey Amalfitano, didn't risk sending Piazza, who was the lead runner, home for the tie-breaking run. Rod Beck, the Giants closer, somehow got out of a bases-loaded, nobody-out jam. He faced only two batters, with Eddie Murray hitting into a 4-2-3 double play. The Giants won the game in the bottom of the twelfth inning and went on to win the division. That 90 feet probably cost Piazza his best chance to win an MVP.

The P in MVP

Should pitchers win the MVP award?

They say that pitching is 90 percent of baseball. But the same guys won't vote for a pitcher for the Most Valuable Player Award. Which is it? Mad Dog untangles this knotty issue.

Would you vote for a pitcher for an MVP award? The answer that most of the baseball writers would give is no—at least judging from the fact that no pitcher has won the award in a decade. The knee-jerk argument that they give for not voting for pitchers is that pitchers have their own award, the Cy Young. I think that does raise the bar a little bit for pitchers, but I don't think it should disqualify them completely.

Three of the last four pitchers to win MVP awards were relievers: Rollie Fingers in 1981, Willie Hernandez in 1984, and Dennis Eckersley in 1992, with Boston starter Roger Clemens, who won in 1986, sandwiched between. That makes some sense, because a) relievers do pitch almost every day, and b) they don't get much consideration for the Cy Young. Looking back, those seasons were a little weird, too. Fingers had a great year, but that was also a strike season. Hernandez won the MVP in '84 and while he had a great year, he didn't really get going until after the Tigers' 35–5 start when they blew away the rest of the league. For Eckersley, it was a bit of a career achievement award: He posted lower ERAs in two of the previous three seasons.

And then there was the 1999 vote between Pedro Martinez of the Red Sox and Pudge Rodriguez of the Rangers. Pedro should have won that award, but they gave it to Pudge instead. Here's one of those rare times when I would have voted for a pitcher. Pedro was so good and so important to that team. He went out there every fifth day and won every huge game, stopped their losing streaks, kept his team afloat. The Red Sox knew that whenever Pedro was on the mound, they were probably going to win. And Pedro's record was the difference between them winning the wild card and being out of contention.

The reason why he lost? Because George King of the *New York Post* (along with another writer) left him off their ballot completely. If a guy just doesn't believe in voting for pitchers, I can respect that. But King had voted for David Wells eighth for MVP in 1998. That's just not right.

Of course, the MVP voting takes place after the season and before the playoffs, but it's funny how sometimes a guy who gets jobbed out of the MVP goes out in the postseason and proves why he should've won it. In the deciding game five of the division series, Pedro Martinez came off the bench, injured, and pitched six innings to beat the Indians in Cleveland. And he dominated the Yankees in the ALCS, handing them their only loss of the postseason. If that isn't valuable, I don't know what is.

Five Aces

Who is the greatest men's tennis player of all time?

They all put their white shorts on one leg at a time. But when it comes right down to it, who is the best to ever whack a felt-covered ball? Mad Dog serves up the answer.

The problem that you have when you're putting together any list of all-time greats is comparing eras. And there's no place where that's a bigger issue than in men's tennis. Where do you put Bill Tilden? Where do you put the Four Musketeers? And what do you do with the fact that until 1968, the best players were professionals and didn't play at Wimbledon, the French, or the U.S. Championships? How are you supposed to evaluate guys like Don Budge and Jack Kramer? I'm going to say that I just can't. Budge and Kramer and Tilden were fantastic players, but they played just too long ago for me to really get a handle on their greatness. I'm going to have to restrict my list to guys who played at least part of their careers in the Open Era.

5. Pancho Gonzalez: Gonzalez is my nod to the old days. Pancho played most of his career during the days of the barnstorming professionals. Every time the guy who won Wimbledon as an amateur moved over to the pro circuit, Pancho killed him. And don't forget that he got to a round of 16 at an open Wimbledon when he was forty-one years of age. He had a huge serve and just refused to lose. Imagine Pete Sampras's big weapon and Jimmy Connors's competitive fire, and that's Pancho.

4. John McEnroe: For a short period of time, from 1980 to '85, John McEnroe was a tennis genius. He had a huge, sneaky lefty serve, great volleys, tremendous touch, and he was far and away the best doubles player in history. And the best U.S. Davis Cup player ever. He dismantled Connors in a Wimbledon final in a little more than an hour, and he basically drove Björn Borg into retirement. At his best he was the best player I ever saw, even better than Sampras.

Now the one knock on him is that he never won the French. He lost the French Open final against Lendl while leading two sets to love and up a break in the fourth. That's a tough, tough loss, but there's a silver lining. It also shows you that he had the game to compete on clay.

3. Björn Borg: Borg's claim to fame is that he won on the two most extreme surfaces: five Wimbledons in a row on fast grass, and six French Opens on slow red clay. In fact, he did the French-Wimbledon double three times. He was a steady, steely competitor, and a remarkably fit athlete—his resting heart rate was 35. But he couldn't win the U.S. Open (see "Of Black Cats and Seeing-Eye Singles," page 71) and that's the thing that keeps him off the top of this list.

2. Pete Sampras: Sampras holds the record for Grand Slam titles, so he's got to make this list. At his best he was tremendously dominant, just mopping the floor with guys like Michael Chang and Andre Agassi in the finals of majors, which is the one big reason Agassi doesn't crack the top five. And he's also had a tremendously long run at the top, winning the U.S. Open at nineteen and again at thirty-one, at a time when only his wife gave him any kind of a chance. The major negative is that he never won a French Open, and never even got to the final. One thing I'll say for Sampras is that he beat Yevgeny Kafelnikov in a Davis Cup Final in Moscow on red clay at a time when Kafelnikov was probably the best clay court player in the world. It was a long five-setter, Sampras was cramping up, but he gutted it out and won the Cup for the U.S. That's a tribute to his greatness.

1. Rod Laver: Believe it or not, Rod Laver is the only guy on this list to win all four major championships in his career. But the Rocket did way more than that—he won the four Grand Slam titles—the Australian, French, Wimbledon, and U.S.—all in one year. And he did it twice. You have to put a little asterisk next to his first one in 1962, where he played against only amateurs. But his second Slam came in 1969, the second year of Open tennis. No excuses there. Laver won eleven majors in his career, but he also missed five years in his prime between 1963 and 1968. If he were allowed to play during those years, you would have to guess that his career total of majors would be closer to twenty and Pete Sampras would still be chasing him. A great student of the game, Sampras considers Rod Laver the greatest player of all time. Who am I to disagree?

SWEET LEW

I interviewed Roy Emerson, who won twelve grand slams, one Super Saturday at the U.S. Open and I asked him this same question. And he said that he would pick Laver as the best player of all time, but at the top of his game, the best player he ever saw was Lew Hoad. Emerson's description: Hoad was an Australian lefty who had remarkable power, great finesse, was very, very strong, a remarkable athlete. He won the first three legs of the Grand Slam in 1956, but lost the U.S. final to Ken Rosewall. Hoad's career was cut short by back injuries, but according to Emmo, on a good day he was untouchable.

Caught in the Draft

Why can't the pros make the right picks?

"With the third pick in the NBA draft, the Los Angeles Clippers select . . ."
It's a moment that some fans wait all year for. Mad Dog tells you why most
years it's hardly worth opening the envelope.

I know that a lot of sports fans look forward to the NBA and NFL drafts. I'm not one of them. I think they're both incredibly overrated events. They're boring, they take forever, and they're a waste of time.

But here's the worst thing. They make heroes out of eighteen-, nineteen-, twenty-year-olds before they've done a thing in professional sports. They're sitting in the green room wearing $5,000 Armani suits, two-carat diamond studs in their ears, a gold Rolex on their wrists. And then they come strutting up on the stage like they own the world.

Teams give players an incredible amount of money based on how they shot layups in a gym in May, based on how fast they ran a 40-yard dash on a carpet in Indianapolis in February. In the NFL Draft I find it very peculiar that the coaches evaluating prospects almost never actually see the players play college football. College football games are on Saturday afternoons, and most NFL games are played on Sunday afternoons. Pro coaches spend half their Saturdays on planes going to road games and the other half making last-minute preparations at home. Coaches will argue that they evaluate players based on film work. Still, there's a lot you can learn from watching a player in a game right in front of your nose.

And, for that matter, a lot of the NFL fans who sit in the Paramount Theater yelling and screaming about a certain pick don't know anything about college football. They wouldn't know Tony Boselli if he fell on them.

"You're big. Who are you?"

"Well, I'm the number one pick of the Jacksonville Jaguars."

"No kidding."

And look at all the great football players who weren't first-round picks. Brett Favre and Joe Montana, two great Hall of Famers, now how come they weren't first rounders? Tom Brady was the MVP of the Super Bowl. He was a sixth-round pick. Kurt Warner was playing arena football, for God's sake. Dan Marino, the best pure passer that the game has ever known, was the twenty-seventh pick in the 1983 draft and the sixth quarterback drafted, behind such luminaries as Todd Blackledge, Tony Eason, and Ken O'Brien.

On the other hand, how did first-rounder David Klingler do? How did Andre Ware do? How did Akili Smith do? How did Ryan Leaf do? Bobby Beathard is a guy who built championship teams, and he used the second pick in the draft to take Ryan Leaf (see "What a Waste," page 147). The great Bill Walsh wanted Rick Mirer. And look at all the quarterbacks that Mike Holmgren's been through in Seattle.

There are more misses than hits in the NFL draft. Look at the Giants in the late 1980s and 1990s. Their first-round picks, whether Tyrone Wheatley, Thomas Lewis, Derek Brown, Jarrod Bunch, or Ron Dayne, for the most part, were all busts. Yet their third-, fifth-, and eighth-round picks were very, very good. They drafted Michael Strahan, Jessie Armstead, and Myron Guyton.

It's not an exact science. A guy gets a stomachache the week of the Senior Bowl or comes down with the sniffles during the draft combines, and all of a sudden he drops to the eighth round in the draft. So I can't take the draft seriously because the professionals foul it up constantly.

The NBA used to be a little easier to evaluate because basketball's more of a one-on-one game. We all felt that Shaq would be a great pro, we all felt that Tim Duncan would be a great pro, because they were great players in college. Still, there were plenty of screwups: Portland fans will never forget the fact that they drafted Sam Bowie ahead of Michael Jordan.

Today in the NBA you're not drafting for performance, you're projecting a player's potential. Teams are using lottery picks to take eighteen-year-olds coming straight out of high school. They're tall, they can jump, and they can score 35 points a night playing against a bunch of pimple-faced kids who will have illustrious careers as accountants and insurance salesmen, so let's give them a couple million dollars and a guaranteed contract. It's absurd.

Or they're drafting these teenagers who are riding the bench on these teams in Europe, thinking that every tall skinny kid who can't speak English is going to be the next Dirk Nowitzski. It's a joke.

So how am I supposed to talk intelligently for five hours about the NBA or the NHL draft when the GM of the Pittsburgh Steelers and the GM of the Los Angeles Clippers are sitting there with a Ouija board, crossing their fingers behind their backs when they make a pick? So that's why I'm not much of a draftnik.

But Is It a Sport?

Can you call a racing driver or a golfer an athlete?

In the age of ESPN, anything's a sport. Lumberjacking. Cheerleading. Rodeo. Mad Dog takes a more purist view of the subject.

I did sports talk in Orlando and Jacksonville for several years, so I took calls from a lot of auto racing fans. I used to have this argument over and over again: Are race car drivers athletes?

Here's what I said. Why don't I drive down I-4, the road that runs from Tampa to Daytona, with the windows closed, no air-conditioning. I'll wear a hot racing suit and a helmet so I'll work up a good sweat. And I'll go 110 mph. I'll be nervous about going 110, especially when I'm passing the little old lady in the Buick with her turn signal on, but I'll do it. I'll make a couple of turns to add to the excitement, and I'll do that for a couple of hours and I'll say I'm an athlete. Oh come on, please, please, please.

The problem I have with NASCAR is that the race car is doing all the work. A great driver in a lousy car is not winning. You've got to have the fast car. Some drivers are a little better than others, I'll admit. But if I'm the best driver and I'm driving a Cavalier and the other guy is driving a Corvette, there's no way I'm going to be able to pass him no matter how great I am. If you've got a fast car, you are going to win, it's as simple as that, which is why NASCAR is not a sport.

Here's what they'd come back to me with. What about the baseball pitcher who has a beer gut and weighs 5,000 pounds. He's out of shape, huffing and puffing when he runs down to first. Is Mickey Lolich an athlete? Is Cecil Fielder an athlete? Is baseball a sport?

First off, the fat pitcher or the tubby DH is the exception to the rule. And I would argue that these guys are athletes because throwing a baseball accurately at 95 mph or hitting a fastball is a supreme athletic accomplishment. He's not depending on the bat or the ball to do the work for him.

I actually think that horse racing is a sport because I consider the horse an athlete. Jockeys aren't athletes in a classic sense, but steering a 1,200-pound animal over a racetrack at fairly high speeds does take some athletic ability. Sure, there's the NASCAR argument—put a lousy jockey on Secretariat and Willie Shoemaker on Arazi, and Secretariat's still going to win. But the difference is that Secretariat wasn't a machine, he was a living, breathing animal.

Is bowling a sport? No way. You're rolling a ball down a lane at some pins. Nobody's playing defense, trying to stop you. The lane doesn't change and the pins don't move. The ball's not that heavy. What's so hard about that? Bowling a strike for these guys should be as easy as hitting a free throw. You ever watch those bowlers on the PBA tour? They're chewing their Slim-Jims and drinking their Pabst Blue Ribbon beer between frames. They are not athletes.

What about the other extreme, something like mountain climbing? Sure the guys who climb Mount Everest are in fantastic shape. So are ballet dancers. The thing is that they're not competitors. They're not racing up the mountain against another team, they're just trying to climb up, see the view, take a couple of pictures for their sponsors, and get down before they get caught in a blizzard or an avalanche and get buried alive.

Is golf a sport? This is an interesting one. It's a competition, it takes some physical exertion, you've got to walk the course, the club doesn't win it for you, the guy swinging it does. And there are plenty of variables. Every course is different. The pin placement changes. The weather changes. The ball bounces six inches farther and you can get a bad lie. So yes, it's a sport.

But is Craig Stadler an athlete? No. I'm not a professional athlete, but I can shoot baskets better than he can, I can run faster than he can, I can hit a tennis ball better than he can. He's forty-five years of age. He is 50 pounds overweight. Just because he can hit a golf ball straight and far doesn't make him an athlete, it means that he has one specific highly developed skill. Considering the fact that Jack Nicklaus can play competitive golf with an artificial hip, I don't think you can say that golfers are athletes. Tiger Woods is an athlete, but he's the exception that proves the rule.

Gridiron Greats

What are the greatest football dynasties of all time?

"On the frozen tundra of Lambeau Field, in front of 60,000 of the faithful, the helmeted gladiators do battle for the ultimate honor . . . the right to call themselves champions." John Facenda's not around to read this chapter aloud, but Mad Dog forges ahead and picks the ultimate giants of the gridiron.

Before you can rank football dynasties, you have to first define what a dynasty is. I looked in *Webster's* and they said "succession for a considerable period of time." Well, the next question is "What defines a considerable period of time?" If you're talking about lines of English kings, that's a couple of hundred years. In football we'll call it three championship appearances with two titles in a four-year period minimum. And that's a tough hurdle in the NFL, because you've got to keep your team healthy, and more recently you're facing the problem of keeping your team together in a league that has a salary cap. Here are some teams that were successful over a considerable period of time.

5. The 1970-73 Miami Dolphins: This is a team that gets overlooked a little bit. The 1970 Dolphins were 10–4, lost in the first round of the playoffs to the Raiders. Fair enough. The 1971 Dolphins lost the Super Bowl to Dallas. In 1972 the Dolphins were undefeated. The '73 Dolphins beat Minnesota in the Super Bowl 24-7 and they were 12–2. Those two seasons the Dolphins were 32–2 with two championships. That's as good a two-year run as anyone's ever had. Over five seasons between 1970 and 1974 they were 65–15–1 with three Super Bowl appearances. That's tough.

Why am I not putting them any higher? I don't think they had the high level of talent that some of these other teams had. Only one guy on that defense is in the Hall of Fame and that's Nick Buoniconti. And their offense could best be described as efficient. They had a great running attack with Larry Csonka and Mercury Morris. Quarterback Bob Griese and his backup Earl Morrall didn't make a lot of mistakes, they played behind and had a very good offensive line. They were a ball control team. But they won football games.

4. 1940–43 Chicago Bears: I called Gil Brandt about this, who's been around the NFL for a billion years, and I brought up all these teams and Gil said, "Chris, don't leave one out." Which one? "Don't leave out those early '40 Bears teams." Back in the old days, George Halas ran the NFL. So he got all the best players whether it was quarterback Sid Luckman or the offensive linemen to protect him. So, I went back to look. The '40 Bears won the Western Division. In the championship game that year they beat the Redskins 73-0. The next year they went 10–1 and tied with Green Bay and then went on to beat them in the Western Division playoffs, 33-14. They beat the Giants in the championship game 37-9. So in two straight championship games they outscored their opponents 110-9. In '42 they were 11–0, undefeated in the regular season, but they lost the championship game 14-6 to a Redskin team that went 10-1. In '43 they came back and played the Redskins again in the championship and beat them 41-21. So, they won three championships in four years. In the three championship games they won, they outscored their opposition 151-30. That's dominant.

3. 1982–89 San Francisco 49ers: They won four Super Bowls in eight years, and you'll remember that they won two of them without Jerry Rice. The '81–'82 Niners were 13–3 and won their first Super Bowl. There was a strike in '82, so you almost have to give them a mulligan on that one. In '83 they lost a close playoff game to the Redskins 24-21 and got a lousy call to boot. They came back and won the Super Bowl in the 1984 season with that great team. And then they came back and won again in '88 and '89. They never lost a Super Bowl. There was some turnover among those teams. Joe Montana, Bill Walsh, and Ronnie Lott were the big constants. Roger Craig gave way to Wendell Tyler, Freddy Solomon was replaced by Jerry Rice, and guys came and went on the defense. The other constant was winning.

2. 1975-79 Pittsburgh Steelers: Chuck Noll's Steelers won four championships in a six-year period. They won two, took two years off, won two more. Actually they hardly took two years off. In '76 they lost to the Raiders in the championship game when their offensive line and their running backs were all banged up. The next year they lost to Denver in the playoffs 34-21. The Steelers were 4–0 in the Super Bowl and that's a big consideration to me. These Steelers and the Niners didn't lose a Super Bowl and that's why they're ahead of the Dolphins and the Bears.

Although there was very little personnel turnover, the team changed character a little—they won their first two with defense and their last two with offense. Their number of Hall of Famers is mind-boggling: Lynn Swann, John Stallworth, Franco Harris, Terry Bradshaw, Mike Webster, Jack Lambert, Jack Ham, Mean Joe Greene, Mel Blount, and of course the coach, Chuck Noll.

1. 1961-67 Green Bay Packers: No other way around it. The Pack won five championships in seven years. They won in '61, '62, '65, '66, and '67. In '63 they were 11–2–1 and didn't make the playoffs because the Bears were 11–1–2. In 1964 they were 8–5–1, still pretty respectable. Then they came back to win three in a row from 1965 to '67. Lombardi's teams were were 9–1 in the postseason. Hall of Famers? They had Hall of Famers galore: Bart Starr, Jim Taylor, Forrest Gregg, Ray Nitschke, Herb Adderley, Willie Davis, Jim Ringo, Paul Hornung, Henry Jordan, Willie Wood, and Lombardi. That's eleven. And that's the greatest football dynasty ever.

BYE BYE BOYS

The one team that I'm not putting in here is the '90s Cowboys that won three championships. They're offense was excellent with Troy Aikman, Emmitt Smith, and Michael Irvin, but outside of Deion Sanders, the defense wasn't really up to par. Although they were very good, it was the era of the salary cap and I just don't think they're in the same league with my top five dynasties.

BEST OF THE BEST

These are the top single-season NFL teams of all time:

5. 1950 Cleveland Browns: Talk about starting off with a bang. In their very first game in the NFL, Paul Brown's Browns beat the defending champion Eagles 35-10. The Eagles had gone 11–1 the year before.

They went on to post a 10–2 record, scoring 310 points and allowing only 144, the best differential in the league. They beat the Giants in the divisional playoffs to snap a tie, and behind Otto Graham and Marion Motley they beat the Rams to win the championship, coming back from a 28-20 fourth quarter deficit.

4. 1972 Dolphins: Yes, they went undefeated. I'm going to tell you why the '72 Dolphins are not the top team of all time. The average record of the teams they beat that year was 8–6. That's not phenomenal. They won the division by seven games. In a playoff game against the Browns they trailed with five minutes left. In the championship game against Pittsburgh they needed a fake punt from Larry Seiple to win the game. In the Super Bowl of that year the Redskins were favored. Although the Dolphins dominated the game, they won by only a touchdown. That's gutsy, but it's not the greatest football team of all time.

3. 1961 Packers: It's the best Packer team out of all of them. They were 11–3. They destroyed the Giants in a championship game 37-0. I can hear it now: "Why don't you put the '62 Packers ahead of the '61 Packer team, because the '62 Packer team was 13–1." A couple of reasons. The 1961 team scored more points and had a better point differential. They were a little younger, a little fresher, a little hungrier. And they were more dominant in the championship game.

2. 1984 Niners: They were 15–1, scored 475 points. They lost in the middle of October to Pittsburgh 20-17 at Candlestick Park. That was it. They dominated in the postseason. They beat the Giants. They mauled the Bears in the championship game. They killed Miami in the Super Bowl, 38-16. The Niners defense shut down Dan Marino, and that year he threw 48 touchdown passes. They had a great young secondary. They had a good pass rush. And they had Joe Montana at his peak.

1. 1975 Steelers: Ask people who know football which was the best team of all time and most people will tell you it was the 1975 Steelers. They were 12–2 and played in a very tough division. Cincinnati was 11–3. Houston was 10–4. They allowed only 162 points, the second best in football. They went out there in the Super Bowl and beat Dallas 21-17. They beat two very good teams, Baltimore and Oakland, in the playoffs. They had a tremendous blend of offense and defense, and the core of this team would win four championships. That, my friends, is the best football team of all time.

The Hatfields and the McCoys

What are the ingredients for a great sports rivalry?

Like the Capulets and the Montagues, like Kennedy and Nixon, like Wile E. Coyote and the Roadrunner, great rivals understand one thing: The only thing more important than you winning is the other guy losing. Mad Dog examines some of the sports world's classic blood feuds.

What makes a great sports rivalry? Well, the first thing a great rivalry needs is the intensity of the fans. You cannot have a rivalry in sports unless the fans are really really into it on both sides. The Giants are coming in, the Red Sox are coming in, the Jets are coming in, Duke's coming in, the Cowboys are coming in, the Islanders are coming in. So you circle the date on your calendar. You wear the crazy colors, make the signs, think up a rude chant. Without fan intensity you cannot have a great rivalry, that's all there is to it.

You know you have a great rivalry when you can never, ever root for that opponent no matter what the circumstances. You're a Yankee fan and the Red Sox are playing the Mets in the World Series. You hate the Mets but you still can't bring yourself to root for the Red Sox to beat the Mets. You actually have to root for the Mets. That's a great rivalry.

To sustain a rivalry, both teams have to have some kind of success against each other. You can't have a one-sided rivalry. You have to have each team be able to win a few. So even in the Yankees–Red Sox rivalry, which is sort of one-sided, the Red Sox have had some years where they've been right there with the Yankees—in the late '40s and early '50s, the mid-'70s, and some in the mid- to late 1990s. If it's one-sided all the time, who the heck cares? How excited can you get beating the stuffing out of somebody time after time? When you win some and then you lose some, when that other team breaks your heart a few times, it builds up hatred for the opponent.

Number three, you have to play each other a lot. For instance, the Jets and the Giants or the 49ers and the Raiders can't have a great rivalry because they play only once every three years. The Dodgers and Yankees, that's not a rivalry anymore either, because these teams haven't played each other with something on the line for decades.

Finally, when I am talking rivalry, I want a little bit of history, folks. I don't want a rivalry that gets hot because both teams are good for three or four years like Miami–Notre Dame or Giants-Diamondbacks, or the Yankees-A's. That's a start, but let's see them keep doing it for twenty, thirty years. I want a rivalry you can trace from generation to generation. The Giants and Cowboys have played twice a year for forty-two years. The Packers and Bears have played since the days of George Halas and Curly Lambeau. Those are rivalries.

And it helps to have a little proximity. Most of your great rivals are relatively close to one another geographically. The Giants and Dodgers weren't that far apart on either coast. The Yankees–Red Sox are not that far. Michigan–Ohio State, not that far. Duke and North Carolina are eight miles apart, practically walking distance. That's important because it allows the fans to travel to see some games in enemy territory.

Let me throw one other thing in the rivalry situation. There are never any deals between the two teams. The Giants are not trading with the Dodgers, the football Giants are not trading with the Cowboys, the Islanders aren't trading with the Rangers, and Duke's not sharing recruiting information with North Carolina. Bo Schembechler and Woody Hayes probably didn't sit around in the off-season and talk about what they planned to do with their offenses. You don't trade with your hated opponent, you just don't do it. The reason is that when it backfires, it hurts twice as much. The Red Sox were burned time and time again by the Yankees, from Babe Ruth to the Danny Cater–Sparky Lyle deal.

Sometimes you'll have players crossing the line because of free agency, or a deal involving a third team—like Mike Torrez switching sides in the Yankee–Red Sox rivalry. Seeing Roger Clemens in a Yankee uniform simply smacks of treason to a Red Sox fan. And it only serves to make the rivalry a little more intense.

Here are some of the sports world's truly classic rivalries:

Baseball, Red Sox-Yankees: It's obvious, but it's a great rivalry. From the 1920s on, Boston has hated New York and vice versa. That's all there is to it. The Yankees stole Babe Ruth. They have played so many times against each other, so many close races, like 1949, when the Yankees were down by a half game coming into the last weekend and swept the Sox in the last two games of the season at Yankee Stadium. Obviously 1978 was phenomenal (see "Down to the Wire," page 190). And while the Yankees have historically had the upper hand, the Red Sox have had enough success to make it interesting.

Honorable Mention: Dodgers-Giants is obviously a classic, too. It's a rivalry that's been sustained for over a hundred years on both coasts. Through the 1950s and early '60s there were some tremendous pennant races and a couple of playoffs (see "Down to the Wire," page 190). Giants fans hate the Dodgers more than the other way around, but I betcha Dodger fans rooted for the Angels in the 2002 World Series.

College Basketball, Duke-North Carolina: That's a rivalry. They're eight miles apart, they can't stand each other. You had two all-time great coaches, Dean Smith and Mike Krzyzewski, and you've got two great teams usually both in the thick of it for the national championship. The universities are very different, and the fans are super-intense, especially on the Duke end of it with those Cameron Crazies. This one has all the elements.

NBA, Sixers-Celtics: The cities are not that far apart geographically, and they are old, established NBA teams. Wilt Chamberlain and Bill Russell squared off in many playoff series against one another. Then Larry Bird and Julius Erving had a chance to renew the feud. Even in the last ten years, when both teams have been up and down, the 2002 five-game playoff series had a little sense of that rivalry. Allen Iverson and Paul Pierce were picking up where these guys left off. That's a very very good NBA rivalry.

Honorable Mention: I would put Lakers and Celtics in there, too, only because they have played against each other so many times. They play only twice a year during the regular season, but they had two periods when they played every year with a title on the line—the 1960s when Jerry West and Elgin Baylor kept losing to the Bill Russell Celtics, six times in all, three times in a seven-game series. Then of course in the 1980s you had Bird's Celtics taking on Magic Johnson's Lakers in three different finals with L.A. winning two of three (see "Do You Believe in Magic?," page 270).

College Football, Michigan–Ohio State: You can come up with a lot of rivalries in college football: Oklahoma-Texas, Oregon–Oregon State, Florida–Florida State, Alabama-Auburn. But the one that I think has the most staying power and the most juice around the country is Michigan–Ohio State. The Michigan–Ohio State game means something to the college football fan around the country. Oregon–Oregon State doesn't mean anything to a guy in Florida. Washington–Washington State doesn't mean anything to a guy in Ohio; even Florida–Florida State, if one of those teams is having a lousy year, it doesn't have a lot of juice in New York. I like Michigan–Ohio State. You know they play every year, and there's usually something on the line: a Big Ten championship, a berth at the Rose Bowl, every now and then a chance at a national championship.

Remember 1968, Ohio State's national championship year, when the Buckeyes went for a two-point conversion on the last touchdown to make it 50-14? Asked why, Woody Hayes said, "I would have gone for three if I could." That's how much they hate each other. I love it.

Pro Football, Raiders-Chiefs: The Raider game is *the* game on Kansas City's schedule. They're not waiting for the Bronco game or the Charger game. The Chiefs could go 0–14 in their other games, but if they beat the

Raiders twice you know a lot of K.C. fans would be happy. It's an annual bloodbath, one that goes back to the old AFL, to Len Dawson and George Blanda. It still rankles John Madden to this day that in 1969 Oakland beat Kansas City in the preseason, then twice in the regular season. But the Chiefs beat the Raiders in the AFL championship game 17-7 and went on to win the Super Bowl. More than thirty years later he still remembers. Take note of the fact that when they realigned the divisions in the NFL, they didn't move Kansas City out of Oakland's division. They moved Seattle out even though Seattle is much closer to Oakland than Kansas City is. The Chiefs and Raiders is a good one.

Honorable Mention: Almost any matchup in either of two divisions: the old NFC Central and the NFC East. Lions-Vikings. Bears-Packers. Giants-Redskins. Giants-Eagles. The Cowboys and just about anyone.

NHL, Rangers and Islanders: This might be the best intracity rivalry in sports. They've been in the same division forever and have played a whole chain of classic playoff series. And Ranger fans, who had been waiting for a Cup forever, really resented the success that the Islanders had in the early 1980s. The Islanders on the other hand have always felt a little like

---

WHAT'S THE HUBBUB, BUB?

These rivalries are overrated in my book.

Army-Navy: I'm sorry, folks, I know people get all wrapped up in Army-Navy. When both teams are 0–8, I can't get excited about it. I know it's got tradition, history. proximity. hatred, and all the things you need for a great rivalry. But the level of competition is just awful. It's Division I-AA football.

Yale-Harvard: If you went to Yale or Harvard it is a big deal. But I didn't, so it's not a big deal to me. I couldn't care less.

Cubs-Cardinals: A very overrated rivalry. When was the last time the Cardinals and the Cubs went head-to-head in the pennant race? Never. These teams have never both been good at the same time.

second-class citizens in New York. Both teams have fallen on hard times a little lately, but the mutual hatred is still there.

Tennis, Martina Navratilova and Chris Evert: This is probably the best rivalry in individual sports. Pete Sampras and Andre Agassi didn't play long enough, and Björn Borg–John McEnroe petered out when Borg quit. Ali-Frazier gave us three fights, two of them classics. But Martina and Chrissie played over and over and over again, almost always in the finals. There was a classic matchup of styles—the serve-and-volleyer versus the baseliner. And while they respected each other, they didn't like each other that much.

Hall Passes

Which statistical thresholds in baseball are most sacred?

"Excuse me, sir, can you tell me how to get to Cooperstown?" Hit 500 home runs, son. When Hall of Fame voters are filling out their ballots, you know their baseball encyclopedias aren't far away. Mad Dog ranks the biggest statistical stepping-stones to baseball immortality.

Careerwise there are three magic numbers in baseball: 300 wins, 500 homers, 3,000 hits. Reach any of those milestones and you're going to Cooperstown. Fall short and you're probably a baseball mortal. Robin Yount and Tony Gwynn got 3,000 hits and they're in. Al Oliver and Harold Baines? Close but no cigar. When Eddie Murray hit his five hundredth home run, he could start packing his bags for Cooperstown. Jose Canseco and Dave Kingman didn't make it to 500 homers, so they're going to have to buy a ticket. In the pitching department it's the same scenario. Don Sutton and Phil Niekro reached 300 wins and they're in the Hall. Tommy John and Bert Blyleven didn't, and they're not.

But which of these milestones is really the most formidable? Let's take a look at each category in two ways. First I'll look back at the players who've already achieved each milestone. And looking forward, I'll project how hard it'll be for today's players to reach these benchmarks.

Looking Back

300 Wins: When I look at the list of 300-game winners, I see a couple, maybe three who just simply don't belong in the Hall of Fame. If these guys had won 294 games, they wouldn't have been voted in, and as far as I'm concerned they shouldn't get in even with 300. Phil Niekro is not a Hall of Fame pitcher. He's a knuckleballer who pitched until he was forty-six. His career winning percentage was .537. Those are not Hall of Fame numbers. Don Sutton is not a Hall of Fame pitcher either. He won twenty games once, never led the league in anything important, and never finished higher than third in the Cy Young voting (see "Rep Artists," page 94). Gaylord Perry is a little better—he won a couple of Cy Youngs—but his career winning percentage is .542. He's a borderline case at best, especially since he has the spitball to thank for a lot of those wins. With these guys already in, the 300-win club has the most riffraff for the time being.

3,000 Hits: Looking at the bottom of baseball's 3,000-hit club list, it's mostly great players, if not immortals. Robin Yount might not be an all-time great player, but he did play shortstop for part of his career. Same with Cal Ripken. Eddie Murray might be a little overrated (see "Rep Artists," page 94), but he did hit 500 homers, and Dave Winfield hit almost that many. Roberto Clemente was probably the best defensive right fielder of all time. Lou Brock stole a million bases. Al Kaline was a fine all-around player. In short, I might not vote for some of these guys on the first ballot, and a few I might not vote for at all, but I wouldn't argue to kick them out either. All of these guys would have a legitimate claim to Cooperstown even with 2,900 hits.

500 Homers: The 500-homer club is as close as you'll get to a list of baseball immortals. Aaron. Ruth. Mays. Bonds. And even on the lower reaches of the list, the quality still stands up. Eddie Murray and Eddie Mathews might be a little borderline, but Mathews was one of the top five third basemen of all time, and Murray did get 3,000 hits. In fact, this is really almost a subgroup. Call it the Dave Kingman Effect, but until about fifteen years ago, every player who retired with even 400 home runs—

Gehrig, Musial, Willie Stargell, Yaz, Billy Williams, Duke Snider—got a plaque in upstate New York. And you can make a case for most of the guys who fell short of 500 being legit Hall of Famers. That's why the current 500-home-run club is the most exclusive in my eyes.

Looking Ahead

500 Homers: The 500-homer club won't remain very exclusive for long. With the offensive explosion of the 1990s, there are a dozen or more active players who'll make serious runs at 500 homers. Some are great, like Jeff Bagwell and Mike Piazza. Some are not so great, like Juan Gonzalez, Fred McGriff, and Rafael Palmeiro. Some started fast and tailed off: Ken Griffey, Jr., and Frank Thomas. Some guys have compiled quietly: Jim Thorne and Manny Ramirez. And some guys are a long way away but closing ground fast: Vladimir Guerrero and Andruw Jones. And there are even a few guys who might hit 700 before they're through: Barry Bonds, Sammy Sosa, and Alex Rodriguez. Not all of these guys are going to make it, of course, and some others will no doubt emerge. But in an era when hitting 50 home runs can leave you 20 behind the league leader, 500 home runs isn't quite what it used to be.

3,000 Hits: The offensive explosion that has raised home run totals dramatically hasn't had the same effect on hit totals. The spate of guys who reached the milestone recently—Wade Boggs, Tony Gwynn, Cal Ripken, and Rickey Henderson—is a little bit of a blip. At the end of the 2002 season there were only two players under the age of thirty-five with over 2,000 hits: Roberto Alomar and Ken Griffey, Jr. A handful of older players—like Rafael Palmeiro, Bonds, or maybe Craig Biggio could make a run. But most of the rest of the contenders—A-Rod, Guerrero, Derek Jeter—are close to a decade away. The 3,000-hit club will grow, but slowly and not for a while.

300 Wins: With the increased use of the five-man rotation, this threshold is going to rise from kind of tough to almost impossible. Among today's active pitchers there are only three who have a decent shot at 300—Roger Clemens, Greg Maddux, and Tom Glavine. That's it. To make this club in a day when 32 starts is considered a full year's work, you're going to have to come up young and pitch very well until you're past forty, without any major injuries. Plenty of contemporary pitchers who were star pitchers with good long careers, like David Cone and Kevin Brown, will struggle to get to 200 wins. Most of the Cooperstown candidates of the twenty-first century—Randy Johnson, Pedro Martinez, John Smoltz—won't get anywhere near 300. In the future, 300-game winners will be the exception on induction weekend, not the rule.

DO THE MATH

To get to 500 homers, you'll have to hit 35 homers a season for just over fourteen years.

To get to 3,000 hits, you'll have to collect 180 hits a year for almost seventeen years.

To get to 300 wins, you'll have to average 17 wins a year for almost eighteen years.

My Back Pages

What makes a great sports section?

For most sports fans, the first exercise they get every day is sprinting down the driveway to get the newspaper so they can read the sports section. Mad Dog examines the role of fish wrapping in the era of electronic media.

In this age of websites and sports news channels, specialty magazines, television, and even sports talk radio, what's the role of a newspaper? When you open your newspaper in the morning, you probably already know what happened to the hometown teams the night before. So what are you looking for in a paper? The newspaper's role has changed. It wasn't that long ago that you relied on the newspaper to inform you—who won, who lost, and what the score was. Today a good newspaper's job is not only to give you the who, what, when, where, and how, but the *why*. It's about intrepid reporting. It's about strong opinions. It's about smart analysis. So here are the things that I want to see in my morning paper.

Send the Writer: You know it's a big-time sports section when in the middle of May you can read a French Open story by the paper's tennis guy. I don't want to read an AP story about the French Open. And don't try to fake it by slapping the wire service writer's byline on there the way the *New York Post* does. You won't fool anyone. If your paper is in a football town but you have a writer from your newspaper covering the Lakers-Kings Western Conference final, you're doing a good job. If you publish in a basketball town yet you have a writer at the Avalanche–Red Wings Western Conference final, you've done a nice job. It's expensive, I know. The *Des Moines Register* probably can't send a guy to Paris, and the *Portland Oregonian* can't have a bureau at the Daytona 500, but it's one way to separate yourself from the pack.

Columnists Who Have Opinions: I want my columnists to have a little bite. I don't want vanilla columnists. Think like a fan. Keep your fingers on the pulse of the local sports scene. Don't be afraid to take a stand. Guys like Harvey Araton, Mike Lupica, and Bob Ryan do that. You see their byline and you know you're going to have something to chew on. That's important.

Be Late: Make sure that you have a late edition. If the Broncos are playing on *Monday Night Football,* I want to be able to go to a newsstand in the downtown area at eight o'clock the next morning and pick up the Tuesday *Denver Post* and find coverage of the game.

All the Box Scores, Please: It's a small thing, but if you can't give me the late box scores in your late edition, I had better see them the next day. If the Angels and A's played an extra-inning game on Wednesday night that ended at 2:45 A.M. East Coast time, I want to see that box score in Friday's paper.

A Sunday Meal: I want a meaty Sunday newspaper. I want to be able to sit down for an hour and really be able to dig in. I want columns on each of the four big sports and some coverage of golf or tennis or boxing. And I don't want it just during the season. I want to be able to read about the NFL in July, about Major League Baseball in November.

Cover the Media: I want a TV-radio column in there. The networks and the broadcasters have become such a big part of the game that you really need to cover them. I love the gossip, but I also want to see some reporting here, too. Be critical if you have to be critical. But cover it.

Be Enterprising: Don't just tell me what happened. If it's a big game, I saw it myself. I don't need to read a description of what happened in the game. I want some reporting. If we're talking about that Monday night game in Denver, I need to hear what Mike Shanahan has to say. If there's a big play, I want to hear from the guys involved. If something happened that the TV cameras didn't catch, tell me about it.

I want quotes and lots of them. That's what a newspaper can give you that television won't. The TV crews are happy with the sound bite. The beat writers should be able to ask the probing question. A newspaper may not be able to be first much anymore, but it can still be best.

JOURNALISTIC DARWINISM

I think in towns that have more than one newspaper, each paper is going to be better. I have been in one-paper towns—Orlando, St. Louis—and for the most part the quality of the journalism suffers because of that. There's no "I've got to top that" mentality. Now you can go overboard with that, where you sort of develop a media frenzy like you have in New York and London and you get a tabloid thing going, in which breaking a story becomes more important than whether it's important or even whether it's true. Tabloids need that big back-page splash to sell papers, so that's another kind of negative. But in general, competition is good.

Money for Nothing

Are professional athletes overpaid?

Remember Richie Hebner? It was only twenty years ago that the Pirate slugger spent his off-season digging graves in a cemetery. If he played to-day he'd probably spend December digging life on his new yacht. Professor Mad Dog looks at the socioeconomics of sports.

I think we can all agree that $10 million is a lot of money. But is it too much? Here are some of the classic arguments that some fans—and a lot of agents—will make when discussing the economics—and the ethics—of sports salaries.

The Harrison Ford Factor: If Harrison Ford can make $20 million a movie, why can't Shaquille O'Neal make that in a season? Or, if the CEO for a major corporation can make $25 million a year, why can't A-Rod? That's the first argument.

The Rebuttal: Harrison Ford is making $20 million a movie because people go watch Harrison Ford movies. There's a direct correlation. "I'm going to go see the Harrison Ford movie." Who goes to watch Kirk Rueter pitch for the San Francisco Giants?

Second, Harrison Ford doesn't have a long-term guaranteed contract. He's an independent contractor. Since he gets a piece of the gross, a lot of his income is tied to the success of the movie. But if Kerry Collins has a bad season and breaks his thumb and plays only eight games, is he going to give back some of his salary to the football Giants? No, he's not. If Harrison Ford makes a bomb, he's not giving that $20 million back either. But that's going to affect his pay for the next movie.

And then there's the budget-quality equation. If a studio spends the ex-tra money to get Nicolas Cage instead of Vin Diesel, that means they might have to scale back on the explosions and the car chases, but the movie will still be better overall. In this age of salary caps and luxury taxes, getting one expensive superstar can actually hurt a team if it means that they have to cheap out on defensive backs or relief pitchers. Look at A-Rod and the Rangers.

The Greedy Owner Aspect: The second argument you hear is that if the athletes don't make the big money, then the owner will, and he's not going to pass those savings along to you, the fan. If Shaquille O'Neal or Mike Piazza or Barry Bonds were to work for half the money, the owners would still charge you the same amount for tickets.

The Rebuttal: Well, my first point is that the owners take the risk. They bought the team, so isn't it reasonable for them to try to make a return on it? The guy who owns the McDonald's down the block isn't there flipping burgers, but he put up the money to build the building and buy the meat. Like it or not, that's capitalism, sports fans.

As for ticket prices, I will grant you that they would have gone up over the past twenty, twenty-five, thirty years—the same way that a movie ticket and a loaf of bread have gone up—even if athletes' salaries hadn't skyrocketed. But, you can't possibly sit there and tell me that there's no correlation at all between higher salaries for players and ticket prices. A Super Bowl ticket ten years ago was not $400. It wasn't. You can't tell me that if the Yankee payroll was $40 million instead of $137 million, that the cost of the ticket would still be $35. Ticket prices would go down if for no other reason than that the fans would demand it.

The Short Career Theory: And finally, they'll argue that an athlete's career is short. In any game, on any play, he can get injured and never play again. He's got to make as much as he can as soon as he can.

The Rebuttal: The first thing is that, except in football, athletes have guaranteed contracts. If they get hurt, they get paid anyway. And with advances in sports medicine, the chances of a career-ending injury are getting slimmer all the time. And let's do the math. If an average fan busts his fanny for thirty years and tops out at $125,0000, that's not even $4 million for a whole life's work. The sports world is filled with players who make $4 million for six months of going to practice and sitting on the bench. That's ridiculous. Plus players have all sorts of other ways to make money, from endorsements to appearing at fantasy camps to signing autographs at card shows. And of course when that player retires, he's not going on Social Security. There's nothing stopping him from going out and getting a job selling insurance or teaching school just like anyone else. So don't blame me if I don't feel too much sympathy for Jayson Williams or Antonio McDyess.

So are athletes overpaid? What do you think I think? The bottom line is that these guys are getting paid to play a game. The average fan wouldn't do Harrison Ford's job or some CEO's job for nothing. But he would—and often does—shag flies or shoot baskets for nothing. I'm not saying that Barry Bonds or Kobe Bryant should do the same. But they should at least appreciate that they've got it pretty good.

Open and Shut

Who is the best closer of all time?

Late and close. Like the bottom of the ninth with the tying run at third and the go-ahead run at second. That's when a closer shows what he's made of. When the game rides on one batter, Mad Dog tells you who gets his call to the bullpen.

Relievers are a little hard to figure. They're vitally important, but only if you have a good team. Do you think that the Yankees would have won four World Series without Mariano Rivera? Of course not. But if you put Rivera on the Kansas City Royals, would they even get out of last place? Nope. If you can't hand him a late-inning lead, your closer's just going to be sitting in the bullpen shucking sunflower seeds.

And I don't think that you can really measure a closer by his statistics. If he lets an inherited base runner score, it doesn't tarnish his own ERA. And I think saves and blown saves are misleading, too. It's one thing to preserve a three-run lead in the middle of July against the Brewers, but quite another thing to come in against the Braves in September with a one-run lead with the bases loaded and one out.

That said, I think there are four relievers who I consider unhittable, guys who would get my vote for the Hall of Fame. The first is Rollie Fingers. He had great stuff and a rubber arm. Dick Williams would bring him in to get out of a fifth-inning jam, and he'd finish out the game. He won an MVP award, and deserved it. Dennis Eckersley was amazing, too. Had a great career as a starter but when he was converted to the bullpen, he came right after guys. No nibbling. Just a great competitor. And you've all seen the ice water in Mariano Rivera's veins. He'll just come in, throw that cutter, and make major league hitters look like Little Leaguers. They're all great, but I saw Kirk Gibson and Roberto Alomar hit some big postseason homers against Eckersley. And while Mariano's been better in big spots, he did give up that dinger to Sandy Alomar in the 1997 division series and that World Series–winning rally by the Diamondbacks.

So I'm going to take Bruce Sutter. That split-fingered pitch of his was simply unhittable. He was great with St. Louis, but I think he might have been at his best when he was with the Cubs at Wrigley, where he won a Cy Young. If he got two strikes on you, the at-bat was over. He was completely automatic. He's not in Cooperstown yet, but he's definitely a Hall of Famer in my book. And if I need a big out, he's the guy I want on the mound.

THE SAVE KING

Lee Smith? Sure, he saved 478 games. An all-time record. But ask anyone who saw him pitch. He was hittable. Steve Garvey killed him in the playoffs. And the baseball writers recognized that at the time. He cracked the top ten in the MVP voting only once, and never came close to a Cy Young. He's not a Hall of Famer, but he might get in because he has the numbers—the voters are going to find it tough to keep him out with the all-time save record.

For the Love of the Pinstripes

Are you a fan of the player—or the uniform?

"And just before the White Sox played the Red Sox in the rubber game of a three-game set, the Pale Hose completed a five-player trade that sends . . ." Mad Dog explores the delicate issue of fan allegiances.

This is a classic chicken-and-egg argument. Are you rooting for the team or the players who play on it? When you isolate it to just one game, one season, it's pretty hard to separate. But to me being a sports fan is about signing on for the duration. It's a long-term—even lifetime—commitment. And when you think about it that way, look at the big picture, it becomes clear: You're a fan of the uniform.

I was a Giants baseball fan long before Barry Bonds showed up, and I'll be a Giants fan long after Barry Bonds leaves. I was a Giants fan long before Dusty Baker ever showed up, and I'm still a fan now that he's gone. You have a connection with the team, with its stadium, with its history, with its tradition, with your fellow fans. It's a lifetime full of memories.

Players come and players go. If Brett Favre got hurt or left the Green Bay Packers, they'd find somebody else to play quarterback. Look what happened to the Patriots when Drew Bledsoe got hurt. Tom Brady started taking the snaps, and away they go. When you see a guy come up as a rookie, there's one thing that's for certain. You realize that one way or another—whether he gets traded, injured, leaves as a free agent, or just retires—there's going to come a day when he's not going to be on your team anymore.

And it is—or should be—about the greater good of the team. Can you tell me right now that if Derek Jeter wasn't a Yankee and Alex Rodriguez was, you would be less of a Yankee fan? Look at Roger Clemens. He came to New York after playing for years for their hated rivals, the Red Sox. Here's a guy who started a beanball war with the Yankees when he was with the Blue Jays. The Yankees gave up a very popular player—David Wells—to get him. Do you think Yankee fans had a problem with Roger Clemens being a Yankee? Maybe for a little while. But I was there that first year when they gave him a deafening standing ovation during the World Series against Atlanta. All was forgiven because he was wearing the pinstripes and helped the Yankees win the World Series. Even though the Yankees were already up three-zip before Roger's clincher.

I'm not going to tell you that you shouldn't be annoyed when a team makes a trade and deals your favorite player. I couldn't believe it when the Giants traded Matt Williams for Jeff Kent. It ticked me off to no end. But because I was a Giants fan, I learned to like Jeff Kent. That's the way it is. I'm a fan of the team.

Now if that team switches cities it might be a little different. If the Dodgers move to L.A., or the Browns move to Baltimore, I can understand a fan saying, "Enough. It's the *Baltimore* Colts, not the *Indianapolis* Colts." But with these rare exceptions, it's a pretty simple equation. Players are there until the end of their next contract, and maybe not even that long. Teams aren't going anywhere.

Touching Them All

Which home run record is the greatest?

From Roger Maris pulling out his hair to Barry Bonds high-fiving his son at home, it's one of the most resonant moments in baseball: breaking the single-season home run record. Dog looks back and ranks the record chases.

There isn't a more sacred single-season record in sports than baseball's home run record. It's simple to understand, and it's barely budged over the course of seventy years. Since 1919, only four guys in history have ever held the mark. (No, we're not counting Sammy Sosa, who held the record for a couple of innings in 1998.) But which slugger had the toughest row to hoe? I'm going to put them in order last to first as far as degree of difficulty:

4. Babe Ruth, 1927: This is going to surprise people, but I'm going to put Ruth fourth. You're going to say, "Hold on, Chris, he hit 60 home runs. The record stood for thirty-four years. How can he be number four?" First off, the Bambino already owned the home run record; he'd hit 59 in 1921. So adding one more to the record in 1927 was no big deal. It was the fourth time he broke the record. I think that everyone, Ruth included, thought that someone would come along a couple of years later—maybe even Ruth himself—and hit 62 or 65. It wasn't a magical plateau at that point. Add in the fact that everybody was rooting for Ruth. I don't think that pitchers or managers were making a special effort to keep him from hitting homers. Was 60 some kind of magical plateau? I don't think so.

Perhaps most important, he had Lou Gehrig helping him. In '27, Ruth hit 20 home runs in the month of September and until the last month of the season Gehrig was right with him in the home run chase. So on the one hand he had Gehrig to kind of pace him, but there wasn't any kind of Maris-Mantle animosity. Ruth also had Gehrig batting behind him, so pitchers couldn't walk him nine million times. You can't ask for better protection in the batting order.

And finally, the conditions were much easier for Ruth. There were no night games. No split-finger fastballs. There was no relief pitching. He wasn't facing a lefty specialist in the seventh inning, and Mariano Rivera in the ninth inning. He was the Sultan, but it was an era where Swat, at least for him, was cheap.

3. Barry Bonds, 2001: Bonds is in the third slot for a few reasons. First off, the record had already just been broken by Mark McGwire, so there just wasn't as much pressure on Bonds. His chase just didn't capture everyone's attention the same way that McGwire's did. Bonds did one media interview before a series, talked after a home run, and that was the end of it. After McGwire reached 70 and Sammy Sosa hit 60 three years in a row, it took some of the mystique away. Bonds isn't exactly Mr. Popularity, so it's not like all of America was waiting with bated breath to see him break the record. The Giants were also in the middle of a pennant race, so that diverted attention from the home run record. And for that matter, so did September 11—after all that happened in New York and Washington, it was a little hard for people to get too excited about Bonds taking a run at a baseball record.

Now Bonds had three or four factors working against him. First, Pac Bell is far and away the toughest home run park on this list, just brutal.

Bonds hit 36 home runs at home and 37 on the road. The second thing is, he didn't have a great home run hitter hitting behind him. Ruth had Gehrig, Maris had Mantle, Bonds had Jeff Kent. Kent was the reigning MVP, but early on teams decided they were going to take their chances with him instead of Bonds. Bonds got nothing to hit in the second half of the year and he broke his own record for intentional walks as well as setting the all-time walks record, which had been on the books since Ruth set it in 1923. And finally, he had the best overall year of any player on this list. And one more reason I put Bonds ahead of Ruth: He hit 13 more homers.

2. Mark McGwire: He gets the second slot based on the fact that 61 was such a tough nut to crack. Maris's record stood longer than Ruth's—thirty-six years. And 61 became one of baseball's most famous numbers, right up there with 56 and .406. McGwire had to go after that.

And Big Red hit 58 in 1997, so he did a million interviews even before the season. Bonds on the other hand caught everybody by surprise—he'd hit only 49 homers the year before. The anticipation surrounding McGwire's run was immense. Plus McGwire had no big hitters hitting behind him. Brian Jordan ain't exactly Lou Gehrig. And he didn't have the pennant race to distract the fans, or the media. The Cardinals were terrible, so the whole year the whole deal at Busch or on the road was to see if McGwire can hit a home run.

On the other hand, I think Sammy Sosa was probably a benefit for McGwire and that's why he's a close second on this list. I think Sosa deflected some of the pressure. Sosa was everything that McGwire wasn't. McGwire was tense about the chase, like Maris. The pressure got to him, it bothered him. Sosa enjoyed it. He was a happy-go-lucky, let's-play-two type, and the Cubs were in a pennant race, all of which shifted attention away from McGwire. And McGwire, for his part, could almost forget about Maris a little and shift his focus to beating Sosa.

Here's the thing I give McGwire a lot of credit for. That last Friday of the season, the Cubs were in Houston, the Cardinals are home with Montreal. Both Sosa and McGwire had broken the record. That night, for about two at-bats, Sosa took the home run lead. We got into a situation where we might have had McGwire be the first to 62, and yet Sosa would win the home run title. It would have been very strange, not clean the way sports fans like it. There would have been an asterisk of a whole different kind on this record. But McGwire responded. Felipe Alou let the Expo staff pitch to him that last weekend, and he put the record out of reach. Remember that McGwire didn't just break the record, he demolished it. He broke the record by nine homers, which is more than Ruth, Maris, and Bonds combined.

1. Roger Maris, 1961: The other three guys on this list are Hall of Fame players, and they would have been Hall of Famers even if they didn't break the home run record. Maris wasn't. He was an imperfect guy doing this amazing thing. He wasn't the sort of guy that America felt deserved to break Babe Ruth's cherished record. We didn't have any problem with McGwire breaking Maris, because he's a better player. And we didn't really have any problem with Bonds breaking McGwire because he was a great player, too. Playing in Yankee Stadium, Maris had to deal with the ghost of the Fat Man. And he had to deal with the guy in the on-deck circle, the great Mickey Mantle. Mantle had a love-hate relationship with the New York fans, but in 1961 almost everyone thought that he was more deserving of the record than Maris. Even opposing pitchers were bearing down against Maris. He didn't have anyone laying in fastballs for him, that's for sure.

In terms of advantages, Maris had Mantle hitting behind him, so Maris

ON THE ASTERISK

The one thing I found interesting in Billy Crystal's great movie *61** is the discussion of the asterisk. Most baseball fans today think that Ford Frick was a total son of a gun for attaching that asterisk to Maris's record. What surprised me a lot in doing research and talking to guys was that before the season began, a lot of baseball players agreed with Frick. The *Sporting News* wrote a big editorial. The 162-game schedule was a new thing, and they thought that Maris—or anyone else trying to break a single-season record—had an unfair advantage with those extra eight games.

didn't get one intentional walk that season. And with that short right field porch, Yankee Stadium was perfect for his swing. But put that aside for a moment and savor this story. Roger Maris was an ordinary guy who did an incredible thing under incredible pressure. That's why he's number one.

The Classic Second-Guess

What are the biggest managerial blunders in baseball history?

As Rocky Bridges once said, there are three things that every man thinks he can do better than every other man. Start a fire. Run a hotel. And manage a baseball team. Mad Dog looks at some managerial moves that will make any second-guesser feel smart.

There is nothing better than a baseball game where the stakes are high, and you can play along with the manager and second-guess him to kingdom come. And baseball allows you to do that much more so than the other sports. In a big NBA postseason game, you can argue about whether a guy should be in or out of the game because of foul trouble, but it's really more of a players' situation. In hockey, you can talk about line changes or when to pull a goalie. In football, you can talk about a coach's decision to go for it on fourth and short.

But baseball is the sport where you can play right along with the manager, pinch hitter for pinch hitter, pitching change for pitching change. Sometimes he's right. Sometimes he's wrong. And sometimes he's dead wrong. In this list is a classic collection of what ifs, couldas, shouldas, and might have beens.

6. 1960 World Series: For some reason or another, Casey Stengel did not pitch Whitey Ford in games one, four, and seven against the Pirates. He pitched him in games two and six, which makes no sense whatsoever. Whitey was the Yankees' best pitcher, and even though he won only twelve games that year, he had a great ERA. But Stengel pitched him only twice in the Series, and both of his outings were complete game shutouts. And in game seven, the Yankees lose 10-9. And remember, there was no league championship series back then and the Yankees had won the division by eight games, so Stengel could have arranged the pitching rotation any way he wanted to. Stengel got fired after this series, in part because he was an old man, and in part because he made a lot of bad decisions in this Series, especially this one. How do you not pitch your best pitcher three times against Pittsburgh? It's mind-boggling. Stengel overmanaged to no end. He drove you crazy. And I tell you, if we had been doing a talk show in 1960, we would have killed Stengel for this move.

5. 1951 Dodgers-Giants Playoff: Dodger manager Chuck Dressen did a terrible job throughout this playoff. Brooklyn won the coin flip but elected to play the first game at home and the next two at the Polo Grounds, giving up home field in the deciding game. Why? Back in '46 in a playoff against the Cardinals, the Dodgers played the first game in St. Louis and lost, then traveled all day back to Brooklyn and played a flat game and got bounced out. Whoever made the decision—Ralph Branca thinks it was a ticket manager named Jack Collins—seemed to forget that the Polo Grounds were a lot closer to Brooklyn than St. Louis. Here are the repercussions of that decision. In game one at Ebbets Field, Bobby Thomson hit a home run contributing to a 3-1 win. And in game three at the Polo Grounds, the Giants won the pennant on the Shot Heard Round the World. If they had played game one at the Polo Grounds and game three at Ebbets Field, both of Thomson's homers would have been just long fly balls and the Dodgers win the pennant. Obviously Dressen should have insisted on having games two and three at home.

And of course, there's no way that Ralph Branca can pitch to Thomson in the ninth inning of game three. Thomson had owned Branca in the second half of the year, killed him, destroyed him. Branca had given up that home run to Thomson in game one. So Thomson's up with the game on the line, and what does Dressen do? He brings in Branca. That is just an asinine decision. Legend has it that Dressen had called down to the bullpen and was ready to bring in Clem Labine, but as he was on the phone, Labine bounced a curve so Dressen went with Branca instead.

That's not the way you run a baseball game. The bottom line is that this doesn't happen today, because with all the stats floating around, everyone and his brother would have known that Thomson beat Branca like a rented mule.

4. 1986 ALCS: Is there such a thing as being too much of a genius? Look at Gene Mauch. In game four of the ALCS, against the Red Sox, up 5-2, top of the ninth, leading three games to one, he totally overmanaged. He did a terrible job. Mike Witt was sailing along, pitching a great game. Witt gave up a two-run one-out homer to Don Baylor in the ninth, and I know that conventional wisdom says you take Witt out after giving up the home run. But if you made a commitment to go to the guy in the ninth inning, and he's been your best pitcher, you stay with him. Witt got Dwight Evans for the second out, so leave him in the game for goodness' sake. But Mauch panics and yanks him. I remember watching the game and saying, "Gene, don't take him out." This game had echoes of that 1964 pennant race, when Mauch pitched Jim Bunning and Chris Short on two days' rest down the stretch and ended up blowing a six-and-a-half-game lead with twelve games left. This ALCS had the same kind of overmanaging.

Mauch brings Gary Lucas in to pitch to Rich Gedman, and he hit Gedman in the helmet on his first pitch. He takes Lucas out of the game and brings in Donnie Moore, his shaky closer, to pitch to Dave Henderson. *Bam.* He hits the two-run homer to give the Red Sox a lead in a game they'll win in eleven innings.

Mauch to me always made too many moves. He made everybody nervous. He made me nervous, rooting for the Angels. When you have a 5-2 lead in the ninth, making two big pitching changes really breaks the momentum of the game. It made you sit around and think about that last out. It's almost like while you were waiting for the game to continue, you had a feeling that something bad was about to happen.

3. 1977 ALCS: For the second year in a row the Yankees and Royals are playing in the fifth and deciding game of the ALCS. The year before, Kansas City lost with Mark Littell giving up a ninth-inning home run to Chris Chambliss. Now the Royals are again just three outs away from going to the World Series. Up 3-2, top of the ninth. This time Whitey Herzog has the brilliant idea of bringing in Dennis Leonard in relief. Leonard had been great in the Series—he beat the Yankees 6-2 in the third game, pitching a complete game.

But Dennis Leonard is a starter. He was a twenty-game winner. He had never saved a big game in his life. Dennis Leonard had exactly five relief appearances in his whole career, and one save. Under no circumstances whatsoever do you bring in Dennis Leonard to pitch that ninth inning. You don't do it. Not with one day off since his last start. I don't think that anyone but Herzog was surprised that Leonard gave up three runs in the ninth inning, and the Royals lost again. Whitey was playing with fire and he got burned.

2. 1985 NLCS: It's game six of the NLCS and the Dodgers are one out away from forcing a decisive game seven against the Cardinals. The situation facing Tom Lasorda: two outs, runners on second and third, and the Dodgers lead 5-4. At the plate is Jack Clark, who was 7-for-20 in the series. On deck is Andy Van Slyke, who was 1-for-10. First base is open. And for some reason or another, Lasorda pitches to Jack Clark. With Tom Niedenfuer, a guy who gave up a home run to Ozzie Smith—his first ever left-handed—the game before. But he's the closer, so Lasorda stays with him in game six And what happens? First pitch, a 450-foot homer to the pavilion in left. Pedro Guerrero smashed the outfield wall, he was so disgusted. That's the dumbest decision in the world. You do not let Jack Clark beat you. Dodgers lose the game 7-5 and lose the series.

1. 1986 World Series: Okay, Red Sox fans, turn the page. As painful as it is, I am obliged to talk about John McNamara's managing, or lack thereof, in game six against the Mets. McNamara ran a seminar of how not to manage a baseball game.

Mets manager Davey Johnson wasn't a genius that night either. He had first and second, nobody out, in the eighth inning of an elimination game, and he didn't bunt. You've got to get the guy to third there. If he did, we wouldn't be talking about this game now. It wasn't easy, but McNamara took Davey off the hook. That's how bad McNamara was.

It starts with taking Roger Clemens out of the game after seven innings, up 3-2. Roger Clemens that year was 24–4. He's young and he's throwing 90 miles an hour. When your franchise is six outs away from winning your first World Series in sixty-eight years, and you've got the Cy Young award winner on the mound, you've got to leave him in the game. It's a no-brainer. You're not saving him for a seventh game. So that's the first thing.

It gets worse. He pinch hit Mike Greenwell instead of Don Baylor late in that game. Only ten days before, with the Red Sox down 5-2 in the fifth game of the ALCS, Baylor hit a ninth-inning home run against Mike Witt, a tough right-handed pitcher at the very top of his game. If it weren't for Baylor, the Red Sox don't even go to the World Series. Why don't you let Baylor hit? It doesn't make any sense.

And finally, McNamara left Buckner in the game in the bottom of the tenth, ostensibly so that he could be on the field for the victory celebration. Dave Stapleton's got to play first base there. I know that Buckner should make that play on the ground ball, but you've got to get your best defense in there at 5-3, bottom of the tenth. Buckner, by the way, hit .188 in that series, so it wasn't like he was keeping his bat in the game just in case. That was a terrible job. So McNamara in '86, that's as bad as it gets.

Okay, all you would-be managers, what's the take-home lesson here? It seems to me that the common thread in almost all of these debacles is managing a playoff game or a World Series game differently than you would a regular season game. Bringing in starters in relief. Yanking a

---

COMING UP LEMONS

I used to think, until I looked at the game a little more carefully, that in game six of the 1981 World Series, Bob Lemon was right to pinch hit for Tommy John early in that game, and Tommy John was a complete jerk for getting mad about it.

The Yanks were down three games to two against the Dodgers, bottom of the fourth inning, 1-1, bases loaded and two outs. Everyone focused on John's reaction on the bench, acting like a baby, showing up his manager.

But we put all the accent on John's behavior instead of studying the situation. You can't pinch hit there. The score is tied. Tommy John is your best pitcher and he's pitched in big games his whole career. He pitched seven shutout innings in game two. Of course, Bobby Murcer didn't make Lemon look good by making the third out. And then George Frazier, who had already lost two games in that World Series, sealed the deal by giving up three runs in the top of the fifth. That's bad behavior by John. And bad managing by Lemon.

starter who's cruising. They committed the fatal error of overmanaging, trying to get cute, thinking about the postgame press conference instead of the game. It's a cliché to say that you should dance with who brung you, but there's a lot of truth to it, too.

Tiger, Tiger Burning Bright

Is Tiger Woods good for golf?

He's golf's answer to Babe Ruth. A savior in a red shirt who's given the game a giant makeover. But is Tiger Woods an unalloyed good? Mad Dog weighs in.

We all know some of the reasons why Tiger Woods is good for golf. Eyeballs to TV sets. He brings the ultra-casual fan to the game. The guy living in the South Bronx is going to watch Tiger at the U.S. Open because it's Tiger Woods and he can identify with him. He has trouble identifying with Phil Mickelson, who grew up at a country club in San Diego, but he can identify with Tiger Woods. So from that aspect you can't get enough of Tiger. It's great for the game.

And you've got to give him credit. He never takes a tournament off. You can go pay your thirty-five, forty bucks in September to see Tiger at the Milwaukee Open, and you know you're going to get your money's worth. It's a nothing event, but Tiger always comes to play. But there are a few negatives with Tiger.

Tiger could be less guarded than he is. Tiger doesn't care about the media, he's not interested in the fans, Tiger is almost too robotic, he doesn't show you what he's about. You talk to him in the interview room, he gives you nothing. He's a lot like Michael Jordan in that way. I think there is a level of mistrust between Tiger and the media and even between Tiger and the fans, and that is bothersome to me because America has been nothing but kind to Tiger.

And Tiger did a terrible job with Fuzzy Zoeller, when Fuzzy blurted out, "What are we going to have at next year's Masters dinner? Collard greens and fried chicken?" Fuzzy was wrong to say that, it was a bad joke that went awry, but Fuzzy's a good guy, great with the fans, good for the game.

Tiger should have taken Fuzzy off the griddle immediately: "He made a mistake, let's let it die." Tiger let it sit for three or four days while he was hanging out with the Nike people in Oregon and let the media grill Fuzzy, and that was wrong.

Tiger, who should know better, also tried to sell us on the idea of the Tiger Slam, that winning four majors in a row over two seasons was a Grand Slam. Sure, what he did was impressive, but he knows the ground rules as well as anyone. Bobby Jones did it in the same year. And Tiger's got to do it, too. He was dead wrong.

And finally, I can't watch Tiger win a golf tournament by 35 strokes. We've seen it three times in his career. We saw him blow away the Masters in '97 for his first title. That was kind of fun, he set all sorts of records. He had a 40 on the front nine in his first day, and came back and finished 18 under par, nobody close. That was a coronation. Okay. The second time we saw it was at the U.S. Open at Pebble Beach, his third major. You want to tell me it's at a historic golf course? You want to tell me that it's impressive to watch Tiger shoot 12 under and everyone else be 3 over? I got bored. I couldn't take it. You're not selling me the British Open when he wins by 10 strokes. I'm off. You're not selling the U.S. Open at Bethpage. I want to see competitiveness in my golf.

I'll take his PGAs. In his first one, he beat Sergio Garcia when he had to make a huge putt on 17 to do so, and in his second he made another big putt to force the playoff with Bob May at Louisville. Those events are more significant to me because the outcome was in doubt. So to me, when Tiger wins by 15 strokes and laps the field, and keeps you at arm's length the whole time, it's boring. And it's bad for the sport.

Staff Reflections

What are the greatest pitching staffs in baseball history?

Pitching is 90 percent of baseball. Well, we don't know about that, but if you can't get guys out, you're in for a long summer. Mad Dog surveys the best pitching staffs ever assembled.

Pitchers will break your heart. Even a good one will get hurt. Or lose his velocity or his movement or his control. Or he'll get Steve Blass disease. But you can't win without pitching, either. However, these five staffs from the second half of the twentieth century are as close as you can get to being ulcer-free.

5. 1954 Indians: Cleveland had five guys who were phenomenal. Early Wynn, Mike Garcia, Bob Lemon, Art Houtteman, and Bob Feller. They were 23–11, 23–7, 19–8, 15–7, and 13–3, respectively. Four guys who were double digits over .500, and another one who was close. Three Hall of Famers. That's just as good as a staff can get. No wonder the team went 111–43. The big knock on them is that in the World Series they did not pitch well. They got swept by the Giants, Lemon lost twice. You've got to complete the deal and the Indians didn't. I can't put the Indians as the best staff ever when in the World Series against the Giants their ERA was 4.84.

4. 1971 Orioles: 20-20-20-21. No, you're not reading an eye chart. Those are the win totals for Mike Cuellar, Pat Dobson, Jim Palmer, and Dave McNally. First and only time it was ever done. In the postseason they had a pretty good ERA of 2.56. They pitched well in the ALCS against the A's, but against the Pirates in the World Series they stunk it up and lost that series in seven games. They won the first two games, but Cuellar gave up three runs in six innings in game three. Dobson gave up four runs in five and a third innings in game four, and McNally gave up three runs in four innings in game five. In the guts of that World Series three of their big pitchers did not get it done. It seems to me that if you are going to be up there with the all-time great staffs, you have to win the World Series. So the Orioles, in a lot of ways, go the way of the Indians. They didn't finish the deal.

3. 1995 Atlanta Braves: You know the names. John Smoltz. Tom Glavine. Greg Maddux. Steve Avery. I love this staff because it combines the best of the early '90s Atlanta staff, when Steve Avery was very good, with Maddux, who came over in 1993.

Maddux was at his very best this year, 19–2 with a 1.63 ERA. Glavine and Smoltz weren't that far behind at 16–7 and 12–7, respectively. Avery didn't have a good year, but he was very good in the postseason, going 2–0 and giving up only one earned run in twelve innings in the NLCS and the World Series. The Braves didn't have the great closer in the bullpen, but in this strike-shortened year it didn't matter so much. They won the World Series, beating a great-hitting Indians team that won 100 games in a 144-game season.

2. 1963 Los Angeles Dodgers: The Dodgers had incredible front line pitching. Sandy Koufax and Don Drysdale at the top of the rotation were magnificent, probably the best one-two punch in history. That year Koufax was 25–5 and Drysdale was 19–17. Johnny Podres was 14–12 and Ron Perranowski was 16–3 with 21 saves. That's a team. And in the World Series they were even better. They swept the Yankees, giving up a total of four earned runs in four games. Koufax was the laggard with a 1.50 ERA. Now that's a pitching staff.

1. 1972 A's: The drumroll please. The best pitching staff I've seen belonged to those early '70s A's. You could split hairs and choose the 1973 team, which had three 20-game winners—Catfish Hunter 21–5, Vida Blue 20–9, Ken Holtzman 21–13, and Rollie Fingers with 22 saves. I'm going to lean toward the 1972 staff, where Hunter, Holtzman, and Fingers were just about equally good, Blue had an off-year at 6–10, and Blue Moon Odom picked up the slack at 15–6. Darrell Knowles also had a great year—5–1, 11 saves, 1.36 ERA—as the first lefty out of the bull pen. What impresses me is what the 1972 team did in the postseason. In the ALCS the Tigers hit .198. In the World Series, Oakland held the mighty Cincinnati Reds to a .209 batting average. Holtzman and Hunter won games one and two by scores of 3-2 and 2-1. Odom lost game three 1-0, and Fingers won game four 3-2. They hit some speed bumps in games five and six, but in game seven on the road, Odom, Hunter, Holtzman, and Fingers combined for a four-hitter to clinch the Series 3-2. That's pitching.

BUT WHAT ABOUT . . .

The *fin-de-millennium* Yankees? Sure the Yankees had Roger Clemens and Andy Pettitte and David Cone and David Wells and El Duque and John Wetteland and Mariano Rivera and Mike Stanton and Ramiro Mendoza and Jimmy Key and Mike Mussina, and yes, even Kenny Rogers. But not all at the same time. I look at these staffs as being assembled out of interchangable parts. Joe Torre ran eight or nine starters out there, two different closers, and a million middle-inning guys. So they don't really feel like a staff to me.

Trade Wins

What are the worst trades of all time?

It all begins with hope, a GM's notion that he's one move away from a championship. Sometimes trades work. And a lot of times they don't. Mad Dog examines the worst deals in sports history.

A trade is a zero-sum game. If it's a bad trade for one team, then it's a great trade for the other. But this is sports, so it's more fun to kick someone in the shins than pat them on the back—figuratively of course. So I'm going to look at this glass as half empty. And while I'm ranking the all-time worst trades, I'm going to stay away from straight salary dumps. Babe Ruth to the Yankees. Wayne Gretzky to the Kings. Mike Piazza to the Mets. In these cases the GMs knew that they weren't getting comparable value, but they were stuck with doing it anyway. No, these are trades that someone, somehow, assumed would make their team better. Really.

Football: Here's a rule of thumb: If you're going to trade a quarterback in the NFL, you'd better make sure that he stinks. Here are three instances in which the team ignored that rule and got burned big-time. In 1950 the New York Bulldogs traded a party boy quarterback who couldn't throw a spiral to the Lions for a receiver by the name of Bob Mann. The quarterback's name? Bobby Layne. He threw for 26,000 yards, won three championships with Detroit, and ended up in the Hall of Fame.

But people never learn. The Atlanta Falcons traded Brett Favre to the Packers for a first-round pick who turned out to be Tony Smith, a running back from Southern Miss, where Favre played. I guess a Southern Miss turns out only one Hall of Famer a century, and Atlanta picked the wrong one. And finally, the Tampa Bay Buccaneers, a franchise that has had such immortals as Gary Huff, Steve DeBerg, and Jack "the Throwin' Samoan" Thompson taking snaps, traded a lefty running quarterback for a second- and a fourth-round draft pick. The QB? Steve Young. Ouch.

NBA: The first lesson if you're an NBA GM. Don't trade with Red Auerbach. Follow this planning. In 1978 Auerbach plays a loophole in the NBA draft, which allows you to draft an underclassman, as long as you let him stay in school and can sign him before the next draft. Auerbach took a chance on a gawky white kid from Indiana named Larry Bird. This en-

---

NOT THAT BAD

How can you trade the rights to a guy who's arguably the greatest player ever at his position and not have it be an all-time disastrous trade? When you get a championship out of it. Because of the NBA's territorial draft, the St. Louis Hawks owned the rights to Bill Russell. Red Auerbach—remember what I said about never trading with him—saw Russell's potential and worked out a deal with the Hawks, giving up Cliff Hagen and Easy Ed Macauley for his rights. The problem with killing St. Louis on this trade is that Macauley and Hagen helped the Hawks win a championship in their first year in St. Louis. Macauley averaged 16 points and 6 rebounds. Hagen averaged 20 points and 10 rebounds and went on to have a Hall of Fame career.

Is this the proverbial trade that helped both teams? No. In hindsight you wouldn't make the trade again, but at least the Hawks got something back in this deal, so it's not as bad as most people think.

---

ables him to let Bob McAdoo go as a free agent to Detroit in exchange for two first-round draft picks. With Bird the team wins 61 games, and one of those picks in the McAdoo deal turns out to be the number one pick in the 1980 draft.

So Auerbach calls up the GM of the Golden State Warriors. He says, "Oh, yeah, this kid Joe Barry Carroll, he's going to be the next Bill Russell. No doubt about it . . . What? You'll give me the number three pick and that seven-foot center kid you've got, Perish, Parish, what's his name again? For my number one? I dunno. Lemme think about it." Takes a puff on his cigar. "Okay, you've got yourself a deal." That number three pick became future Hall of Famer Kevin McHale, Robert Parish became one of the best centers in the league, and the Celtics won a championship that very next year.

Major League Baseball: Baseball 101: Think twice, no three times, about trading a young everyday player for a pitcher. The Cubs traded away a skinny young singles-hitting outfielder to St. Louis for veteran starter Ernie Broglio. Broglio went 7–19 for the Cubbies. That outfielder— a guy by the name of Lou Brock—went to the Hall of Fame. The Red Sox traded away a young third baseman who couldn't quite crack the lineup behind Wade Boggs, and got Larry Andersen in return. Andersen pitched very well, posting a 1.23 ERA in fifteen games and helping Boston win the AL East before departing to San Diego. The third baseman? The Astros moved him to first, and Jeff Bagwell blossomed into one of the great hitters of the 1990s. And for that matter, if you're trading away a washed-up position player, make sure he's washed up. The Reds dealt Frank

---

KILLING THE MAD DOG

In my job I get to do a lot of second-guessing. Here's one time I was wrong on the first guess. On the air, the day it went down, I told anyone who would listen that the Mets made a great trade getting Juan Samuel for Lenny Dykstra. Boy was I wrong. Dykstra was a great spark plug for the Phillies, leading them to the World Series in 1993. Samuel hated New York and was a bust among busts. The Mets got burned and so did I.

Robinson to the Orioles for Milt Pappas. Pappas was 12–11 the next year. Frank Robinson won the Triple Crown and led the Orioles to the World Series. Lest you think that only position player-for-pitcher trades can detonate, I give you these two words: Nolan Ryan. The Mets traded Ryan, a wild, young pitcher who threw 100 miles an hour, for California third baseman Jim Fregosi. It's not even like Fregosi was coming off a good year. He had 5 homers and 33 RBIs and hit .233. Does it get any worse than that? Here's an honorable mention. Pedro Martinez for Delino Deshields. What were the Dodgers doing? They had Pedro's brother on the team, and he had been a great pitcher until he hurt his arm, so they should have had some idea of how good Pedro was. Sometimes the best deals are the ones you don't make.

Motivation by Armani

What makes a great NBA coach?

It takes more than just a great suit to win an NBA championship. Mad Dog discusses the finer points of motivating seven-footers.

An NBA coach is in an unusual position. His players are more important than he is and they know it. In basketball you only need two stars to win a championship. Jordan-Pippen, Tim Duncan–David Robinson, Shaq-Kobe. That's not the case in the other sports. In football you need more than two running backs, in baseball you need more than two pitchers.

In the NBA, a coach has to be able to develop a partnership with his stars. He almost has to treat the Shaqs and the Kobes as equals. You have to get them behind you. Get them to believe in you and everyone else will follow. That's why you can't bring Kurt Rambis in to coach the Lakers. He doesn't have the credibility that a coach like Phil Jackson has.

When Pat Riley or Phil Jackson walks into a new situation, you bet he's wearing a ring or two that first day of practice. He's sending a message. "See what I've got? Want one? Then listen to me." To get the attention of these players—guys making tremendous amounts of money, with fifteen cars, huge entourages—you've got to have the hardware.

You have to build a partnership with your stars, and that's what Phil

Jackson has been so unbelievably adept at. He walked into a Chicago situation that was perfect. They had gone through their growing pains with Doug Collins, making some advances in the playoffs before losing to Detroit a couple times. Phil came in with a new voice. He made a partnership with Jordan. In L.A. he did the same thing with Shaq and Kobe.

Jackson's secret is not the triangle offense, which I think is overrated. How did the triangle offense do when Jordan wasn't there? Game seven against the Knicks in 1993–94, they couldn't throw the ball in the ocean. The Bulls scored 14 points in the fourth quarter of game seven. Where was the triangle offense then?

No, the great coach is creative psychologically. It's the little things you do to get a player to perform at a high level, to pique his interest, whether it's giving him books to read on road trips or dunking your head in a bucket to make a point. You've got to get your star engaged. To play defense. To rebound. To pass the ball. To just show up at practice. Do that and the rest of the team follows suit. Red Auerbach had Bill Russell, a player who couldn't survive without winning, and Auerbach was smart enough to know how to capitalize on that. Riley made a pact with Magic Johnson. Jordan was practically a coach on the floor. The great coach is defined in terms of working with a great player.

And once the game starts, the coach's role is to set the tone. In game seven against Portland in 2000, down 15 in the fourth quarter, Jackson didn't yell and scream. He just sat there. And at that moment, Phil Jackson was worth every penny that Laker owner Jerry Buss was paying him. Young players take their cue from a coach, and they needed to see that he wasn't panicking.

Chuck Daly used to tell me, "I'm the pilot of an airplane. We'll take off at the beginning of the season, and there are going to be some storms, some bumpy rides, some smooth sailing. But I've got to land that plane." How can you tell if a guy is a great coach? He lands the plane—sometimes even with a couple of engines burned out.

Here are your top five NBA coaches:

5. Jack Ramsay: His 1976–77 Portland championship club was a picture-perfect team that was loads of fun to watch. If Bill Walton hadn't been injured, you know that he would have won a couple more titles. And I think you can measure a great coach by his offspring. Chuck Daly, Paul Westhead, Jack McKinney, Pat Riley, Jim Lynam all got their start under Dr. Jack.

4. Chuck Daly: He managed to win back-to-back championships in 1989 and 1990 with one great player and a bunch of pretty good ones. And those Pistons were one of the few teams to beat Jordan in his prime.

3. Phil Jackson: I spent a lot of time talking about Jackson's strengths. Here's the knock on Jackson. He never went to a bad team and turned it around. The Bulls and the Lakers were teams on the verge of greatness, and he just helped to push them over the top. I'm not saying he couldn't win with a bad team, but he hasn't, so that's a negative.

2. Pat Riley: Sure he walked into a championship situation with the Lakers—after all, Paul Westhead won that first title, and if it weren't for that Jack McKinney bike ride, who knows how this list might be different. But after he left the Lakers, Riley took over messes in New York and Miami, and after winning with offense in L.A. won with defense and toughness with the Knicks and the Heat.

1. Red Auerbach: He won nine championships. Eight in a row. His Celtics were the greatest dynasty of all time. He was a master motivator. And wearing the GM hat, he built the team from the ground up, from the 1950s through the 1980s.

VCR Classics

What sports moments are worth watching again and again?

What's a VCR for? It's not for taping Days of Our Lives. *Mad Dog tells you which games you should be looking out for on ESPN Classic.*

To be fair about this, I'm going to give you games that I watched live and can recall firsthand. So I'm not going to give you Bobby Thomson. I'm not going to give you game seven of the 1960 Pirates-Yankees World

Series. That would be like when Ken Burns asks Bob Costas to talk about Stan Musial on his baseball documentary. C'mon, he didn't see him play in his prime. I'm not going to do that. I'm going from the mid-'60s on. That said, here are some all-time great games that I'd watch again just about any day.

Nebraska-Miami 1984: This game really had a little bit of everything. It had the Cinderella team in Miami, who lost badly in the first game of the year in August at Florida, so they were under the radar all year long. Bernie Kosar was the quarterback and Howard Schnellenberger was the coach, and it was really him—not Jimmy Johnson—who got things started for Miami football.

They were taking on a Nebraska team that beat everybody up. They had the triplets in Turner Gill, Irving Fryar, and Mike Rozier. They had a tremendous offense, great speed. They were just an unstoppable machine, they went through their conference with no trouble whatsoever. I think they won a game that year against Minnesota 84-13.

In the Orange Bowl that year, January 1, a night game. Nebraska was the heavy favorite, double digits. But Miami attacked Nebraska. They didn't sit back and play ball control, play keep-away, try to run the ball. They threw the ball all over the place. And they put Nebraska on their heels in that game and jumped out to a big lead.

Nebraska came back late and scored a touchdown with time running out.

And Nebraska coach Tom Osborne went for two. Had to do it. Remember, if he gets the tie, he wins the national championship. A tie, they win. Still he went for the two-point conversion. Nebraska didn't run a great play. The ball got knocked away in the end zone. 31-30 Miami.

Yankees-Diamondbacks 2001: In keeping with the upset theme, I really liked game seven of the 2001 World Series. Coming into the Series, nobody thought the Yankees could lose. They were this incredible dynasty, four World Series in five years. And coming back to Arizona, up 3–2 having won those two dramatic come-from-behind wins at Yankee Stadium, we all thought it was in the bag. But it all came apart in one inning.

It was an intriguing matchup with two huge pitchers—Curt Schilling, pitching on three days' rest, and Roger Clemens. And they both pitched great. Alfonso Soriano's dramatic homer in the eighth put the Yankees ahead 2-1. Randy Johnson comes in to get four huge outs after he pitched the day before—winning games six and seven back-to-back. And then the unhittable Mariano Rivera let it slip away in the bottom of the ninth. The D-Backs hit Mariano fair and square. Mark Grace hit a line drive to center. Womack hit a line drive down the right field line. And then those fielding plays. On the last chance of his career, Scott Brosius had the opportunity to get the double play on the Jay Bell bunt that might have helped get the Yankees out of the inning. But he settled for the sure out. Bad play. And Mariano Rivera up to that moment had made one error in his career. And he throws the ball into centerfield. I'm not a Diamondback fan. I hate the Yankees. But I'd watch that game over and over.

Celtics-Suns, 1976: Two words: Triple overtime. There are a lot of great NBA games, but for my money you've got to go with Phoenix-Boston, 1976, game five. Phoenix had knocked off the defending champion Warriors. And this game was a classic—you knew that the winner of this game was going to win the series.

The Suns were down 22 in the second half and came back to tie after John Havlicek missed a couple of free throws. At the end of the second overtime, the Suns were down 3 with about ten seconds left. Paul Westphal made a shot, then stole the inbounds pass and threw it to Curtis Perry, who made a shot to give the Suns a one-point lead. The Celtics called a time-out with five seconds to go. And Havlicek made a 15-foot running leaner. Westphal then called a time-out that he knew he didn't have. The Celtics made the free throw to go up two, but the Suns got the ball at mid-court, setting up Gar Heard's basket—a point that Tommy Heinsohn has rightly complained about over the years. Phoenix was rewarded for an illegal play. The NBA changed the rule the next year. Heard's shot with one second to go forced another overtime. So in a span of twelve seconds you had four baskets. Westphal, Perry, Havlicek, Gar Heard. That's amazing.

And then there's the phantom time-out. After Heard made a shot in the first OT to tie it at 101, Paul Silas and three other Celtics called time-out even though the Celtics had used their last one. The referee Richie Powers was looking right at them and elected not to acknowledge the time-out. If he calls it, the Suns send Westphal to the line, he makes one, and the Suns probably win it. It's a moral dilemma. What do you do there if you're Richie Powers? His explanation was, "I was not going to mar this classic game for the ages, having it won on something like that." On the other hand, a rule's a rule, and that's part of the game. A very, very tough call—or noncall.

Georgetown-Villanova, 1985: I like upsets, and that's why I'm picking the Georgetown-Villanova national championship game. This was a huge upset. Georgetown was a real powerhouse, with Patrick Ewing in his senior year. Villanova knew how to play Georgetown, played them in the Big East. And Villanova that year had played very poorly. They got blown out at the end of the season by Pittsburgh by 23 points. They were surprised that they got an NCAA bid. But in the tournament they got on a roll. And in the final they played an absolutely perfect game. They made just about every shot in the second half. The thing you like about this game is that both teams played very well. Despite the fact that Villanova won 66-64, Georgetown played a good game. Georgetown didn't collapse. It's just that Villanova had a great game plan, made every shot, played great ball control, and most of all were not intimidated by the Hoyas. If those teams played ten times, Georgetown would have probably won nine. But Georgetown got them on a night when they were just unstoppable.

Dallas–Green Bay, 1967: I'll start this one with a disclaimer. I was only eight years old. I don't want to pull a Doris Kearns Goodwin and tell you, as she did in her book, about how she analyzed the classic '51 Dodgers-Giants Series when she was seven. That drove me nuts. So I want to get that out on the table. But the fact that I remember the game pretty distinctly all these years later tells you what kind of game it was.

I had Tom Landry in here once in the studio on a Saturday morning and he told me that he went to bed on that Saturday night and didn't think anything of the weather—it was 25 degrees that afternoon. But when he got his wake-up call Sunday morning in his hotel in Green Bay, the lady said, "Welcome to Green Bay. Your temperature outside is minus

15 degrees." Landry could not believe it. It's 17-14 Dallas, late in the fourth quarter. Dan Reeves threw the option pass to Lance Rentzel, to give Dallas the lead, but the Cowboys don't get the first down to run out the clock. They punt. Green Bay gets the ball back. Ray Scott called this "the greatest mind over matter drive in NFL history." You watch ESPN Classic, and I don't care if it's four o'clock in the morning, and you wake up and go to the bathroom, you see that this game is on, you watch that last drive. Chuck Mercein sliding on the ice out of bounds down the left sideline. Lombardi going for it on third down with no time-outs left instead of kicking the field goal that would have tied the game. The great block by Jerry Kramer (see "No Guts, No Glory," page 169). That's got to be the best NFL game I've seen. Now I was eight, so I can't give you specifics on every single play, but it's a classic.

The All-Century Team

Who are the greatest baseball players of all time?

You built it and they came. It's a real-life field of dreams, and you get to fill out the lineup card. So who's on first? Mad Dog gives it up.

When you try to narrow all the great players who've played the game of baseball down to eight, let's face it, it's just about impossible. When you see my list you're going to say, "Oh, Chris, you're leaving out the all-time home run champ? You're leaving Willie Mays out? You're leaving Honus Wagner out? Honus Wagner!" This is just one man's opinion. Let's start with an easy one:

Right Field, Babe Ruth: We've gone through this a million times (see "100 Years of Swat-i-tude," page 280). Ruth's the best offensive player of all time, and a great pitcher. And you forget, this is not only a guy who hit more home runs than whole teams, he hit .378 while he was doing it.

Left Field, Ty Cobb: I don't know how you could leave Cobb off, so that's why we're moving him to left and slotting him in ahead of Ted Williams, Stan Musial, and Barry Bonds. You can certainly make the argument that he's the greatest player of all time. He's got way over 4,000 hits, he's got a .366 lifetime batting average, he scored a million runs, and even though he didn't hit a lot of home runs, he drove in 100 plenty of times.

He's got a couple of things you don't like. He didn't win a World Series. He was a dirty player. And off the field he was an irascible SOB and a bigot. But we're not running him for Congress, so I don't see how you can keep Cobb off this team.

Center Field, Joe DiMaggio: This is the real debate. A lot of people are going to say Willie Mays. I had Hall of Famer Larry Doby on a year ago and he saw both Mays and DiMaggio, and he thought Mays was a little bit better than DiMaggio: equal in the outfield, a little better because of his speed.

Here's how I see it. Mays had a longer career, hit 660 home runs. But Mays never hit .381. And Joe D had a lot of intangibles. His teams were 9–1 in the World Series. He owns an important record—the 56-game hitting streak. And you've got dramatic moments, like the one in Fenway in 1949 when he came back with those bone spurs in his foot and hit all those home runs. Joe D gets the edge because he's just a better hitter than Mays.

First Base, Lou Gehrig: You could put Jimmie Foxx there. You could even put Mark McGwire there. But I'm going to go with Gehrig. Sure, he played in 2,130 consecutive games (see "They Call It The Streak" page 81), but mostly he was an unbelievable hitter. Look at his RBIs. He's third or fourth all-time. Another thing you like about Gehrig is that he spanned two Yankee eras. He was on the Ruth teams and he was on the DiMaggio teams, too.

Third Base, Mike Schmidt: When you look through the Hall of Fame, there aren't a lot of incredible third basemen out there. You've got Brooks Robinson. You've got George Brett. And then you've got Schmidt. He was a tremendous hitter, a phenomenal defensive player. Dominated in 1980, got the Phillies through that pennant race. I know the batting average isn't great, but he walked a ton. He won back-to-back MVPs, ten gold gloves. He's not as good defensively as Robinson, and if you're down in the ninth inning and you need to get a hit, you're going with Brett, but as far as the total package, there's nobody better than Schmidt.

Catcher, Johnny Bench: I'm taking Bench behind the plate. There are a few guys you can consider—Yogi. Bill Dickey. Even Mike Piazza or Pudge Rodriguez. I've got to go with Bench. The home run he hit off Dave Giusti in 1972, ninth inning game five, 3-2 Pirates, is still one of the classics. How about the base hit he got in the ninth inning of game two of the '75 World Series against the Red Sox? He changed the way the game was played defensively, too. Remember what Ted Williams saw in Bench way back in 1968? Bench asked him to sign a ball and Ted wrote, "To Johnny Bench, A Hall of Famer, for sure, Ted Williams." In his rookie year.

Shortstop, Alex Rodriguez: Okay, if you're doing this right now, Honus Wagner's still the greatest shortstop of all time. But I'm going to take A-Rod on projection. His numbers are just mind-boggling. Forget about comparing him to Nomar Garciaparra and Derek Jeter. He's better than Cal Ripken, better than Ozzie Smith, better than Robin Yount. There's no telling what kind of numbers he might put up. He might hit 700 home runs, maybe even 800. As a shortstop. When he's all done, we might be calling him the greatest player ever to play the game, at any position.

Second Base, Jackie Robinson: You've got Rogers Hornsby, who hit .400, but he played in a big offensive era when everybody was doing that. And he's not known as a great defensive second baseman. I'm not putting Roberto Alomar there, at least not yet. You can also throw in Eddie Collins, the only player who was clean during the Black Sox scandal of 1919. He gets a little forgotten. The two guys I would consider at second base would be Joe Morgan and Jackie Robinson. Jackie Robinson's career numbers don't compare very favorably to most of these other guys. But he broke in when he was twenty-eight. And he was such a competitor. His speed, his daring on the base paths, the big plays he made in big spots, the diving catch and the home run in the fourteenth inning to win the last game of the season in '51 against the Phillies, for example.

As far as Morgan is concerned, he had only a .271 career average. But look at it another way. He was the best Red on two great teams, a team filled with MVPs and Hall of Famers. Tony Perez. Johnny Bench. George Foster. And Pete Rose. Look at Morgan's walks. His home runs. His defense. His smarts. The great catch and throw he made down the right field line in the 1972 World Series. The hit that won the World Series three years later.

I'd say that Morgan and Jackie Robinson are tight. In 1999 at Turner Field, before game six between the Mets and Braves, we had Morgan on for the first time ever. Tremendous spot. He's a great guest. We talked about the All-Century team. He said, "Let me tell you something right now, if they vote me on that team, I'm giving my spot to Jackie Robinson for what he went through in 1947." It was a very emotional moment, with tears running down everybody's face.

So there's your team. I think people might argue about the catcher, the shortstop, the second baseman, and I can see some arguments in favor of Willie Mays in the outfield. But any way you cut it, that team's going to win.

The Erasables

Which sports moments don't hold up under repeated viewings?

The tape doesn't lie. Your memory tells you it was an all-time great game. But your television tells you it was dull and mistake-filled. Mad Dog names the most overrated classic contests.

There are some sports moments that just take on a life of their own. We talk about them constantly. We build them up in our minds. We remember them mostly because they were unique. And we make the short leap from unique to great. Here are a few sports moments that just don't hold up for me.

1975 Reds-Red Sox: Yes, we know it was twelve innings. The great Bernie Carbo homer with the Red Sox down 6-3, which was far more remarkable than Fisk's game winner. George Foster's great throw to the plate in the ninth to keep the game tied. And Carlton Fisk trotting down the line, wishing his home run ball fair. It had just about everything you could want in a baseball game. Just about.

The problem I have with this is that the Red Sox lost the World Series. Do you think the Reds would trade places with the Red Sox in the Series, winning game six and losing game seven? Don't you think a Red Sox fan wouldn't rather have won a ho-hum game six and won game seven instead of having this classic game they like to talk about forever in Beantown?

Its hard for me to consider a game an all-time classic when the team that won the battle ends up losing the war. I can't do that.

Tennessee–St. Louis Super Bowl: Super Bowls get overrated because the games are usually so bad that when it's a half-decent game, we automatically elevate it to classic status. A good example is the Titans-Rams. Okay, it was close. But the first three quarters were boring. It was an awful game, and Tennessee did nothing. They didn't score in the first half. I just never got the feeling that the Titans were going to win that game. And yes, Mike Jones made a nice play saving the touchdown. But people forget that a last-second touchdown for Tennessee would have just tied the game. Mr. Jones didn't save the game, he saved overtime.

1993 Toronto-Philadelphia World Series, Game Four: I'm not talking about game six when Joe Carter hit the walk-off homer. I mean the game in Philadelphia when both teams scored a billion runs. It was like 15-14. I know people who loved that game. Lot of runs. Back and forth. Toronto came from behind. The most runs ever in a World Series game. You see that game on ESPN Classic all the time. I was in the park, and it was a terrible baseball game. There was absolutely no pitching. It was like watching batting practice. That game did nothing for me. It bored the heck out of me.

USA-USSR Hockey: Now people are going to kill me for this, but I had a huge problem with this game. First, the Russians really didn't play well (see "Heimlich Time," page 171). The other big problem was with the broadcast. The game was played at four-thirty, five o'clock in the afternoon, but ABC tape delayed it until eight o'clock at night. So that's a major problem. And here's the big negative. When ABC came on that night, there was a party in that booth. There were American fans with the flags right behind Jim McKay. He was all happy and smiley. If you had stayed away from the score all day so you could watch the game without knowing who won, McKay ruined it for you. It was like someone reading you the last page in a whodunit.

Do You Believe in Magic?

Who's tops in the Lakers-Celtics rivalry?

It's Bird and Magic. West Coast–East Coast. Showtime vs. the Victory Cigar. But who comes out on top in the basketball world's best matchup? Mad Dog gives it up.

D uring the 1960s basketball had an annual rite of spring. The Bill Russell–John Havlicek Celtics and Elgin Baylor–Jerry West Lakers would play for the NBA championship. And the Celtics would win. All six times. If that great rivalry was a little one-sided back in the '60s, it wasn't the 1980s.

It all started with the draft. In 1978, Celtics GM Red Auerbach watched teams ahead of him draft legends like Mychal Thompson, Phil Ford, and Purvis Short, and while he was cagey enough to use sixth pick to draft Larry Bird as a junior (which was legal back then) and let him play out his senior year at Indiana State, Red was then able to deal Bob McAdoo for some draft picks that he was able to turn into Kevin McHale and Robert Parish on draft day 1980, (see "Trade Wins," page 256).

The Lakers lucked out in their own way, getting the number one overall pick in the 1979 draft from the Jazz as compensation for signing Gail Goodrich. Their pick? Sophomore point guard Magic Johnson.

The NBA got the biggest break of all with these two superstars coming into the league at the same time and making an immediate impact. The league was in a lot of trouble back then, dealing with drug rumors, and the perception was that only the last five minutes of a game mattered. It got so bad that in the late 1970s and even the early 1980s, the NBA finals were on tape delay. Remember game six of the 1980 finals between the

Lakers and 76ers in which Magic fills in for Kareem and scores 42 points, grabs 15 rebounds, and has 7 assists? Only the people in the Philadelphia Spectrum saw it live.

The antidote? Magic and Bird, two great contrasting players renewing their rivalry—the pair had faced off in the 1979 NCAA championship game—in the pros.

While they entered the league at the same time, there was a little bit of delayed gratification that I think enhanced the rivalry. The Lakers topped the Sixers in Magic's rookie year. The Celtics beat Houston in 1981. The Lakers again topped the Sixers in 1982. And the Sixers took the title in 1983.

So in 1984, you had a tremendous buildup for what was to be the first of three great matchups between these two franchises. And that magnificent final lived up to its billing. The Celtics had the home court in the 2-2-1-1-1 playoff format which, as we'll see, was very, very important.

These were two magnificent teams. Think about it, folks. You had six Hall of Famers on the court at one time—Magic, Kareem Abdul-Jabbar, and James Worthy for the Lakers, and Bird, Robert Parish, and Kevin McHale for the Celtics. A Hall of Fame coach in Pat Riley. And I think Dennis Johnson should definitely be a Hall of Famer. And if you're so inclined you can even kick in Bob McAdoo, who was an important role player for the Lakers between '82 and '85, and Bill Walton, who came off the bench for the Celtics in 1986.

Of the three finals in which these teams met during the 1980s, the first was the one in which the two teams were most evenly matched. The difference in this series? Magic choked. There's no other way around it, Magic had a terrible series. He forgot the clock situation in one of the games in L.A. when they lost in overtime, he wilted in the heat in game five, he had a terrible game seven, when he shot awfully. Of course the Celtics won 111-102. I have always felt that Bird at his peak was better than Magic because this one time when both guys played against each other at peak form, on equal terms with no excuses, Bird was better.

A couple of things made this a great series. First off, the Lakers got a split in Boston and won the third game at the Forum. The Celtics were way down in the fourth game, came back, and tied the game late. On the last L.A. possession, Magic essentially dribbled out the clock with the game tied, they didn't get a final shot off, and the Celtics won in overtime. They get even 2–2, a huge game in the series because you're not going to beat the Celtics in Boston Garden. In game five, Auerbach kept the temperature at about 97 degrees, which wilted Kareem and the Lakers' running game. Los Angeles came back in game six and blew Boston out in L.A. In game seven it was almost as if the teams had picked up where they left off in the 1960s. Magic choked, shot terribly, did nothing, and after the game he and Michael Cooper were sitting in the shower for hours, wondering how this could have happened, while the Celtics were celebrating across the hall. Remember that up to that point, the franchise had never beaten the Celtics in the NBA Finals.

The next year provided a rematch, and the key difference between '84 and '85 was the playoff format. The NBA changed it from 2-2-1-1-1 to 2-3-2. In the first game the Celtics blew the Lakers out in the Memorial Day Massacre, 148-114. It was almost a continuation of the seventh game the year before. But while everybody wrote Kareem off after that game, there were three days off before game two, and Kareem came back and scored 30 points and grabbed 17 rebounds to even the series. The teams returned to L.A., and it was déjà vu all over again. The Lakers blew the Celts out in game three, and in game four, Boston was way behind, came storming back in the fourth quarter, and the series is tied 2–2. If this was 1984 they're going back to Boston for a game five. But in 1985 they're staying in L.A. for game five. What's the big deal? If that series goes back to Boston for game five, the Lakers probably lose another seven-game series. The new format of the '85 NBA Final got the Lakers over the hump against the Celtics, and anybody who argues differently is not paying attention. The Lakers had that terrible loss in the fourth game, eerily similar to the one in '84, but they got that fifth game in their building and grabbed that all-important 3–2 lead.

How come the Celtics couldn't win these last two games at home? It's hard to beat a great team twice in a row. In these two series, only once did a team win two games in a row. The Celtics looked old in game six, and the Lakers exorcised a lot of ghosts with that win.

In 1986, that great Celtic team, (see "Hoops Hierarchy," page 36) beat the Rockets in the Finals. In 1987 it was rematch time. That great Laker team took the first two games from the Celtics, lost game three, won game four in the famous baby hook by Magic. The Lakers lost game five, but the Celtics had no chance at the Forum in game six.

The difference in this series was health. By 1987, Magic was better than Bird because Bird had suffered a chronic back injury. He just wasn't the same after that. I always found it interesting that the two of them became such good friends, because I always thought, watching them go at each other in the mid-'80s, that they were mortal enemies. I always thought that Bird kind of enjoyed seeing Magic melt down in the '84 finals, Larry waving that white towel on the bench at the end of game seven.

Who gets the edge in the '80s? I'm going to go against the grain and say the Celtics were better than the Lakers. I know Laker fans are going to kill me for this. "How can you say that, Russo? We won five titles. We won two out of three head-to-head." I think Boston's better for three reasons.

First, the format change. If that fifth game in 1985 had been in Boston, the Lakers would not have won that series, they would have lost in seven games. The second difference is that Boston had the best team out of the era because I think the '86 Celtics were better than the '87 Lakers (see "Hoops Hierarchy," page 36). And the third theme is that Bird was better than Magic head-to-head, at the peak of their games in 1984. But any way you slice it, this was an all-time great rivalry.

Guilty as Charged

What are the greatest guilty pleasures in sports?

Foreigner albums. Filet-o-Fish sandwiches. Small-college basketball tournaments. Life is full of slightly guilty indulgences. Mad Dog shares his.

In sports, there are certain things you've got to do. The World Series. The Super Bowl. The NCAA Tournament. But I must say that some of my favorite events throughout the year are downright weird. I'm sitting in front of the television, having a great time, and then I wonder, "Is anyone else watching this, too?" And some of my favorite story lines don't play out on television or the front page of the sports section, but in the agate type of the standings pages. Here are my guilty sports pleasures.

The Australian Open: I know it sounds wacky, I love this tennis tournament. It often provides a respite from the two weeks of hype before the Super Bowl. I love the retractable roof; you don't have to wonder if it's going to get rained out. The incredible heat—remember that Jennifer Capriati–Martina Hingis final where it was 115 in the shade?—adds an element of drama. And there's just been some great tennis there—Agassi and Sampras hooked up in some great matches, and Andy Roddick played a couple of classics in 2003. And ESPN2 does a tremendous job with their coverage. They basically go on live every day at 9:30 P.M. and take it until 11 or 11:30 P.M., which fits perfectly into my schedule.

NHL Western Conference Playoff Race: Let me confess something. In the last four weeks of hockey season, I find myself obsessing about the NHL Western Conference playoff race. Yeah, I know that's weird. Why would Christopher Russo in New York City care about where L.A., Edmonton, Vancouver, Phoenix, and San Jose finish up? Well, first I like the little guy aspect of it. There are a lot of small-market teams there. Second, the travel there is mind-boggling, those long Dallas to Vancouver flights. Edmonton plays at L.A. one night, Calgary the second night, and the last night they are home against Vancouver. For some reason I get a kick out of that. And finally, the real heavyweight team in the NHL—Detroit, Colorado, Dallas—is usually in the West. So it's not only important who gets the eighth seed, you also want to keep an eye on who can move up to six, seven, and five to avoid Detroit and Colorado.

Small-College Basketball Tournaments: In the middle of February, I go straight to *USA Today,* and I cut out the schedule of when Austin Peay and Florida Atlantic begin their conference tournaments. I love it. Win and you're in the NCAA Tournament. Lose and you pack up the balls and go home. The atmosphere in these games is great. They play in these small home gyms, packed to the rafters, real juice in the building. Most of the kids are going to stick around for four years, so they're really into it. And the team that wins has ten days to bask in the glory, waiting for Selection Sunday when they see their name go up on the board. Then it's a reality check when they have to go out to the Far West Regional and play big bad Duke in the first round.

NFL Tiebreakers: There is nothing I enjoy more in November and December than poring over the NFL schedules and all the tiebreaker scenarios. On Thanksgiving, I can tell you the net point differential between the fifth and sixth seed in the AFC. I know everyone's schedules, when their bye-weeks are. I have memorized it. I know what the common opponent record is. I know the tiebreakers by heart. I love figuring this stuff out.

Nothing drives me crazier than listening to the announcers who can't figure out for the life of them how the outcome of a game is going to affect the team's playoff positioning. It drives me nuts. I even found a loophole in the NFL playoff format. A couple of years ago, Detroit finished with the same record as New Orleans fighting for the wild card. And the first tiebreaker is where you finished in your division, so Detroit was out and New Orleans was in. Not fair. Why should Detroit be punished because they were in with good teams like Green Bay, Minnesota, Tampa, and the Saints are in a division with tomato cans like Carolina and Atlanta? I think I've thought about this more than the NFL has.

Announcing Tandems: Nobody gets more wrapped up in announcing tandems than me. So Mike, who do you think is doing the Red Wing–Panther game on Fox on Saturday afternoon? Who do you think is doing the Charger–Cardinal game Sunday on FOX at five? Are they sending Ian Eagle and Jim Spanarkel to Sacramento for the first round of the NCAA Tournament? Are they going to send Jim Nantz and Billy Packer to the Friday regional in Baltimore so they can do the Sunday five o'clock game right up to *60 Minutes,* or are they going to let them do Duke because they're the best team in the country? Is Joe Buck doing the Thanksgiving Day game Thursday in Detroit? Is he working Sunday afternoon, four days later? Is Marv Albert going to double dip and do a game Saturday and a game Sunday? Or is he doing only one game? Are they bringing Bob Costas in? Why do I get into this so much? I guess I'm living vicariously, because there's a part of me that wishes it were me out there traveling around from game to game.

Heartbreakers, Dream Takers

What are baseball's most crushing defeats?

T. S. Eliot argued that April was the cruelest month, but September and October can be pretty rough, too. Mad Dog revisits baseball's ultimate close-but-no-cigar moments.

The crushing loss is more painful in baseball than in football, basketball, or hockey. That's because baseball season is the longest. It unfolds on a day-to-day basis like the pages of a book. You live with the team every day, day in and day out. The crushing, franchise-altering, sticks-with-you-for-generations defeat is a baseball thing.

In compiling this list, I'm looking for the loss that still haunts a franchise. And with the Angels winning the World Series in 2002, that eliminates the ghost of 1986. It's over. You scored eight in an inning to beat the Yankees, ten in an inning to beat the Twins, and came from 5-0 down in game six to beat the Giants. Donnie Moore is no longer applicable.

If you've won a championship since the franchise-altering loss, it's no longer a big deal. If you've won a lot of championships—Mariano Rivera throwing the ball into center field in the 2001 World Series, the A's in 1988 with Kirk Gibson—losing one is just not a tragedy. And it doesn't have to be a World Series. Sometimes a playoff loss can be just as much of a knife in the ribs—stick it in and twist. So here are some really ugly baseball moments.

8. 1980 Astros: This is a franchise that has never won a playoff series. In game five against the Phillies they had a 5-2 lead in the eighth at home with Nolan Ryan pitching. The Phillies loaded the bases without hitting the ball hard and scored five runs. The Astros tied the game in the eighth, and then they lost in the tenth. And the Phillies went on to win the World Championship. That's criminal.

7. 1981 Expos: Why the Expos? They had a period from 1978 through '82 when they were very good. A lot of really excellent players—Andre

Dawson, Gary Carter, Tim Raines, Steve Rogers. They lost a lot of close pennant races. In 1981 they beat the defending champion Phillies in that first round of the strike-induced playoffs. In the NLCS they had a 2–1 lead in games, coming home to Olympic Stadium. In game four they gave up six runs in the last two innings to lose 7-1. In game five, two outs in the ninth, 1-1, Rick Monday hits that big home run to right center off Steve Rogers. Big home run. They were *that* close to going to the World Series and they haven't even been able to smell it since.

6. 1985 Cardinals: They won the first two games in Kansas City, were up 3–2, and had the lead going into the bottom of the ninth in game six. Then it's Freddy Krueger time. Don Denkinger's bad call on Jorge Orta. Jack Clark misplayed a pop-up down by the first base dugout. And Dane Iorg's two-run single. They were three outs away. That stings. And then the Cards get bombed 11-0 the next night. John Tudor didn't have it and Andujar goes crazy. This was much worse than the Yankees of 2001, who had no business even playing in the World Series after being dead and buried against the A's and then again in games four and five against the Diamondbacks. Not so with the Cardinals.

5. 1997 Indians: They weren't an incredible team. They won the division with 86 wins. And they never had a lead in the Series—they were down 1-0, 2-1, and 3-2 in games. But they had a ninth-inning lead in game seven, and they hadn't won a World Series since 1948.

Two things about this game. Everyone forgets what happened in the top of the ninth. First and third one out, Cleveland up 2-1. That's a huge third run. And Robb Nen gets Marquis Grissom to hit a ground ball, and in the bottom of the ninth Mesa lets it slip away. Charles Johnson has a big hit and Craig Counsell gets the sac fly to tie it up, and then, after the normally reliable Tony Fernandez makes an error, Edgar Renteria gets the hit to win it in extra innings. Just awful.

4. 1992 Pirates: Want to send shivers down the spine of a Pirate fan? Just utter these words: Francisco Cabrera. For the second year in a row the Pirates had the Braves on the ropes. In 1991 they had a three games to two lead going back to Pittsburgh and lost two in a row. That was bad.

In '92 the Pirates fight back from three games to one down, and have Doug Drabek pitching game seven with a 2-0 lead in the bottom of the ninth. Then the wheels come off. There were a lot of factors at play here. The Pirates didn't have a closer that year, so Jim Leyland had to stay with Drabek. The normally reliable Jose Lind makes an error. And then there's the umpire situation. In the third inning, home plate umpire John McSherry fell ill and Randy Marsh moved behind the plate. Marsh calls his strike zone as tight as a drum, and in that bottom of the ninth the Braves had two walks, and I'm telling you, every single pitch could have gone either way. The Pirates didn't get one call. I'll give Braves manager Bobby Cox a lot of credit, though. With the bases loaded down 2-1, 2 out, a 2-0 count, the Pirates were walking the ballpark, thanks in part to Marsh, but he let Cabrera swing away. Barry Bonds always gets blamed for being a smidgen off line on his throw to the plate. That's absurd. The Braves won it fair and square. That ninth inning was the end for the Pirates in more ways than one. Bonds left. Drabek left. Leyland left a couple of years later. And the Pirates haven't been the same since.

3. 2002 Giants: What can you say? 5-0 lead. Eight outs away. There's no Leon Durham here, there's no Bill Buckner or Bob Stanley. There's no Don Denkinger. There are no real goats here. You've got a 5-0 lead bottom of the seventh, with your relief pitchers who had done a magnificent job getting you to this spot. In the postseason, Felix Rodriguez, Tim Worrell, and Robb Nen were virtually unhittable. Yes, Dusty Baker took Russ Ortiz out too soon. But in the space of seven hits over two innings, the Giants lost the World Series.

That's tough to take. Scott Spiezio's home run is one of the most dramatic homers in the history of the World Series. Jim Leyritz's home run in 1996 against the Braves wasn't in an elimination game. The game was tied when Bill Mazeroski hit a homer against the Yankees in 1960. It was just like Bernie Carbo if the Red Sox had won the 1975 World Series. That was an unbelievable defeat for the Giants. I can live with it because I can't find a goat. I can't kill my manager too much. But it's still one of those slow torture games.

And there are two other things I thought about. Barry Bonds is in two of the games on this list. And how about Thanksgiving at the Worrell household? Todd Worrell against the Royals in 1985 and Tim Worrell against the Angels. Tough.

2. 1984 Cubs: That was as ugly as it gets. They had the NL MVP in Ryne Sandberg, and guys like Ron Cey and Gary Matthews and Lee Smith. They had the Cy Young Award winner in Rick Sutcliffe—having traded away a young Joe Carter to get him. This excellent Cub team held off the Mets, and all of Chicago—remember, this is before the Bears and the Bulls, so the city hadn't had a championship team in like forty years—was going nuts. Just getting to the World Series would be huge. The Cubbies won the first two games of the five-game series against the Padres. Had a middle-inning lead in game three, let it slip away. No big deal. In game four it was 5-5 going into the bottom of the ninth when Steve Garvey hits a homer off Lee Smith to win it. In game five, Chicago scores two in the first, one in the second, and have Sutcliffe going on full rest. A 3-0 lead in the fifth inning with your best pitcher pitching. The Padres get two in the sixth, and then Leon Durham lets a grounder go through his legs to score the tying run in the seventh. The Cubs lose 6-3. That's losing ugly. And the Cubs haven't gotten this close to the World Series since.

1. 1986 Red Sox: You know about this one (see "The Classic Second Guess," page 247). And it was every bit as bad as you remember. Sure, the Red Sox helped out the Mets. And actually I think the Bill Buckner grounder is a little overrated. Remember that the score was tied there. The wild pitch from Bob Stanley that scored the tying run was even more damaging.

But they got to within one strike of ending sixty-eight years of futility—twice. That's as bad as you're ever going to get. The Mets had conceded. The champagne was on ice. They flashed "Congratulations Red Sox" on the Shea Stadium scoreboard. Keith Hernandez is already in the clubhouse with his uniform off, with a beer in one hand and a cigarette in the other. Talk about snatching defeat from the jaws of victory. It doesn't get any worse than that, sports fans.

100 Years of Swat-i-tude

Who was really the top athlete of the twentieth century?

Forget Y2K, the biggest joke of the millennium was ESPN's Sports Century. Great idea. Great programs. And they picked the wrong guy. Mad Dog gives props to the main man of the last one hundred years.

When ESPN did their *Sports Century* a few years ago and named the top athlete of the twentieth century, I couldn't believe it. It was a joke. Michael Jordan? C'mon. I think it was just ESPN trying to ingratiate themselves with Jordan. And they figured, hey, at least we can talk to him every now and then.

The criteria for a player being the athlete of the century, or something like it, are pretty simple. First, the guy needs to dominate his sport. There shouldn't be any question that he was the best player in the game when he played, and on the very short list for the best of all time. You shouldn't be able to open the record book without seeing this guy's name all over it. It's as simple as that.

The second yardstick? Winning. You need championships, multiple championships.

Third, you've got to transcend the sport. Be bigger than life. Fifty years later people still have to know who you are. Finally, you've got to change the sport in some way. Joe DiMaggio or Willie Mays didn't have that kind of lasting impact. They were great players. They had a lasting *image*, but the game of baseball isn't different than if they had never played.

All that said, who makes my top five? And who's my number one? I'll give you a hint—it's not Michael Jordan.

5. Jim Thorpe: Thorpe might just be the best athlete the United States has ever produced. He excelled in three different sports: football, baseball, and track and field. His problem as far as our list is concerned is that he played so long ago. He played before World War I, and football was an entirely different game and the level of competition wasn't nearly what it is today. And time has passed him by just a little. In 1950 he was voted the top athlete of the first half of the twentieth century ahead of guys like Babe Ruth and Jack Dempsey, but a lot of people don't know who he is today. I'm sorry to say it, but Jim Thorpe is not bigger than life, at least not anymore.

4. Wayne Gretzky: In a lot of ways, Gretzky is hockey's answer to Babe Ruth. He rewrote the hockey record book. He's the greatest offensive player of all time, the best goal scorer, far and away the best passer, and he really revolutionized the game. Before Gretzky, scoring 50 goals or tallying 100 points was a big accomplishment. In 1981–82 he scored 92 goals and 212 points. Of course, he was a winner—four Stanley Cups. He's also got that larger-than-life personality. When Gretzky is on with Mike and the Mad Dog, my wife, who isn't a sports fan, tunes in.

But the problem is that he's a hockey player, and sorry folks, but hockey is a distant fourth among sports in the United States. If we're doing this in Canada, he might come out first on this list. But we're not.

3. Michael Jordan: Let's get something straight. Michael Jordan did not save the NBA. That's a myth. It was Magic Johnson and Larry Bird and David Stern who saved the NBA in the early '80s. Nobody but die-hard

---

THE FOOTBALL FACTOR

Sorry, football fans, but there's no NFL player on my list. The best candidate is Jim Brown. He was a dominant running back and he was also a great lacrosse player. But he wasn't loved by his teammates, much less all of America. He was a sour guy. Never blocked. And he played only nine years and won only one championship. And he didn't retire because he was protesting the Vietnam War—he quit because he was ticked off that Art Modell fined him for being late to camp when he was off filming *The Dirty Dozen*. None of the quarterbacks make it either. They pretty much fall into one of two categories—guys who dominated statistically like Dan Marino or Dan Fouts, and guys who won without putting up huge numbers like Terry Bradshaw and Joe Montana. And that isn't enough to crack this very tough list.

basketball fans cared about the league. The Bird-Magic rivalry saved the NBA (see "Do You Believe in Magic?," page 270). The league was already on its way back by the time Jordan broke in.

So he doesn't get that intangible that Babe Ruth gets, that Muhammad Ali gets. He was a great player no doubt, and you can certainly make an argument for him being the greatest basketball player of all time. And there's no denying that he was bigger than life. The Nike commercials. The jerseys he sold—two different numbers. *Space Jam*. And the fact that he went back to the Wizards and sold out every building. But the greatest of the century? I don't think so.

2. Muhammad Ali: Nobody transcended his sport more than Ali did. His stand against the draft wasn't a sports story, it was a *news* story. He also changed boxing forever. Until Ali came along, heavyweights were expected to just stand there flat-footed and slug it out. He brought grace and artistry to his weight class. He also brought his own "Float-like-a-butterfly, sting-like-a-bee" brand of showmanship to the world of sport. Every Ali fight became a real event. And of course, you've got these great defining images of Ali. Standing over Sonny Liston. The Thrilla in Manila. The Foreman fight in Zaire. Carrying the Olympic torch.

My one knock on Ali is that, unlike Ruth, he's not without a doubt the best ever at his sport. He was a tremendous warrior, but there are four or five guys who were as good or better. He might not even be the best heavyweight of all time. Joe Louis, Rocky Marciano, even Jack Dempsey would have given him all he could handle.

1. Babe Ruth: No question, he's the athlete of the century. He dominated the game. Changed the game. Transcended the game. We all know what a great home run hitter Ruth was. But he was a lot more than that. In 1921 he hit .378, scored 177 runs, and drove in 171. His career batting average was .342—14 points higher than Wade Boggs's.

And let's not forget that Ruth was a pitcher. And a darn good one. Take a look at the Red Sox record book and you'll be surprised. You'll find Ruth's name all over it, ahead of guys like Cy Young and Lefty Grove and Roger Clemens in a lot of categories. If he'd stayed on the mound, Ruth probably would have made the Hall of Fame as a pitcher. That's like Wayne Gretzky being an All-Star goalie, too, or Joe Montana leading the league in touchdown passes and sacks.

But just as important, he changed the game of baseball. Ruth ushered in baseball's live ball era. Before Ruth, pitchers were throwing spitballs, all brown with tobacco juice, and players were choking up, bunting, happy to hit singles. He was the first guy to make the home run a weapon. In 1920 he hit 54 home runs. The Cleveland Indians, who won the American League pennant, hit only 35. Think about that.

After Ruth, baseball became a power game. Because pitchers knew that guys could score a run with one swing of the bat, it changed baseball. They threw harder, pitched to guys more carefully, and really adjusted their approach. And that's all because of Babe Ruth.

And finally, he was bigger than life. The poster boy for the Roaring Twenties. He made more money than the President, and when a writer pointed it out to him, he said, "I know, but I had a better year than Herbert Hoover." And he did. The most famous ballpark in sports was built because of Babe Ruth.

You'll remember that Ruth's rise came during a real black period for baseball. It was just after the Black Sox scandal and just after Ray Chapman had been killed by a pitch from Carl Mays. The same way a

---

WHO'S NEXT

If you're doing this list ten or fifteen years down the road, who could crack the top five? One guy who's playing today: Tiger Woods. He's on his way to just demolishing golf's record books. He's changed the game in all kinds of ways. He's bringing minorities—and athletes—to the sport of golf. The most venerable golf course in the country—Augusta—was redesigned because of the way his distance off the tee threatened to turn it into a pitch and putt. And he's a big-time celebrity. People who never watched a golf tournament before are tuning in to see Tiger. If I'm doing this kind of list again ten years down the road, I think it's bye-bye Thorpe, hello Tiger.

great player can carry a team on his back for a couple of weeks, Ruth carried the game on his back for a couple of years. It was as if in 1895 in Baltimore, God said, "In twenty years baseball is going to have some really tough times. And I'm going to create a guy to help pull the game through." That guy was Babe Ruth.